# MAN, THE REGENERATIVE EVOLUTIONARY SPIRIT

# MAN, THE REGENERATIVE EVOLUTIONARY SPIRIT

By
Ruth E. Norman (URIEL)
and
Charles Spaegel

UNARIUS Educational Foundation
145 South Magnolia Avenue
El Cajon, California 92020-4522

# MAN, THE REGENERATIVE EVOLUTIONARY SPIRIT

### FIRST EDITION

Copyright 1988 by Unarius Educational Foundtion

Copyright under International, Pan American, and Universal Copyright Conventions. All rights reserved. No part of this book may be reproduced in any form, except for brief quotations (not to exceed 1,000 words) in a rcview or professional work — without permission in writing from the publishers.

Printed and bound in the United States of America

ISBN 0-932642-95-0

Unarius Educational Foundation
El Cajon, Calfiornia 92020-4522

Ruth E. Norman and Ernest L. Norman
Founders and Channels
Unarius Educational Foundation

**CHARLES SPAEGEL**
Subchannel / Class Moderator

# CONTENTS

| | |
|---|---|
| Foreword | i |
| What is Life? | 1 |
| The Music of the Spheres | 26 |
| Man, the Enigma | 53 |
| Music, the Symbolic Logic of the Whole Note | 81 |
| Chaos and Cosmic Time | 109 |
| Entropy and the Interdimensional Cosmos | 133 |
| The Singularity of Energy — A Fourth Dimensional Physics | 158 |
| The Joining of Science and Religion | 183 |
| Man, the Regenerative Evolutionary Spirit | 209 |
| The UNARIUS Science of Life | 236 |
| The Great Chessboard — Life | 263 |
| Rational and Irrational Numbers and the Sylogism of Man | 288 |
| Man and Spirit — Coefficients of Energy | 315 |

Foreword

"This book is addressed to all seekers who are concerned with the unification of the basic elements of the physical and spiritual dimensions of themselves. It is a book for all man, and yet necessarily, as it is couched in the language of science, it will be more easily understood by those who have developed certain expertise in the disciplines of science.
"Hence, physicists, anthropologists, archeologists, astronomers, biochemists, et al, will find in these pages, certain similarities in the common denominator of their work.
"At the same time, the information of this book, as it posits the truth of man as a regenerative, evolutionary spirit, will carry the reader beyond the tenure of his present recognizable, third dimensional world. This is so because man is not a third dimensional object, solely encompassed by a five-sense physical anatomy, a cardiovascular system and neurological brain system.
"It is the intent of the Author and with those whom the Author communicates on a high frequency of a fourth dimensional plane, to develop an understanding of the extraterrestrial nature of Homo sapiens and of his interdimensional characteristics.
"This book is a continuity of other books of the Unarius Academy of Science, describing the nature of man and society, how the spiritual nature of man is sustained from environmental

factors that are predicated as the forces that engrave themselves into the electronic body of the mind of man, molding the contours of the individual in his evolutionary trek through time and space; from life to life and planet to planet, both in the third and fourth dimensional universes.

"It is then the purpose of this book to dialogue with the reader to reveal the interdimensional nature of himself and to extend his understanding of the physics of energy beyond the third dimensional framework. The window into a larger Infinite is opened to the light of fourth dimensional wisdom and reflected into the minds of the Seeker of Life. The reader is thereby attuned to the higher frequency of minds freed of the time-space dilemma of the earthman! Such individuals live in an extended manner on non-atomic planets and in worlds whose society is governed by the unifying forces of an Infinite Creative Intelligence (as it is on Earth) but expressed to a higher degree by their recognition of the grand, unified field equation of energy. In this space-time continuum, there is no separation between the mind and the body, but a joining in spirit!

"The present dilemma in both physics and cosmology, in the attempt to integrate the four presently known forces of energy, the gravitational force, the strong force, the weak force, and the electromagnetic force, is due to the ignorance of the fifth force of energy. This fifth force is truly the

Mind, which contains the equation that has baffled the scientific community in the present 20th Century. The fifth force is nothing else but the reality of the mind as an interdimensional field force, dual in its nature, containing the alternate movement of man in his ability to transmit from a fourth dimensional plane and to receive from a third dimensional plane; in the intermixing, to determine the logic and reason of his local environment.

"However, in this admixture of two environmental forces, the basic thrust is to recognize the continuity of consciousness as an evolutionary expression of this ever-moving synusoidal expression of energy. The reality of the electromagnetic nature of energy will therefore be seen to be the very sum and substance of consciousness, which is the writing on the blackboard itself, the reality of the mind, carrying with it the accumulated material of life experiences inscribed upon the electromagnetic-computer body that is interdimensional in its ability to input all factors of life expressions.

"You will therefore find in the chapters of this book, the logic and reason that is etched and abstracted from the various disciplines, of mathematics, philosophy, psychology, including present research into particle physics and cosmology, in the attempt to gain an understanding of the evolutionary design of Homo sapiens.

"It can therefore be recognized that the information in each chapter was not based upon the physical bases of present physics, philosophy, or psychology and all other attributes of man's present knowledge of his physical environment, planet, solar system and galaxy, but was transmitted by Advanced Scientists from higher stations in their evolutionary positions. They are the true Authors of this book and who speak from a higher perspective of life's paradigm.

"The reader will note that he will experience a transcendency that will provide him a clearer perspective of those factors of himself that he has wished to understand - notably, the answers to the enigma of the nature of those unanswered problems relative to social conditions involving crime, disease, poverty, environmental polution, etc., and the desire to equate oneself psychologically and spiritually in his expressions of life.

"Hence, the thrust of this book is to open up the mind of the individual to the spiritual factors that contain the answers to all problems which have dogged the individual in his daily life. The principle of frequency and harmonics, as they resonate within each individual life-after-life, is the common denominator that, as a thread, will unify the disparate nature of man in his isolation from his spiritual, creative intelligence.

"The grand, unified theory is therefore the enigma that is resolved when the individual recognizes that he contains all necessary factors within himself that will unify the four forces of energy, and of the atomic nature of life with the higher atomic factor of the fifth force; if you will, a fourth dimensional agency. This will, to all intents and purposes, reveal the essential protonic catalytic, binding force of the interior man and the electronic nature of the mind!

"This, therefore, is the purpose of this book, to acquaint man with the regenerative, evolutionary nature of spirit, and spirit being the interdimensional energy system that contains the creative intelligence of an omnipotent, omnipresent force.

"The Unarius Academy of Science is a coalition of Master Minds, of personages who once lived on planet Earth, comprised of all humanists in all disciplines of life, whose sole purpose is to advance the progressive evolutionary intent of Homo sapiens.

"Read, therefore, with renewed spirit and with an open mind, realizing in your attempt to understand self that you are embarking upon a journey that will take you out of the narrow definition of science. The Science of Life is interdimensional in its scope, and contains the logic and reason for life and of life, enabling the individual to function from the higher position of his mental self, rather than from the past, unpolarized by the higher mechanics of evolutionary physics.

# Chapter 1

# What is Life?

"The evident nature of life is the apparency, the contradiction and the wholeness of Infinite Intelligence. Life is an apparency to all peoples, because each individual is feeling the pulse beat of his life, which is being reflected from the nature of life. Hence, each individual is receiving a special touch that works into the interior, the nether-nature of himself. Each individual is therefore an apparency of life, gestating the many facets of such a person who develops the individuality of himself as he becomes aware of and capable of sensing the organism that has been shaped within the pulse of life.

"The contradiction of life is that in these many individualizations which are the reflection of the apparencies of life, there is a contradiction; a contradiction which is the movement of life as it touches people who, in their differences, having been shaped by their own development, provide a contradiction within the vast features of life. These are contradictions which are the inherent nature of the great mirror of life. The apparency of life is that which is shared by each Homo sapiens, as the Homo sapiens is the pulse of this apparency. It is an apparent factor of life because the Homo sapiens has not yet developed the viable nature of this pulse which is invigorating his mind; invigorating the extensions of the mind in its physical appurtenances.

"It is an apparency that is taken for granted and shared by all human beings. It is the invigorating nature of life per se, not thought of, not considered, not truly understood as to the nature of this invigoration, but sufficiently so that it is taken for granted as each individual sees the reflection of the apparency of some life that is invigorating another individual. It is because the nature of this pulse, the appearance of a human being is not fully understood that there are contradictions within the common denominator, which is the fact of life.

"Life is a word pertaining to living. Life and living are word structures but what do they truly mean? What do they stand for? It is a retorical statement that can engage two or more people in arguments pertaining to the meaning each has as to the nature of life. The contradictions are therefore the very interpretive values that are taken from the nature of this vast system which can be validated on the basis that there is a development within the sphere of physical life. There is a validation of this process called life as it can be seen in its gestation, in the budding of a flower, in the growing of grass, a tree, a crystal. But to the fullest extent is it shown in the fertilization of a human egg, which becomes a full-bloomed, thinking being - a Homo sapiens!

"The eternal question that has

been asked by all people throughout the ages, 'What is life?' It has been further answered by masters; those individuals who have mastered the elements of this process of the cyclic movement of energy. But what of the contradictions in this process of life shared by all human beings who breathe the same air? - qualitatively, of course, depending on what part of the globe of Earth they are presently stationed.

"The contradictions of life are the nature of life; life being a process of growth. Such masters have spoken and have correctly spoken in the clearest of manners, and have pointed out, 'Man of Earth, you are life; you are growth; you are both the spermatozoa and the egg. You are both the gene and the formed structure which is the shape of the finite character of Infinite Intelligence. You are man, the all, and you are the finite. You contain within the organs of your amoebic self the vast concourse of the Infinite Mind of the Cosmic Intelligence. You are gestating Infinity! Yes, you are gestating Infinity, because Infinity is ever and anon, evolving and becoming infinitely Infinite. You hold the secrets of life's mighty reflection within the palm of your hand, within the fingertip of your finger. Every tissue of your body bespeaks of the intelligence which is the mirror reflection of a factor of this face which is the illumination of the vast panorama that contains for man a visage and a vista of his originality.'

"Man is both the beginning and the

end, the alfa and omega, because he had no beginning and he has no end. He is both the spermatozoa and the egg. He is all that is contained within this Infinite. Man is the egg of the Infinite, which is one of the infinite, so-called eggs; a cellular structure of the vast infinite organism which is this Father that has been related in the historical narratives of Earth people. How else could man understand the nature of himself if he did not have a developmental statement within the growth of his amoebic self?

"So it is that a family contains the basic ingredients which is the fertilization of the cell of man. And through the various relationships that are the associations of the members of such family, affirmative action is taken , providing each amoebic cell of the Infinite an opportunity to begin that ever-developing statement as to its identity.

"It has been stated by physical scientists that the physical universe began with one mighty explosion of a primeval atom; that this atom was the singularity of the entire known universe and its billions of galaxies. There is some truth to this to the extent that the entire nature of the physical universe was contained in its egg, a fourth dimensional prerequisite for the birth of the universe. The birth of the universe was an orderly development, a gestation, so to speak, which had its causal basis from its parent; that the egg which contains the entire characteristics of the ninety-two natural atoms is the regeneration from this primeval so-called atom. They are the children, so to speak, that have matured through the development in the plasma of the third dimension.

"In this respect then, each of these atomic elements have in their own evolutionary development, regenerated additional characteristics and factors which have given in their maturation, new perspectives and newer relationships in their individualization. It can be said then, that the two hundred million galaxies have been spawned from the same Father and that they are children of this, their parent. In this respect then, we see in the two hundred billion galaxies contradictions in the different appearances which have been the statement of the differences in their individual development; contradictions in that the developments have indicated different forms, shapes, and other vagaries which have been a factor in the reformation of the energy which has completed a phase in the development of these galaxies.

"The galaxies are then again a regeneration of individual solar systems. Again we see contradictions, because of the innumerable changes that have been the statement of the evolution of the individual forming solar systems within the galaxy. We see then, that the contradictions are truly a basic statement of the ever-expanding nature of energy, and the ever-descending or contracting nature of energy, and that life as we had pointed out as a basic function in which all Homo sapiens function, is the Force that contains within it the contradictions of its own nature.

"It is in the large array of the hundreds of countless trillions of forms which are the development of the expanding movement of energy in the physical universe that provides the great learning as to what this movement called 'life' is all about. As the parent has regenerated from itself through its own energy process, compliments of its own characteristics, these compliments and characteristics have become the individual members of a family, gestated from the cellular structure of the atomic nature of the parent. As the physical universe is a rendition and a statement of such development, so is each individual a statement of this process in the divisibility of an egg which, when hatched, indicates a complete and full-grown human being.

"The entire nature then of the Infinite, which we have been speaking about, is the process of regeneration; a process in which the Infinite, as it is contained within its finite reproductions is the entire essence and function of Itself within the cellular nature of its reproductive self. As man is a product and is, in every essence, a function of the third dimension, he has likewise been born through the same medium as the suns and planets!

"Man has gestated from a singular energy form; singular in this respect, that the present understanding of himself has a parental causality. Thus the contradictions, which are the nature of the apparency of life, are the unknowable factor of man's life Force which he takes for granted and accepts, because he is that life Force. But he hasn't yet developed the means by which he can see into the mechanism which fibrillates every cellular factor of his organism. It is in this manner that the greatest of philosophies, the theories which have inundated the physical, social, psychological statements of life have attempted to understand the whys and the wherefores of life.

"The contradictions that have inundated the many dissertations from noted philosophers and scientists, and those who issue their statements from the pulpit, are in every respect, interpretations from the eternal, the infinite film, the picture that all peoples see and take their proper resolution. However, they see from a perspective which is different, according to the eye which selects, according to the interpretive concept that has been a factor in that individual's development.

"But it is in this very factor of the contradictions which are the nature of this life that is lived by man on his earth world, on his astral world, that the life which is the consciousness, permeating into the basic electromagnetic spectrum of every planet, gives the opportunity for the children of this Father to develop. In their individual development which may seem to be a contradiction with respect to other people's development throughout their planet, there is the growth in the gradual understanding of the vast differences which are the individual reflections of the greater Infinite. In other words, the finite variations of the species: man, animal, plant, vegetable and mineral, is in itself, the proof of the infinite nature of life.

"So if the question was to be asked, 'What is life?' Is it a finite factor? Is it an infinite factor? Is there a singular intelligence that is responsible for all that is the apparency of the contradictions that one sees in his civilization? And are these contradictions, which are the basic breakup and fragmentation of society a consideration that there is no overall intelligent Force responsible for the individualization and the contradictions in the life of man?'

"In every respect then, the understanding of the physical universe, of the paradoxical nature of this universe as it is resolved from the astrophysical movement of the galaxies, the suns, planets, and other refracted appearances of the latter, provides a certain statement of the appearance of life. The physical nature of man, on the other hand, provides from a lower perspective in terms of the refraction of man's eyes to be able to see the movement of the energy which is life within his refracted physical anatomy.

"And here are the great contradictions which have not been resolved, but which are the essence of this life Force. The contradictions are the actual movement of the electromagnetic field itself, as it is consistently resolving into a base plane statement, carrying the knowledge of its own intelligence in equivalency, which is the refraction of itself from the movement of its own internal intelligence.

"The consistencies of life that have gained a basic latitude whereby there is a balance in the apparency of life in which the many millions of peoples are living and refracting from life's mirror, is the resolution of the contradictions which are the very developmental nature for mankind to recognize within himself. These opposites which live within all life, within the galaxy, and which is the complete and sometimes utter chaos that can be seen to function on the surface of a planet; or it can be seen to be the great balance and peace, a recognition of the alternate fields of energy that function in this great biological plasma. That is man! That is the universe!

"Yes, the universe is a biological plasma, because the universe is the gestating field in which the spermatozoa of man develops. In many respects, the physical universe is the giant egg in which the physical characteristics of itself are developing and which becomes the atomic plane of life for a human being.

"That atomic plane of life is its physical organisms, and these physical organisms have been given their equivalency from the very atomic elements which are the characteristics of the physical universe. The schematic then for man to become aware of in the great and broader configuration of evolution is the realization that he has been born, as has the universe, from a parent atom! The parent is an infinite, yet finite factor of the greater Infinite. It is infinite in that it contains every specific characteristic necessary to reproduce itself. It is finite to the extent that the reproduction of itself must develop over evolutionary cycles into the recognition of its infinite properties from which it had been derived.

"The eternal question therefore, 'What came first, the chicken or the egg?' is the paradigm that contains within the question the answer, the entire statement of the Infinite Creative Intelligence, and does explain what life is. It is not a singular property that can be understood in the environment of a physical universe. It cannot be completed in its understanding from all measurements so taken from an instrument that is measuring the characteristics of this physical universe, including man himself in his physical anatomy.

"The purpose of man emerging from the egg, which is his emergence from the womb of woman, is to determine for himself and to gain the strength in the development of those energy structures of which he has been constructed, which is his life Force. And in the development of this life Force, through all the contradictions which he apparently sees around him in his growing as a child into adolescence and adulthood, he gathers the evidence and applies the facts that are the gathering of this evidence and instruments this within himself. Thus, according to his success, he learns who he is.

"His success is of course, tantamount to recognizing the puzzle that life provides for him in the innumerable differences, and sometimes similarities he spots as he develops in his young years and evolves into his latter years. He is wiser because of his capability of perceiving the reality of the apparency of his outer environment.

"He becomes wiser in each and every successive emergence from a newly-hatched egg, carrying with him additional clues that had been gained by him in previous emergences into the physical universe. His egg, he finds, is not just one dimensional, two dimensional or even three dimensional but is fourth dimensional! Then he begins to resolve that enigma of what life is as he finally recognizes a truth that he has been emerging from the egg from two opposite doorways; in essence, that he had already been born but was learning in the fashion of birth and death in the physical statement of life, and birth and death in the spiritual statement of life.

"He begins to recognize the contradiction that lies within his own field, the energy self. As he gains additional clues in his movement throughout the firmament of some earth world and recognizes that in the contradictions are the answers to this puzzle, he realizes that he is seeing the nature of his own duality in the reflection of his so-called physical reality. Then he knows that what came first, the chicken or the egg, is a paradigm that had been developed by those who were not aware of the construct of this fourth dimensional puzzle. They were but seeing only the singular face of birth and death and were unaware as to its inner statement and the continuity of the energy which was the form of some man or woman into a new birth in the ever-moving, ever-developing, ever-cyclic change from the non-atomic to the atomic form.

"So eventually a man or a woman sees the fullness of himself in the non-apparent nature of life. But in the reality of life he realizes that he contains within himself the egg; that this egg is the reconstructed Infinite Force that has been shaped by himself, which now reflects the circular nature of himself! He sees that life is a constant movement of energy that is the containment of his own interpretation, based upon his own involvement in his ever-developing concerned desire to know of himself.

"Then the puzzle has been resolved to the extent that he now can develop those very necessary characteristics which contain the balance in the evolutionary design of himself as a constructive factor in the ever-expressionary movement of the Infinite. The Infinite therefore becomes not a question of absolutes, but it becomes a very actual presence of knowledge that has been gained of the interior mechanism, which is the cell structure of man's mind.

"The wealth that lives on one planet is astounding! That wealth is the very nature of life. Life is the appearance of Spirit because it is everywhere. It functions in the deep core of the earth, under the mantle; it functions in the atmosphere; it functions throughout the interplanetary nature of the galaxies; it functions intergalactically! Life is therefore the ever-present nature of Spirit because Spirit is an interdimensional movement, a Force that knows no obstacle, knows no barrier, is not restricted by man-made measurements of time and space.

"Spirit *IS* therefore that Life Force. Spirit is the Infinite, the Creative Intelligence that is cosmic in its breath and breadth. It is an Interdimensional Force! But that Force lives within the very cellular structure of each egg, which is the manifestation of this Spirit! It lives within the many individual forms that have been the maturation of the egg.

"Man therefore contains within himself, the maturation of all of those gestating characteristics that have been formed in his spiritual birth. The spiritual birth of man took place on a fourth dimensional plane. In this sense then, and in this reality, man is a Spiritual Force. Man is Spirit, spawned by the Father of Spirit. What then is the physical body that is the apparency of man's life? If man is Spirit, how is this Spirit and its characteristics revealed? In what form does it take, and what actions are its rendition on the plane of life?

"The physical universes are the birthing pangs for the growth of understanding of this, the spiritual nature of life. Man lives in physical dimensions as a means of developing the higher physics of himself to realize that as a spiritual being, he is an energy field. As an energy field, he is therefore a reflection of the Cosmic Mind, in the rendition in which this energy field has been so constructed as such a reflection. He is a small eddy pool in the larger eddy pool of the regenerating Infinity.

"But as an infant he must learn by the means in which learning takes place from an infant's mind, to learn of the senses of his spiritual self. Therefore, crudely at first, he learns in the crude fashions which are the associated reflections of this physical structure called the atomic body. By handling those objects which are the refractions of the physical universe, he gains his first rudimentary understanding through the development of his five physical senses, which are the basic refractions of this atomic body. But as man is an energy system, he begins to realize as his mentality develops, and as he is a product of billions of years of physical evolution, his physical anatomy has attained to that development whereby it is capable of becoming oriented through the prism that has been developed - a prism which is the brain structure, capable of interpreting the higher sense factors of its spiritual self.

"The physical evolution of mankind has come to its highest development, whereby the sense structures of this anatomy is an instrument which had been purposely created by the Cosmic Intelligence, the Father, to provide for the beginning of all sentient beings who occupy such bodies, to reach a point in their constructive development through evolutionary epochs of time, to gain the latitude whereby they could apply knowledge of their true identities.

"Man, as we said, was not born in a physical anatomy; man was born in a spiritual anatomy. The physical anatomy was basically a learning device, and as the butterfly emerges from the cocoon, man also emerges from the cocoon, which is the temporal home of his spirit. He emerges in his full-winged splendor, having developed the realization of his purpose, to move to higher grounds and to take up his proper position in his evolutionary development, to become a value to the ever-expanding movement of life.

"Man's purpose is therefore to develop the civilizations in the spiritual worlds to recreate the higher statement of the Infinite Intelligence in the dimensions which contain the entire refracted nature of the Infinite as a unified function. The separate and divisible picture of life that is the basic breeding ground for mankind in the third dimension is but the formative features of life, and the apparency of life. Therefore, it is not full and conclusive to any man who is Spirit, living in the cocoon of a physical anatomy.

"When he does learn in a manner which is his full consciousness of his true identity, at that moment he becomes aware of the answer to that enigma, 'What is life?' He thus knows that he is life which has been gestated from an Infinite Force and that he is the responsible, determining element that will open himself to his real home, and where he will return, to furnish such a home with the knowledge that he has gained.

"This knowledge is the entire purpose of third dimensional life, to develop the electronic sensitivity whereby as an energy system, he can properly function within the greater and higher frequency structure of his new home, his environment which is radiating the basic higher intelligence of the Infinite, so rectified and so balanced in the rectification that his city and the people living within it, are all constructive and are functioning in a balanced manner, so polarized with the knowledge they have of themselves as factors in this great chessboard that is life. Each know their own positions but not restricted, realizing the broad nature of evolution and the eternal development that is the prerogative of each individual spiritual being, to generate a greater application of himself in the movement of all of those component parts that make up the relationship of people in a civilization.

"Homo sapiens is a word that connotes a thinking animal. Homo is the nature of a homonide, and a homonide is an ape-like being. The ape-like being is the nature of the physical atomic organism containing, as it does, the basic features of a biped and all of the characteristics so associated within its cardiovascular and brain system.

"The sentient part that occupied this homonide is responsible for the completion of this physical, mechanized, atomic body to take on an intelligence that is non-physical to the extent that it can function beyond the associated factors of five lateral senses that can give this homonide its ability to secure the necessities of its physical nature: food, clothing, and associated needs. The sentient factor, therefore, of man which is now Homo sapiens, is the spirit that contains the intelligence that functions within the physical anatomy of this construct of such a physical body.

"This is the basis of learning. Man enters into a lower organ, learns how to function this lower organ and therefore, to propel and direct it so he can gain the necessary knowledge of the environment in which such a structure functions. This environment is the finite reflection of the Infinite Intelligence. Man is down in the lower depth of the great oscillating vortex, and is no different than the life forms that function deep below the oceans, having gained the knowledge of their lives, their function within the plasma of these ocean seas. But they are developing factors of the Infinite nonetheless, developing in the natural, so-called way of evolution in the environment which has been their spawning ground.

"Man has emerged organically from these lower depths into a slightly higher relationship. He is still functioning in the lower frequencies of the spiritual dimensions and therefore, must function within the confines of such a physical structure in order to protect his higher senses from being harmed. This is the entire purpose of physical life, to provide for the spiritual body, a proper containment so this spiritual body can learn of itself.

"The spiritual body of man is his mind! The mind has nothing to do with the physical anatomy, which will return to the elements of its universe. Since the mind was not constructed from the 92 natural elements of the physical universe, it will return, as it always has, if such is the case, and become conscious of its true home. But the home that man lives in, as it is his true spiritual nature, his true spiritual body, the electromagnetic energy field that is sometimes called the psychic anatomy, is also developing. It is constructing new homes, beginning with one room and then adding to these rooms, where in some future time, according to the knowledge of that being of his spiritual body, he will be able to constructively add rooms to his home. In this case, he will have gained a greater degree of his recognition of his spiritual, infinite nature!

"At the present time, man is living in his physical larva state, learning of the true understanding of his birth. To that extent, in the learning he has dissociated himself from the truth of this identity as an interdimensional construct of energy and has contravened his own life. He has contravened his own life because, in the evolutionary periods of time in which he emerged into the physical body to learn additionally of the nature of his spiritual organism, he took for real the appearances of life, refracted from the 92 atoms. To that extent, he regenerated an artificial body and created for himself in this regeneration a prison, the bars of which were stronger than any atomic element.

"Man, who therefore took to be real, the temporal world of the atom, became loose and weak in the recognition and in the strengthening of his understanding as to his true energy body, and the true identity of this energy body as a force in tune with the Infinite Father.

"The contradictions, therefore, that were meant for the gestating of man so he could learn in this fashion, through life's experiences, the opposite of himself, were lost in the maze in which his life's processes had been gained. To that extent, the great trial and tribulation of man began millions of years ago; in fact, hundreds of millions of years ago, because there have been homonides and Homo sapiens ever recreating, regenerating, evolving in the constant movement of the Infinite from its nuclear self to its infinite, expanding nature.

"The great contradiction is the contradiction of materialism which is the belief in the refracted nature of physical substance as a need or security to stabilize an individual's belief in his life. The knowledge of the true identity of man, as he was born in a spiritual dimension, a fourth dimension, resolves into the understanding that man is a fourth dimensional structure. Therefore, there is a great contradiction that lives within humanity and which has been caused by the lack of knowledge or by the regeneration of misunderstanding or unfactual evidence that had been substantiated as being truth.

"The truth of the present nature of any individual's present apparency of life has been given the basic construct that he is dependent upon the material structures of his world to the greater extent than any other espousal in the theory as to the nature of life's existence. Hence it is, that in the ordinary common sense, logical and reasonable realization of the nature of life, taking all factors that each individual has substantiated for himself from his life-to-life incursions into the schoolroom of his third dimensional planet, he has been *DERAILED FROM THE TRUTH!* Not that he can be if he were to accept the reality of himself and examine his own structures, but that he had given the greater determination as to the security of himself to other peoples and had allowed himself to be moved away from a recognition of his inner senses.

"The broad picture then of evolution is that there is no strength to a Homo sapiens, male or female, in the espousal of life from his third dimensional environment. That is to say, there can be no security to such an individual who believes that the 'laying up of treasures in his bank and the accumulation of material properties' will give him the security he seeks. Yet, it is just on that basis that the great contravention against the essential nature of life is being regenerated!

"The great conspiracy, to all intents and purposes, functions secretly because it is an acceptance by those individuals who have lost their senses and their memories as to their true beginnings. In this respect then, having been lost to some extent on a desert island, they have attempted to secure for themselves the essences that would give them the sense of aliveness, seeing through the reflection of all of the physical appurtenances of their environment. This is essentially the basic problem that lives within each individual, his society and his civilization. The true knowledge of each individual as a spiritual being, and Spirit containing with it the answers to all the enigmas which have been his contradiction, renders obsolete the opinions and any interpretation of anyone who does not himself carry the same understanding.

"Eternal life is a simple proposition. It is a recognition that each individual contains the organs to perpetuate his energy structure, and that he can fan these organs to regenerate its stimulus so it will be stimulated in this fashion. He, and he alone, is capable of learning the operation of this spiritual anatomy! It is pure science! It is a science that can function with anyone beginning in his larva-state while still learning of the nature of himself in the physical anatomy. It must begin in that dimension. It must have the realization to each individual that he is expressing the *NEGATIVE POLARITY* of his internal energy system, and that he is learning of his spiritual origins when he begins to develop the knowledge of the schematic through which his life force functions.

"Hence it is, that in the physical anatomy in the physical universes, purposely regenerated by Infinite Intelligence, does man become a thinking being. He learns in the lowest possible part of the Infinite, in the lowest frequency and through a physical organ, the opposite nature or the dual nature of his spiritual identity. In this fashion does he begin to reciprocate, and in this reciprocity does he gain the lateral understanding of the higher senses that are the stabilizing factors of his energy body. He realizes then that he is a higher refraction of life than is the physical anatomy, and thereby he develops the capacity to stand outside of the artificiality, in a sense, although it is a natural development of evolution, but an artificial body which is a third dimensional substance, the lower nature of the developmental spiritual organism.

"Therefore, the entire purpose of life is one in which each individual living in his physical body must accept and appreciate the many contradictions which become the appendages of this body, by the very nature that the physical universe is itself, an expression of the negative polarity of life; that the positive polarity is the parent, the fourth dimensional egg, so to speak, which spawned the nature of itself, but from an opposite perspective!

"As the scientists have spoken, matter and antimatter are the opposite natures of the characteristics of matter! It is essentially that the atom is the matter of the third dimension and the antimatter is the isotope which has a positive charge; the atom has a negative charge. Man in his physical body is therefore negatively charged because the physical anatomy is a construct of the 92 atoms which are negatively charged in the third dimensional equivalence. The positive charge is his spiritual or fourth dimensional energy body which is biased, so to speak as an isotopic refraction of energy.

"In all respects then, the contradiction of life is the great learning of man as he becomes aware that the infinite nature of himself as it is learned in these opposites, develops the greater knowledge of the evolutionary development of life as an interdimensional restatement of energy, functioning constantly, recreating the opposities of itself as dimensional equivalents of the Infinite Creative Source.

"Hence it is, that as a third dimension, as it has been called, is the negative polarity of a fourth dimension, so is a fourth dimension a negative polarity of the fifth dimension. We see in this constant duality in the constant oscillation of energy as electronic wave forms, the interrelationship, the cyclic movement of all expressions that is called life. The logic here is that the apparency of life that is taken for granted, is only the beginning development of some homonide who has gained or is gaining the more intelligent refraction of itself and is beginning to become aware of the processes of its own recreated nature which eventually will speak to him. Thereby he will hear of the true birthright that has always been its history.

"Man must therefore realize that he was first born regenerated as a spark from the cosmic egg, and that this regeneration called birth contains within it the entire history of Infinity! The entire process of life is therefore the learning of these very infinite factors that are contained within the finite subtraction of this spark which learns of itself as a functionary process of energy and that energy is a process, a function, a never-ending movement of Infinity."

## Chapter 2

## The Music of the Spheres

"Throughout the Old Testament, there are ascribed approximately one-sixth of the number of pages to inspirational verse. This inspirational verse is poetry that has been suggested as being of the highest merit because the words speak of man's spiritual nature, of his Infinite Self, and touches the warmest recesses of mankind, the humanness and the compassionate nature of himself.

"One-sixth of Truth that had been relayed from the higher stations of man's true Infinite Self found a receptacle in the physical worlds. Throughout the great stresses and strains of man's clamoring for the acceptance of his ego as being the most important effigy in the Infinite, such poetry has remained as a basic foundation, speaking of the universal nature of love and of the great importance of life as this Universal Force. Yet there are volumes of texts that are crammed full from cover to cover that speak of this infinite knowledge that diagrams the basic philosophical statements and the inspirational feelings that bring out the most positive qualities in man.

"The teachings of man as a universal statement of the Infinite, have both a finite and an infinite structure and have been relayed throughout the galaxies in this great physical department of Infinite Intelligence.

"Do you think that your planet, stationed as it is, three radial lines from the sun, a small dwarf sun, is the only planet that has been visited by compassionate people who have been the authors of these verse? Do you think that an universal knowledge such as has been spoken in these verses and in the many additional verses in these other texts that we have spoken of, including Shakespeare and the many metaphysical poets, are the only verse that contain the validity of interdimensional life - infinite life? It would be a great contravention and a hypocracy to think so!

"Man is an individual beat frequency, containing the many different shapes, forms and colors, and the variety of characteristics that make up the outward appearance of his physical structures counted in the billions on one planet, and as man is an energy structure that is a continuity from a central nucleus, does that not speak of the infinite number of beat frequencies that have extended from this central nucleus that are occupying some placement on some planet, on some part of the universe?

"It is the nature of this apparency of life to recognize its reflection from different barriers; barriers that in some respect, have been purposely erected, not to hold man within a limitation in his life learning, but as a means of strengthening the mental structures of which he is a complete containment. These barriers can be seen in the scientific sense to be time and space, and it is just on that development that the evolution of the infinite character of the central nucleus is begun for those emanations from its central self.

"The sparks that emanate as laser beams of light of intense radiation, contain the entire sum and substance of the nucleus. This nucleus that we speak of is the Creative Infinite Mind shooting out with an intense Force from the Central Core. These pulse beats of the Infinite Mind are projected to the furthermost frontier of this radial, moving structure; the centermost, the innermost, the cosmic egg, the Fountainhead. And as a father is responsible for the development of his children, so is there a responsive cord that is the linkage between the nucleus, the Infinite Force, and all of its radiations which find themselves on the periphery of the dimensional statement of this, the great Causal Force.

"This great Causal Force, this great Causal Mind, this Infinite Regenerative Creative Intelligence functions in radial lines of electromagnetic vortexal energy wave forms. The pulse that emanates from the central nucleus is deposited as a larva into the lowest and furthermost section of the Infinite. This is another nuclei; a nuclei, however, that is the recreated and regenerative substation of the great Cosmic Minds. This is the furthest that the Infinite Creative Intelligence has projected itself in a contracting fashion, demodulating the great, intense Intelligence into a factor of itself, but on the lowest frequency that is the basic demodulation of that great macrocosm, the Fountainhead.

"The opposite nature of the great Cosmic Mind therefore finds itself in its most divisible polarity. The opposite nature of itself is the negative content of itself, and that negative content is the third dimensional atom; it being the nucleus for the gestation of all of the Force that is the characteristic of this emanation. This emanation contains the exact configurations of the central nucleus in its lowest depository in a structure that allows the emerging Homo sapiens to look about him and to develop the necessary science so that he can begin to balance the forces that lie within himself. These are the opposite electromotive factors of his energy structure that are the reflection of the greater Infinite; the positive and the negative polarities of his life force.

"So we see that the universe that man lives within on the negative polarity of life is a great reflection and refraction of the Infinite, which lies on the opposite side of the spectrum in a field of energy which is the containment of the unified positive forces. This is the beginning development of man to realize. That unified field, known as the Creative Infinite, cannot be resolved by any one individual who is still learning to walk, mentally speaking. He cannot understand the mathematics, the geometry of a unified field where time and space is melded as a continuum, so joined that the apparency of life is of a different nature, different in its mental content.

"The quotients are therefore of a new relativity and they have resolved themselves into a new spectrum where life takes on a new equation. Just as it is, in all schools where learning takes place, a child learns of the whole by having the whole separated into parts with the intention, of course, of giving the child the opportunity to rectify the individual parts as increments of the whole, to retrieve the characteristic of the mystic that becomes a new revelation to that child, as to an awareness of his own being. This is a development within the entire panoply of life in which different aspects of this Life Force is viewed from its component parts.

"The third dimension is the atom. The atom is the lower nucleus of another nucleus that evermore regenerates into another nucleus. So all dimensions which contain these nuclei are another developmental statement of the equation of the Infinite as composite parts of it. The knowledge, therefore, of the nature of life: What is God? What is the Infinite? Who is God? or who is the Infinite Creative Intelligence? can only be resolved through each individual's interpolation from his base plane life experiences. These life experiences, as they have gained alacrity in the ability of each individual to add newer and newer or fresher and fresher concepts, are the result of the complimentary relationship of different parts that have been the nature of his experiential life.

"The great poetry of man is evidence of the perception that had been gained by the authors of these verse. Such authors have completed certain developmental learnings and have begun to recognize the inherent truth of themselves. They have realized they are a complimentary note in the great harmonics of life. This is truly the first great learning for man to realize: that if he is (and he is) a complimentary note in the great harmony of the Infinite, which certain poets have described as 'the music of the spheres', then man is out of tune if he has not been attuned to the composition, which is the harmonic notes of the Infinite Intelligence.

"That composition was written by the Infinite Mind. What that Infinite Mind is cannot be determined by any one of the musical notes. There is only one way in which a musician can understand the nature of the composition with which he is presently involving himself as a participant in the score. That is by participating in the score of the composition in such a way that in his participation he so melds himself and receives the answer to the enigma of that question.

"By the very involvement of man in his life, he gains the answers to his constant questing because it is in each individual's participation in the music of the Infinite that the music speaks to him and explains to him the very nature of his beingness. How this is done is a factor of each individual's individual development. How this takes part in each individual's discipline is in the asking of the question and in the accompanying rectification of all of the anomalies of life which are basically his inability or inexpertise in tuning his musical instrument.

"Life can therefore be seen to be a musical chord structure in every respect, but music itself is based on a great science. That science is the interrelationship of the infinite electronic, energy wave forms which make up the musical score. Music is a pleasing sound and all factors of the greater Intelligence that is the Infinite Mind of man, is located in the lower demodulated note which is his third dimension.

"The physical universe contains within it the entire rendition of the score of the Master, but the barriers that make it difficult to read the score are those which are man's method of learning. Time and space may be considered to be a barrier because not only is time and space a physical factor of life, whereas the body contains a certain association of atomic energy, tuned to a certain frequency, but the mind contains a certain degree of energy that is also attuned to a certain frequency.

"So we see in this very evident factor of time and space that the physical anatomy is the ingredient which contains both the barrier and the answer to that enigma. How can man move through so-called physical space and so-called physical time, and unite himself with some other individual in some other space or time, in another part of the universe or in another part of his planet?

"Homo sapiens is an atomically created structure; created from the nucleus that had its home and origin in a higher dimension, a fourth dimensional field. Man's home is in the fourth dimension because man is a spiritual field force who was emitted from the central nucleus, the regenerative, creative Infinite Intelligence - the Force behind the force - the Omnipotent, Omnipresent, Eternal Mind!

"The physical body is the apparency of the life of the atomic universe. That is to say that man is *NOT* the physical anatomy but that the physical anatomy is the construct and the structure of the atomic forces, which had been regenerated from the primary atom; the basic result of its emergence into a lower frequency field. The entire abstract nature of this has been the work of innumerable philosophers and philosopher-scientists to ascribe to life some understanding that could explain the apparency of life in its contradiction; whereas, we see the physical anatomy and all apparencies of life moving through a cycle of birth and death.

"And so the first meaning of life that is attained by mankind from the base plane window in which he looks out through his physical anatomy, is to ascribe to life the beginnings and endings of some reflection, whether it is in the corn in the field or whether it is in the plant and animal and vegetable species. But in man, the entire contradiction of himself is seen to be fully reflected.

"Hence, birth and death is a cyclic movement of the energy that is known as the atom and its component associations as the molecule, its cellular structures, and which become the basic characteristic of an outward, observable form: the mineral, the plant, animal and Homo sapiens. Hence, in the early development of man, all ascribing factors of life were related within these basic boundaries. And all determinations as to how to contain one's life and live it within these boundaries is ascribed to the beginning of a life of a fetus and the completion of the life of the same fetus after it had gained a number of years in the development in the physical anatomy, which culminates in the completion of the life process, whereby all of the organs seemingly have lost their association and have been terminated.

"The so-called seven score years ascribed to the bodily processes of a physical anatomy have been the limitations in which man has functioned to learn of the various functions that take place in this process. These limitations are seemingly a statement of the short duration of life and that one has to give all he has in order to enjoy that duration of fleeting time. And yet that is a barrier itself, which gives a certain basic lesson to man; that in the recognition that he has X-number of years to live, he will attempt to form his life in accordance with certain prerequisite understandings that must be resolved, and to provide some completion in this resolution; the fulfillment of an objective.

"The various statements of each individual's life, therefore become a development in the fulfillment of certain purposes that have been his determination. It is in the life to life living in these basic short durations that the knowledge contained within the true nuclei of each individual is developed. It is in the testing and the constant retesting within the environment of other human beings and in the grouping and regroupings of individuals as they change places and relationships that a wider and wider diaphram is developed in the lens of each individual.

"That lens is his intelligence, and as he gains greater and greater understanding as to the so-called durability of time and space and realizes that it is the association of only one dimension of life, the physical dimension, and that physical dimension is the structure of the atomic body which has a certain cycle as he gains greater and greater knowledge, factually developed from his involvement in the many fields of endeavors in his life, living in many different ways, associating himself in the many different aspects of society, he begins to recognize the widening diaphram of life!

"This realization is the recognition of another life force that exists within the physical apparency of life. As he sees his father completing the cycle of his physical life at some advanced age, and as he sees other people in his community terminate their life at a so-called young age, he also has the many different experiences of the varieties of associations where birth was a developmental beginning factor in some new life of a physical anatomy. He sees the many different changes that are the interferences in the maturation of some individual occupying a physical body. It is in these barriers, the very self-inscribed forces that function within the physical society where all factors of life are ascribed to the security of the atomic body, that Truth finally seeps out; that the Force that provided the life for this body was an *ETERNAL FORCE*, that it was *NEVER* terminated, nor could it ever be terminated! and that this Force constantly regenerated a new body.

"The child recently emerging from the womb of his mother, is the attested proof and the validity of this Force that never changes, does not have a birth or does not have a death! It is the eternal, causal, Infinite Force. As man is living within the atomic definition of life, he is the smallest component factor of this Force, gaining his awareness of its nature through the window of the negative polarity of this Force.

"The negative polarity is a frequency that has been demodulated into the minutest form and structure so that in its lowest denominator and its slow motion, the learner could gain some understanding of the structure of himself. The third dimension is therefore a slow motion picture of the fourth dimension, slowed down to such an extent that composite factors of the fourth dimension can be seen, can be worked with and can be interrelated and sewn together as intelligence.

"Intelligence is the sum and total of the polarization of individual energy structures that now form in a lateral network as a spider web has been woven by the spider. Now that this web can function as a literal part of the spider, so is man's electromagnetic force field sewn together so that it is a functionary factor for the individual, to use in its association in accomplishing a deed; to weave into life in its relationship with other people some factor that reveals the movement of the Infinite. It contains in this movement a beat frequency of intelligence which is adding to the interlaced energy network of electronic wave forms, and attunes the individual to the positive polarity that is the nature of this electronic structure.

"The abstract nature of the Infinite is indeed abstract, because it contains energy that is moving at a frequency beyond that of the polarized consciousness of the beginning Homo sapiens. Spiritual man is called Homo sapiens whilst he is still functioning through the physical atomic structure which is his larva state. It is in this larva state that he gains the knowledge of the mechanics of his true spiritual body, where he can spread his wings and metamorphose, as does the butterfly, to move away from the restriction of his primary development. But it is in this primary development that mankind is learning of the true identity of himself.

"It is a development that does not necessarily function automatically, where all of the sparks of the Infinite that have been depositied into the atomic structured universe will grow, mature, and metamorphose into the free and open spiritual being, who will fly away, so to speak, from the lower gestating universe. But there are many difficulties besetting each individual.

"The difficulties are the test of his own developing knowledge and the contradiction that he finds himself in, as an evident, moving life force, containing the complex mechanical equipment of a physical anatomy that breathes, that has a pulse, and where the organs are seemingly automatically functioning; having been recreated many billions of years ago.

"Man, who is residing in this sensitive electronic system - as the atom is an electronic function and each cell of the physical anatomy is an electronic process - he accepts the apparency of the life force that moves this physical instrument and therefore believes that this is the entire nature of his life.

"Hence it is, that one can take advantage of this apparent life where the physical body provides a great deal of the pleasantries of the life of the individual; pleasantries which are associated with the five physical senses. He can and has regenerated this apparency of life as a physical picture, and has given to his consciousness the reality of this life and wishes to live it as long as he can, in the deepest manner that he is able.

"The life cycle of an atom is only one hundredeth of a billionth of a microsecond! Man is not yet aware that during every micro-instant his physical body is being recreated from the fourth dimension and 1,500,000 cells are born and die in just one second! This is the reappearance of life that had and can only be had from its primary source! The physical anatomy therefore has a life cycle and it cannot live beyond that life cycle. Whether it is seventy years or 700 years, it eventually must terminate. But that is not the most important part! The physical dimension carries within it the important learning factors of life as a development for other learning stages for the spiritual being so he can gain the trajectory to move back into the infinite, creative nature of his birth.

"Man is moving in this progressive

manner, evoluting and reinstating himself into the Eye of the Infinite, so to speak, and this evoluting is adding to each of those sparks which emerge from the central nucleus, greater and greater energy fields which it grows through its acknowledgment of its existence. And its growth is the development of the finely tuned statement in the rearranging of the electromagnetic energy structures of itself! In the cognizance of each individual, he develops a nucleus which is consciousness.

"Consciousness is therefore the basic shutter of each individual. He can open the lens of his eye and see in greater and greater speeds. The faster the shutter, the more will he see, in that he will be able to make out the many different ratios and appearances of the Infinite in the different ways and shapes in which that Infinite appears in its energy construct. The mind is the polarization that is the development of each individual of his spiritual nature, the electromagnetic field that is that spark. It is in this manner that man's purpose is inscribed in the very birth of himself - a purpose which is to rejoin the Father in evolutionary periods of the cyclic movement of this, the Creative Intelligence.

"That is a very abstract statement and is of course, beyond the comprehension of any one individual in his present nuclei state while still developing the purposes of his life. Yet in each stage that the larva matures, it begins to integrate various processes that are the makeup of its body, and this is the nature of that species. But the larva of man is of the highest species in the evoluting of all structures of the Infinite, which are really and truly the supporting foundation for the emergence of man so he can furnish the necessary propellant energies to the minutest of the fauna and flora of its world.

"The difficulty which is the present emergence in the 20th century of man, is in the discrimination within himself of the contradiction that lies within himself and the evidence of those many millions of individuals who have chosen the physical apparency of life, who have given this physical life a greater belief in the fact that it provides some complacency to the individual.

"Hence, the contradiction that is each individual's nature, the physical factor of his present body and the spiritual factor of his future body, are regenerated into the myriad of individuals who contain the same apparency of life. The contradiction is regenerated in society where there are the adherents to the importance of living a physical life and 'living it up', saturating that individual with all of the ingredients that are the makeup of man-made society.

"On the other hand, although it is not a clear, distinct separation, there are those individuals who have learned in previous lifetimes, and who have gone through the larva state and are beginning to emerge in their true state as butterflies. The roseate nature of their electronic structures are being revealed in the many higher frequencies associated with these colors. These individuals are those who have attained to a greater recognition of the Infinite, as they have learned they are responsive chords of this Infinite. And the music they make individually, is a very important additive to the great composition of life.

"So within the gestating, developing stage of spiritual man are the theaters upon which this gestation takes place. The individual notes of the great harmonic of the Creative Infinite had been recognized by other Homo sapiens, who had emerged from the larva state and had progressed and added greater music to the composition. They had attuned themselves as beat frequencies in the musical score, and as they were man, they are now spiritual man. As they were Homo sapiens, they are now Universal sapiens or Homo Spiritualis. They are universal in that they are not restricted to the dimension of time and space.

"As the fourth dimension is the true home of spiritual man, it has a greater integrated relationship to the Infinite Vortex, which is the breathing in and the breathing out of this mind. Hence, it is to attain to that integrated state where the knowledge of the alternate structure of the Infinite had been recognized in the finite structure of one of its children. So that child becomes an adult, and therefore as adulthood, it has its own maturation.

"The fourth dimension is a dimension, a spectrum, in which great galaxies function for adults; those individuals who have matured and who realize, having recognized their part in the great orchestra, that they are functioning in tune with the orchestra. In this functioning, they are adding to their own individual development because they realize they cannot progress without their involvement in this progression of other beat frequencies, other spiritual beings. Therefore, singularity, considered to be a merit in the third dimension, is an unknown quality in the fourth dimension; unknown to the extent of course, that the responsibility is the realization of that individual in his ability to live as a part of a community.

"The fourth dimension is an expression of the higher meritorious accompaniment of a society that functions in one accord and realizes the individual differences in the development of each individual's knowledge of himself; the lower and the higher function of an accompaniment where the minor chord and the major chord are not rivals but are relationships. In this sense, there is in the fourth dimension, a world of spirit where there are no rivalries, for the rivalries are only within the minds of individuals who have not gained this great understanding and lesson of life in their own development.

"The fourth dimension, therefore,

has within itself contradictions of a different note than there is in the third dimension. In the third dimension, as we have pointed out, is a factor of a physical anatomy that has an energy structure made up of atoms that have a duration of X-number of so-called years, the measuring method of that dimension.

"In a fourth dimension, where time and space have been unified, the grand unification theory is a fact, and all the forces that are seemingly separated in the third dimesnion have been reunited. But man is evolving yet to the homes of his Father, and he is still learning of self. His true learning is just beginning in the sense of his recognition of his spiritual nature, the properties of this electromagnetic field and the 'tuning up' of it so that the orchestra will take on a greater and greater harmony.

"The mind that was beginning to be recognized as the Central Force of life, in the gestating third dimension, is an actual and a factual statement of life in the fourth dimension! In a third dimension, the physical body is the primary motivating factor. It is the apparency of life. It is given the greatest of potency, the greatest of admiration and concern, because it is still the 'yet developing' recognition that one cannot live if his body does not function in its proper relationship. That is well and good up to the point when it is realized that the physical parts of that body are instrumented by a mental force, and that mental force is the developmental learning of each individual of his Infinite Self called the Spirit Self!

"The Spirit Self is a realization of anyone who is able to exist on a fourth dimensional planet, that he must be able to play his own musical instrument. The ability to do this is the understanding of the strings of his instrument. The strings of his instrument are the associated electronic movement of the parts of his electronic body. Therefore, each and every individual who is living upright and able to breathe without the cardiovascular system, and walks without having to bring knowledge of past associations from his physical lives, would have to be a Master or the beginning of one who is mastering himself - mastering the mechanics of his electronic structure or else he cannot survive in the world where the physical atom does not function.

"The fourth dimension is a world of an atom, but it is an atom that does not have the radius of a physical atom. It is an atom that has a new property and its weight is of a different nature. Its movement is of a frequency so advanced that this would need to have been learned by the Homo sapiens in his many different schools where he had gained these lessons.

"Again, as man is a fourth dimensional property of the Infinite, he has and is constantly gaining knowledge of the fourth dimensional physics of himself, whilst he is living in these fourth dimensional worlds! The contradiction, therefore, of life is that man, Homo sapiens, lives in two worlds! He lives in the physical universe through a physically dominated energy structure, and he lives in a fourth dimensional, spiritual world through a dominated spiritual structure! The energy, therefore, that is functioning on both worlds is the Force making possible his life.

"The apparency of life on his third dimension is the reflection from the denser lower-frequency, physical body. The higher frequency which is his energy or electronic structure, the psychic anatomy, is not yet known to him. He has taken for granted or accepted the movement of his atomic body, and as he moves over to the other side after his physical body dies, he is functioning through his true electronic body without the physical structures to support life. He is learning in this sense, the reality of his mind which is still a gestating, developing nucleus, not sufficiently strong or capable enough, as it is a child who cannot stand alone and does not have the security and confidence of its own abilities. Hence, man moves laterally as he is an Infinite Force, not known to himself, and functions on two dimensions.

"Birth and death are therefore synonymous to life in the physical body and life in the non-atomic, spiritual body. Man is born into a physical anatomy as a fetus and occupies that structure when it is sufficiently matured, and where the organs have been grown for his spark to occupy these atomic constituent parts. Then he is born again into the spiritual side or the fourth dimension. So death is the termination or the completion of a cycle. So the death of man is truly a misnomer, because the physical anatomy terminates and can be said to have completed or finished its cycle. It *NEVER DID* have any intelligence! The intelligence ascribed to the physical body is the motivating force, the mind of that spiritual man or woman that reflects through the various cell structures of the body. And through the eyes can the spirit of that individual be recognized!

"The spiritual structure of man or woman in its fourth dimensional home has a completion of a cycle as well, because that structure, that body, has not yet been matured, and it cannot survive beyond a certain so-called number of cycles or cyclic time and must again move in its oscillatory manner to the physical side of life. This is the great sine wave movement which is the inherent characteristic of the Infinite.

"This is the pulse beat of life, and man learns of himself in this movement from life to life. And we speak of this manner as from life in the physical body to life in the spiritual body, until he learns of the evidentual nature of the reality of the spiritual structure of himself, which is his mind! When he has developed this understanding to a greater degree, then he gives lesser consideration to the needs of the physical body, above and beyond its necessary purpose, to provide for the completion of some project, which is the carrying out of the functions of his progressive evolution, to inform other individuals who are living in the Homo sapient structures of their physical lives of their spiritual nature.

"So the physical anatomy contains many forms of the Infinite. It contains the children of the Infinite; it contains adolescence, and it contains adults. It is the adults who have been the responsible precursors of the great poetry of mankind which alludes to and adds to and validates his real purpose. It validates the reality of himself as a component part of the Infinite Creative Force. It speaks in this fashion and amplifies the higher notes which are the structure of each individual's creative Infinite Self.

"That spark that was born from the womb of the Father is now developing in the many different accompanying manners of each individual beat of this greater Mind. It is truly beating and is revealing its beat in every aspect of life that is the revelation to Homo sapiens and to spiritual man.

"As it is in the natural environment of man on a planet that he sees the sunset and sunrise; he is witness to volcanos and earthquakes, hurricanes and tornados. He has been a close witness and has had close encounters with fire, with death of the physical body. He has seen wars between rival communities. He has been witness to the vagaries of his contradiction in life where he has lost his spiritual direction, because of the overabundance and satiation of his physical body. He has had a reflection of the Infinite in every way and every manner, as it has been spoken to him in the supposed seemingly contradiction.

"And still man asks, 'What is life that God should punish me?' and, 'What is life that justice has not done?' It is in all of these interpretive manners through the test when the barriers that are seemingly the contradiction, close in on an individual that he truly begins to make his first beginning in the realization that any barrier that is the conformity of life, is the nature of his own interpretation. Hence, his lack of analysis has therefore not given truth to the statement that the Infinite lives within him. And should he be capable of recognizing it in one small aspect, he will have immediately dissolved that barrier which was his consideration, as it was an apparent obstruction to him.

"In this way, through all of the contradictions, through all of the supposed restrictions that meet mankind through the very restrictive nature of these experiences, does he realize they are mentally conceived and are energy structures that he has created from his own psychic anatomy. His mind, therefore, which is the polarization of this psychic anatomy, contains limited understandings, and it is in this limitation that he has lacked the attunement which would give him the open sesame and unrestricted appearance of life. He would be in tune with the energy force fields, the interdimensional function of this Life Force.

"So in its tiniest and most remote region in this great Infinite, man is living within the smallest facet of this Mind, which is the Father of the Creative Force. It is the Creative Force he is seeing - a reflection of this Force! So who can say that in the many splendid appearances that are a reflection of the Infinite, that it cannot be a means to open up the restricted nature and appearance of life to those who are moaning and groaning and have not realized in the highest and most evident manner, that they, and they alone, are the responsive chords of what they consider to be the appearance of life, because each individual is a beat note of the Creative Infinite and can recreate any appearance of life they wish!

"The lower dimensions (and the third dimension is called the lowest dimension) do have the recreated appearances of life, formed from the restricted acts of mankind as he has functioned in a group manner. It is therefore the restricted nature of the appearance of life that lives within society and which is the picture of life that is the basic curriculum in the schools; courses that have to do with the understanding of international relationships and the breakdown of the family unit; the nature and cause of the variety of enigmas that have to do with the physical nature of the planet; the occurrences of volcanos, hurricanes, the anomaly of weather, the fractures within economic and political life. All of these are fractions of the Infinite that have gained a fracture because of the over-concern given to the nature of the atomic appearance of the physical anatomy.

"Hence, the spiritual man was restricted, considering that his importance was greater as a leader and as an individual, whose security was of the utmost importance to him. It is not the security of his awareness of the continuity that he would experience, as he cannot and could not ever die to himself, but that he would die to the APPARENCY that he gave to life as an importance; whereby his body and therefore the mind that was so interpreted from the body, became the all-important vessel of life!

"Therefore, the various problems that have been associated in life are problems that have taken on a greater disharmonic, and yet a harmonic but on a lower frequency; disharmonized from the progressive higher developmental statement of the musical score. Hence it is, that planet Earth has been considered to be a planet 'out of tune' with other planets within the universe of this physical dimension.

"You must know that there are people who have gone through their evolution and are continuing in their evolution but have gained a greater and higher beat frequency, whereby their mental statements of life have given priority rather than the evident need to obsess and control other people in the domination of their own importance, given to their seemingly physical life. Because in this understanding and in this knowledge they have attuned their communities, their societies, their civilization, their planet, to the frequencies which are being emitted from other human beings on other planets. But more importantly, they are in tune with their fourth dimensional nature which is the all-important understanding of life!

"It is this great importance which is the enigmatic nature of physical life, the recognition that all physical properties of life that give the apparency of aliveness are only capable of having this aliveness from the Causal Motivating Force.

"Would it not then be the more intelligent act to become aware of and concerned with the knowledge of this Motivating Force? Its structure and how it is able to function in the myriad of countless finite relationships? This would naturally be the first and foremost study that should be the basis of all school systems; the knowledge of recreative, motivating, Infinite Force, because that is each individual's mind. And each individual's mind is linked to a Mind that carries the beat frequency of each minor chord!"

## Chapter 3

## Man, the Enigma

"Man, the eternal quest! Time, the eternal puzzle! Man and time! Life, a geometric equation that includes time, its equivalence of space, and man as the central enigma of all! The timeless nature of the Infinite, the finite nature of man are the eternal questions that have been the life to life developments of the greatest of philosophers, scientists, artists, musicians and above all, those who are the common man who function within the great panoply which is the umbrella of their lives, the skies above them and the firmament below them, and man placed directly in the middle.

"What can be said of time and what can be said of man who has the great contradictions within himself; the doubts, the separations that he feels from the magnanimous macrocosm, where he feels as a pinch of snuff, and is affected by the components of these elements? Man contains the derivatives of a timeless, spaceless, abstract Infinite, and yet within it all, he is a being in his atomic body, imprisoned within the nature of time.

"The enigma then, that has been the basic statements of philosophy and science, art and music has been within and without this barrier that has, on the one hand, constrained man, and on the other hand, has given him the security and the knowing that he can function beyond time at certain intervals of his life.

"The great enigma then is this: that in the spaceless-timeless nature of man, as he is an infinite energy field, is the apparency of his appearance of life as a separate condiment of this spaceless, infinite abstraction. He sees that he is truly locked within the tethers of physical time and the entire measurement of his conscious statement of life is geared to physical time. His life is a ruler marked off in the increments of seconds, minutes, hours, days and years; each a sixteenth, a thirty-second of an inch that marks that much of his life, and he comes closer to the conclusion of the seemingly conscious appearance of himself as a living, breathing organism.

"All around him he sees the entire nature of this measurement of the timeless-spaceless statement of life, and he senses in another perspective of himself from the real nuclei of his true identity as an immeasurable and yet component part of the Creative Infinite Intelligence. He realizes that he is not a part of time and space; yet the contradiction stares him directly in the face and he sees that his very life that is the breathing through the lungs and the ability to hold consciousness, is directly attributed to his ability to learn the calculations of his time and space dimension. Not to do so means his death; at least to the extent that he has no consciousness and is not aware of his physical environment.

"Hence, the greatest conundrum of thinking man has been the understanding of this enigma time. Theories are plentiful; hypotheses are innumerable, and because of them the sciences are the rectification of these thoughts of man. Physics is a method of resolving the apparency of the time-space dimension into some measurable statement. The entire purpose of physics is therefore to render into the component parts of time and space, the basis of some measurable aspect, the characteristics which would give the entirety in the answer to this entirety; the whole of this life that man is living as a component part.

"The fields of science contain many glimpses to the answers of this great enigma, of how to recognize the surface nature of life, which is the reflection of the physical universe, where time and space became the basis of its reality. The universal science that man is questing has surely been known before the quest of Homo sapiens began, even in the billions of years previous to this 20th century!

"Surely thinking man, in his philosophical inquiry into these strange contradictions he sees as the evidence of finite life and of infinite life, has already been resolved, else how did life come about? And whence came man? What of the innumerable appearances of life in the minutia of the sedimentary deposits on this one planet; the sedimentary deposits on the moon, Mars, Venus,

Mercury, and the beginning understanding of the gaseous nature of the outer planets in the Earth's solar system?

"Surely the name, 'thinking man', and we mean by that, those who are the pioneers attempting to resolve the contradictions of life into its holistic pattern, have come to the awareness that there have been the resolution of this apparency of this finite life by other human beings who have traveled the same pathway and who have gained their stance and their intelligence through their own overcoming of these perplexing geometric relationships of the great energy structures that are the parallaxing appearances of the solidity of third dimensional life.

"We read through others who are functioning on these many different relative levels of life; those who are involved in attempting to understand the microscopic, biological system of the cell; those who are functioning to make sense out of the cosmos and the many contradictory appearances of the astronomical objects in the Heavens or in the electromagnetic field, which is a more proper definition of the Heavens. As an aside then, in early man's development, the heavens were related to him as a state of consciousness upon which man had graduated and had advanced to the recognition of his unified consciousness, and he resolved the puzzle, the eternal puzzle, of man and his exterior environment. He saw the duality in the whole.

"Yes, it is a great puzzle; yet

that puzzle is the basic wisdom of Infinite Intelligence. That puzzle is called evolution, and it is an evolution through which man is gaining the direction of his understanding of who he is. It is true that several biologists have come to the same understanding of the development of the species of life as an evolutionary step in the bifurcation of the cosmos into its separate component finite species. It is in just that manner that man can be understood that what has been called Heaven is a holistic or unified statement of the separation of energy in the third dimension when the fourth dimensional atom was resolved into its opposite characteristic, and the positive and negative polarity of itself moved out into a field separated; separating the polarities in respect so that they took on a new characteristic - time and space.
"Again, the separation, which is a bisecting or bifurcation, is the great anomaly that is the need for each individual to resolve for himself in which he is given the opportunity of his evolution. Evolution means growth; it means evolving, and to evolve means to put together the various countless complexities of these separations that have been attended to by the demodulation of a higher frequency energy structure into a lower frequency.
"It is in this change that bifurcation takes place, and it is in this complexity that the many species are

the resolution. But in each evolution as the primary atom is demodulated to the lower expression of itself, in which its central nucleus has been separated into two halves, the two halves that become a rendition of the parents themselves, contain the essential similar characteristics of the parents, its positive and negative polarity. But now they resolve into a time-space relationship - a point to point relationship, so to speak, which gives the appearance. It is in this resolution that again there are the complexities of the Infinite restated in its finite and smaller ingredients.

"Each species therefore, that is the aspect of the father, the parent of itself, contains the basis, as a child contains the genetic structure of both mother and father. Every atomic, element, in this respect, contains its positive and negative polarities, but now expressed as a lower frequency. It is in this respect that man is attempting to gain the realization and recognition of time, because time is that bifurcation; that is, it is a separation, a bisecting of the cyclic unified movement of life which man realizes. He has pondered and touched upon it in his own inner and quiet moments where he realizes that he is an integral part of the whole. He feels it; he senses it; he knows it and gains his great sense of security by it with that knowledge that he is an essential feature of the Infinite Intelligence. That is the infinite nature of man.

"But the infinite nature of man is when he becomes aware to the greater extent of his separation from the fourth dimensional nature of himself, and he is aware of the many contradictions, the pulse beat of his physical body; the many different messages or signals that reflect to him from his brain structure, and which speak of the finite nature of himself: the sun coming up over the horizon, opening up a new day; the sun retreating and night falling, calling on the end of the day; the passage of the seasons indicating the movement of the planet about its sun; and the changes that are indicative of the growth of his crops; the varieties of pressures that are attendant upon the seasonal changes; the climatic changes as well, which cause higher and lower pressures, making necessary man's concern for his body.

"The complexity then of life is the result of the third dimension. The third dimension is the component factor of the fourth dimension, and since the third dimension contains all of the complexities that it does, it comes down to the basis that each individual has a physical anatomy and that physical anatomy is functioning according to the regularity of its organs; that its organs are naturally conducive to the health of its parts.

"A regeneration of many different factors have developed to attend to and provide for the health, the welfare of the physical body to make possible the association of man to man so he can create for himself the real picture of life that will release or induce him to stay.

"He feels these many pressures in the separation of himself from his integrated knowledge that there is a reality of another nature that lies beyond his conscious, rational mind; all the while man is living, attending to the innumerable complex factors that are involved in his stay upon his physical planet Earth. It is all he knows to the greatest extent, up to a point in his evolution, and that point is when man begins to realize that there is sense that can be made out of the seeming chaos.

"The complex contradictions of physical life are, in every respect, chaos, because if the vessel of the vehicle does not have its navigational instruments so controlled, it will move in a chaotic manner. It will move from left to right, up and down, and it will veer in circles, never truly completing its objective to the point which it was attempting to reach.

"In this respect then, it could be understood why there is such a great desire of intelligent man to understand the vehicle that he presently occupies and to gain control of this vehicle so it will function within the great abstract sea of energy which he knows is infinite, that has always been there and will always be there; that it has the force impinging upon his tiny vehicle spaceship. He knows that his planet is receiving the many different forces of the electromagnetic envelope with which it is surrounded. He knows that he himself, in his physical anatomy, is being affected by the many pressures as well, from the hysteresis of these great energy systems.

"He is being radiated from his own sun, from its interaction with his planet, and as a result, man is a resistant factor in his physical vehicle of his atomic body, in this great hysteresis and heterodyning of great energies; all being resolved through the nucleus of the sun and through the coronas that is the result of this movement of energy through the interior of the sun to its surface. Then the awesome spectacle that is related to the man of science is established, and the reality of life then begins to make its mighty statement!

"Man is a protoplasm that is moving through a great electromagnetic field force, containing many unexplained movements, the intelligence of which was the manifestation of a greater field force that recreated the sun. So it is that the 'Day of Awakening' is coming to mankind, as he is becoming that much more aligned with the realization of the true Transmitter. What it is and how it functions is the next step in man's development, but the establishment of its identity is the first and greatest beginning in the quest for the mind.

"Because the mind cannot be understood until the vehicle that is man is realized as the essential correlation between the exterior atmosphere and the great hysteresis of life, which is the interior atmosphere. The great contradictions, the enigmas of life will be resolved and the resolution is that man has been his own worst enemy! He contains within himself the evident nature of the answers to this great puzzle which has been a game of chess and checkers to man so long as he believes he is a basic physical protoplasm and did not understand at that time that the very protoplasm contained the essential secrets of his identity. Then he has *NOT* progressed himself!

"Man has been looking for the answers as to who he is. He has been a foster son, looking for his father; yet he need only to have begun that introspective research and to discover the essential factors that speak of the Father. True, it is an evolutionary development because each and every individual must add the ingredients of each life, disseminated from his life experiences; experiences which he gains by reflecting the many seekings and searchings in his relationship with other people and with his relationship to himself as he is, in every respect, seeing himself projected from and reflected from the faces and the actions of those with whom he has taken on some personal statement of life.

"Science is attempting to understand the resolution of the abstract nature of life, looking into the interior of the atom and attempting to measure the increments of every finite factor of the particles that are the fragments of his cyclotrons as a means of adding up these particles as components of the atom, saying, 'Ah ha! We have now the entire measurement of this great force of energy, and we know all of its parts from its fingers down to its toes! We have examined the essential nature of the atom, and we can now say that we know that this atom is a composite that explains the entire movement of life within man in the firmament of this physical universe!'

"Of course, that is the intent of the particle physicist; yet their attempt is frought with failure because of the essential factor, in that the object that is examined, the exterior environment, cannot be separated from the examiner, who is man himself. Until a physist (or whomever is doing the examination of some biopsy of some characteristic of the physical universe) knows the essential nature of his own subjective consciousness; not as a metaphysical statement of life, but as a factual statement of science; until that can become a valid statement in the scientific school, science will be SEPARATING MAN from his environment! And since man is the essential ingredient of the physical universe, man is the only means through which the negative and positive polarities of the finite third dimension can be understood.

"This understanding is thrown back to: 'What is man himself?' rather than, 'What is the nature of the movement of the planet around its sun?' By itself it has no meaning, for such as measurement is a tangible evidence of the objective nature of the Infinite, and it is a function that is beyond each individual atom. It is a function of a higher intelligence, which intelligence is a completion of the duality of energy. It is a completion of it, because it is functioning on a synthesis, an integration, a complete coupling of the polarities where they had gained a great balance. It is this *BALANCE* that provides the ability for that energy to function in its higher frequency or on its forward movement, a progressive statement of evolution.

"Man must know then, that the complimentary parts of himself are moving in the exact same manner as the planets revolve around their suns, and in this respect, the greater understanding gained from any equation of life, in the exterior understanding of the macrocosm, is to relate this picture in terms of its meaning and application to the protonic element that is man, to realize that he has discovered some essential guidelines as to the movement of his infinite energy structure. He is learning that his mind is the sun in some respects, and that his body, his physical anatomy, revolves around his mind. The force for his physical structures comes from his mind, as the force from the sun is providing the stability and the organism for life of the planets! In this manner can there be a greater understanding of the entwinement between man and his universe.

"The statements of scientists in all fields, if they are not related to the understanding of man in terms of his daily involvement with life on his physical plane, do not establish the validity of that science, because as we have indicated, it is our proposition that science must be a science that dissects life in all of its component parts, examining the surface nature of physical life and resolving the many irregularities that have found their presence within the organism that has been malformed.

"Science must understand the continuous nature of the interrelationship of man and his environment; man and society. Man, as an evolutionary statement of energy is therefore never separate from the complex nature of the protonic elements that are discharged into him. Therefore, as the sun is a central source of interest in astronomy, so should the mind be a central source of interest to all scientists, to man who is and will become a scientist, concerned in understanding the complimentary nature of his own complex nature.

"So once again, whomever has been recognizing the inherent nature of the mind of man as the essential source of answers to life, must begin to realize that this mind, as it is interdimensional, contains all factors of understanding within its attributes. Mathematical physics, astrophysics, atomic physics are statements of mental discoveries, because those individuals who are applying the characteristics of these evaluations are using the evolutionary development of their own mental understandings.

"Their intelligence is the recognition that THEY PROJECT OUT into the seeming abstract time-space DIMENSION a factor of some previous understanding gained and which, through their questioning, resolves back again into the present in terms of their updated instrumentation, capable of evidencing a greater rectification of this polarity situation and the negative polarity, stationed in a time-space dimension. Man, the positive polarity, is stationed in a spaceless time-space continuum, the fourth dimension!

"Pioneers who land on a distant planet and who carry with them many advanced instruments which are capable of revealing the reality of hidden energy, are capable of revealing the cities of ancient civilizations that have been buried under the sands of their planet. They who are capable of revealing the nature of the interior of the physical body and indicate on oscilloscopes, the movement of energy that cannot be seen by the physical eye, are not always welcomed and cannot always be understood because they come from a future.

"As all life is an evolutionary development where each individual gains the ability to reconstitute the complexities of his life and to resolve it into some understanding form, he may not have the ability to resolve into his mental self the higher mathematics which present new resolutions of life. This has been true in many respects in earthman's history when Spinoza, an advanced thinker, a philosopher, advanced a schematic of evolutionary life, a design which was geometrically related in his texts, spelling out the essential nature of the fourth dimensional characteristics of man and of his third dimensional, physical expression - all within the basic mathematics that the lower numbers must be understood as simple arithmetic and basic algebra before the higher calculus could be reconstituted in the individual's psychic anatomy.

"The principles of the Pythagoras teaching, of Socrates' teachings, of Akhenaton, and the complete unification of the teachings of Jesus of Nazareth, contain futuristic concepts which need to be and are being mathematically derived through the individual experiences of man, whereby he is seeing the proof of these basic algebraic symmetries of life. The symmetry which is a synthesis has been demonstrated by these teachers, as well as many others, but these, as a whole, have been in every respect, relating the clues for many to realize that he is a syllogism and is now able to take from his basic experience and resolve into his own present consciousness, to ratify the essential statements that man is a spiritual being who derived his first birth pangs in a fourth dimension and that his birth was the beginning of an evolution.

"Evolution then can be understood to be truly a spiritual development. To understand the enigma that is the basic statement of third dimensional life, is to understand that third-dimensional life, the life of the atom, life that is attenuated by time and space, is a resolution of this spiritual voyage. In this respect then, no researcher into the sense of life, could come to any conclusive understanding until he realizes the truth of man as energy, or energy as man, and of the polarity association of the regenerative, infinite statement of life.

"It must be understood that this time-space dimension, known as the third dimension, containing all of the direct pictures of the objective evidence of an atomic frequency, is the negative polarity of an energy force field, a dimension, and an essential factor in the evolutionary movement of life. That force, that energy which stemmed from a higher Creative Force *MUST KNOW* of itself by coming to grips with the alternate nature of itself!

"Man is therefore seeing the reflection of the alternate nature of life; that which has been called bifurcation by certain advanced thinkers; another statement of polarity, the separation of one into two. It is in this sense that the essential beginning can be a reality because all things can be separated into their alternate polarities. That is the essential proof of energy, that it contains and will always contain its positive and negative field, no matter how it is separated. Man himself has been separated to learn of the negative field that is the important aspect of himself. To learn of his positive field, in his separation he is living within an alternate field which is a lower expression of this duality.

"Positive and negative lives within the lower and lowest frequency of the atom and man is constantly seeing the opposite natures of himself from different vantage points, until he gains the realization in this life experience that truly if there is day and night and up and down, male and female, there are two kidneys, the right and left hemisphere of his brain, the north and south pole of his planet; there is bifurcation in all elements of life! This is the first learning!

"Taking that up an additional step in the intelligent assimilation of such information, we see then that there are the opposites in all reflections of life, from the lowest to the highest, but the positive and negative take on newer and higher indices of the intelligences that are functioning in this constant movement.

"Evolution in this respect, is a continual association between alternate hemispheres, and that is what most metaphysicians have been speaking about, the basic statement that there is a higher frequency dimension than the third dimension. Not that it had not been related by those futuristic pioneers who had landed on these lower planets and who had pointed this out, that the fourth dimension, the higher dimension, the positive dimension or the positive polarity of the third dimension, is an integral part of the third dimension!

"There could be no third dimension if it did not have its complimentary positive polarity, known as the fourth dimension. There could be no man, known as Homo sapiens, if there were not the complimentary spirit or psychic anatomy that contains the positive equivalence of a higher frequency field! It is the battery moving; it is the battery which essentially is the construct of two poles where the electronics that provide the power that is the movement between the two poles of the battery that are energizing the cells and which regenerate a current.

"There can be no electricity if there were not two polarities to exchange their intelligence. In this respect then, how could it be otherwise, that man who is attempting to gain the knowledge of who he is, not to accept on the basis of evidence from his surrounding electromagnetic field, from the smallest to the largest factor in this field, the realization that he is a polarized factor in the function of the movement of energy?

"The problem comes down to the nature of polarization. Polarization, as we have stated in previous chapters, can be biased to the negative pole or to the positive pole. As we have indicated, is man's regenerative, evolutionary or fourth dimensional, spiritual, energy field, which had been and is the polarization of the Infinite Creative Intelligence, the Regenerative Cosmic Mind.

"Evolution has as its purpose, to constantly regenerate the species of the protoplasms of life so that they regenerate successively by gaining new derivatives of the exchange between their positive and negative polarities, so that in this exchange they gain a greater momentum to attune to the fourth-dimensional, polarized nature of itself, as it was a factor in the eye of the Infinite in the evolutionary momentum of life.

"Man knows in his inner awareness that he has a prototonic polarized self, the pressure which speaks to him and provides him with a certain momentum in operating his physical anatomy in the lower pressures of the third dimension. This is his libido, his drive, and it is the beacon that is held forth by Infinite Intelligence. Although Infinite Intelligence is the abstract statement of the Cosmic Mind, it does have a system of objectifying Itself to mankind in the evolutionary placements of the Infinite on planets that are the recreative statement of this Intelligence; planets that have been formed from the regenerative energy fields that are the expressions of each of the dimensions. So in this way, the third dimension is a regeneration from the force fields of the fourth dimension.

"As man has learned of the essential nature of his polarized Infinite Self and has moved through life to life and life experiences in these lifetimes, gaining the knowledge of the enigma of life which was his first beginnings of Spirit, he has attained to a higher realization of his spiritual self and has generated an electromagnetic field, rectified through his own development in the polarity relationships in the third and fourth dimension; progressing successively into the fifth, sixth, and seventh dimensions. He has regenerated an energy similar to the corona of a sun.

"It is this regenerative nature of energy that has been constructed through the hard work, we might say, that is progressive evolution. Man has become a relay and has been capable of regenerating his spark so that it becomes a Beacon of Light, so polarized that it can be reflected into the beginning dimensions! It is this reflection we speak of, as those who are pioneers, who have come from the Future World and have brought information to the striving Homo sapiens in the lower worlds, and to striving man in the lower worlds of the fourth dimensions, for each dimension is successively an evolutionary development of worlds.

"It is not possible to discuss the basis of the principles of science without involving man, and the basic problem of the physical sciences up until the present has been divorced from the evidence of human potential! Scientists have been playing a game of chess, but as they have kept their appearances as placid as possible in order not to give evidences of the moves that they would make on the chessboard, so have scientists been playing a game and have been relating their games to their own associates; separating any and all people from the nature of this scientific game of life! They have not involved themselves, but have been looking out the window into the macrocosm or the microcosm of the electromagnetic field; yet they, themselves, have been left in some vacuum whereby there was no involvement within their own psychic anatomy. At least, they thought so!

"They have not objectively made any statements in terms of the truth of the continuity of all factors of their research within the nature of the history of their own evolution! They haven't discussed their own emotional reactions to the works of other scientists in other fields. They have not given any truth to the inner and deeper reactions they have kept from their associates as to their belief systems. And if they have, they have done so in a subjective manner. This has been the story of many who have been attempting to consider what is the construction of this energy field called life!

"Fortunately, there are pioneers who have, in the ordinary manner of life as an evolutionary statement, involved themselves in the physical bodies, the natural way of birth into a physical organism; however, carrying with them the advanced technology, not of the third dimension but the advanced technology of the higher mental dimensions where the mind is the resolution of life, and the body is still the training vehicle for the mind; the physical body not yet having been resolved as a reflective factor of the mind.

"As important as it is and as complex as its instrumentation is, the physical anatomy is nonetheless a secondary anatomy, and it does itself contain within its own machinery the evidence of the abstract Infinite. It attains the perspective again of the manner and way in which the finite is resolved into its infinite parts. Again, the physical anatomy takes on its polarity relationship, which is of a lower frequency; yet resolving itself into its alternate movement. Each cell structure contains the ingredients of the regenerative field of a higher structure that is the Father.

"*SO THE ENERGY BODY OF MAN, THE INVISIBLE FORCE, IS THE CONSTRUCTIVE, REGENERATIVE BODY OF THE PHYSICAL ANATOMY!*

"The scientists of today have not yet completely determined, nor have they accepted the appearance of this higher energy structure. Why have they not accepted it? It speaks to them in all manners and all ways! No life form can exist without its backup system! No life force can exist if it *DOES NOT*

*HAVE* a constant projection from a transmitting Force, an input. Yet science is still separated on this basic understanding.

"This is the hub of the entire statement of time and space, which is the frequency of the third dimension, which is a lower frequency of the fourth dimension, and which in every respect, resolves itself into a separation of all species of life, from the integration of all energy structures as unified, containing a higher perspective and a higher awareness; a resolution that adds to the nature of man as a real - and with capital letters REAL in the sense that it *CANNOT EVER* lose its Force, because this energy body cannot decay in its fourth dimensional structure because it is *NOT* a limited cyclic movement, as is the atomic anatomy.

"The next step in the advancement of science is therefore through the help of those pioneers who have landed on earth and who have interpolated through the means of earth methods, an understanding of the fourth dimensional physics of life, pointing out, articulating, and diagramming the evidence of the invisible fourth dimensional structure that is the entirety of man, which will resolve once and for all, the enigma and the separation in the fields of science, philosophy and religion, the knowledge of man as an energy system.

"As energy is a *RECREATIVE, REGENERATIVE FORCE*, stemming from the abstract Infinite, the nature of this abstract

Infinite Force will begin to be understood in the future, in a greater intelligent manner than ever before, because man has been separated from himself. He has only seen one-half of the movement of this Infinite Creative Force! He has been seeing the negative polarity of this great oscillatory system of life.

"The great abstract Heavens, as he has called it, is in reality, the many-faceted appearances of the face of the Father in its lowest possible gradation. Yet, even in the lower frequency of a physical universe, the substance of this Infinite, the Father, in its great awesomness, provides the balm and the healing attributes for man, as it indicates that he has the ability to live constructively and can take from the evidence of his life what he wishes, according to his desire. In every respect, there is never any completion in the recreation of knowledge as to who he is.

"It remains, therefore, for those who have gained the higher understanding, to realize the responsibility of their position in their recognition of this evolutionary design, for each and every human being presently involved in the beginning development of his spiritual evolution, is as important as the other. When Truth is learned of in some aspect, some function, some statement of life, that truth must be divulged and shared by any individual so capable of having gained the higher perspective, because he then is a brother of humanity and has the responsibility of adding the force of his own mentality to the ever-widening arch that is the environmental nature of progressive development!

"We speak in this manner then, of the new science of man - a universal science that explains and diagrams not only the nature of the evidential, physical geometry of the universe, but also of the spiritual geometry of this universe, that integrates the seeming separate appearance of life that resolves, once and for all, the enigma of society, the many breakdowns within the pattern of societal man.

"This science then explains the apparency of life from the perspective of the physical or negative perspective and the reality of life, from the recognition of the interrelationship and the constant movement of the two polarities of man, seemingly moving in opposite directions and yet, functioning at all times, to integrate man with his time-space dimension and also, with his fourth dimension.

"Time and space will have been seen on the one hand, to be an objective evidence of the third dimension from the ratification of the physical senses. But at the same time, time and space will be seen to be a subjective factor of man as he becomes more aware and biased to his fourth dimensional self, realizing that he can move away from his third dimension according to his understanding of the factors involved in becoming biased to his

spiritual self. He will then let go of
the training wheel and stand up on his
spiritual legs, no longer being restrct-
ed by the time-space dimension or being
restricted by his physical anatomy, but
free in his mind which has gained the
strength to function because he has
learned the technique of attunement.

"He has become an electronic engineer and has developed his anatomy to
that position whereby he has gained the
ability of selecting the higher channels of the timeless-spaceless dimension in which he will live in his future!
But this is the present, and the present
is a time and space in which man lives
in his physical body and is still grop-
ing for these futuristic understandings.
Unarius provides the mechanics for such
future development, and the future is
each and every moment that each individual so occupies any station in the
vast Infinite.

"Hence, Unarius is presented, not
as a distant future but as a present
statement of the opportunity to gain
what would seem to be a distant future,
where the enigmas of life and all of
the pressures of life are attendant in
this enigma. The lack of understanding
of the continuity of the past, etc.,
will be resolved. Unarius presents the
knowledge of a corrective, preventive
discipline to add to each individual's
awareness of life, the objective evidence of the evolutionary cosmos, to
add to each individual's consciousness
the evidence of his own perverse, past
negative life expressions. The two can-

not meet, because of the opposite nature in which the bias has been so set.

"Hence it is, that science must be an understanding of the corrective element that must be applied by mankind to change the energy wave forms which have been polarized on their negative placement. In order to gain the objective statement of the reality of life in the fourth dimension, as a moving energy force field, he can polarize the field force within himself that has been fragmented and has therefore not allowed him to regenerate his own consciousness of his spiritual nature from his opposite self, his higher Self.

"This is the statement, and how this statement will be resolved is therefore the basic function of science. Yes, science is a technique of measuring energy, but as we shall see in the further dissertations, this measurement will not be on the basis of resolving the fragments of energy as it has become some piecemeal appearance. But we will integrate these fragments which are the negative spectacle of mankind, and show how these fragments have gained their basic resolution and have therefore given the appearance of life to the many billions of earth people.

"It will be shown what the true science is - a science that is the unification of the right and left side of the Infinite - a science that displays the interdimensional statement of the spectacle of life, revealing not through rose-colored spectacles, but through a clear prism, the evidence of life that is lived by those who have attained to a higher intelligence!

"This has not been the statement of science and has been the difficulty of those individuals, because they have not been willing to accept the truth of their own inner awareness of their own spiritual self. They are fearful that they will become captives of an unaccepted school of thought. But until the man of science does state the truth of man as an important and, in fact, the *ONLY* importance in his essential desire to provide evidence of the electromagnetic nature of life, he himself loses his own strength, and his own progressive development is imperiled. Let us not be concerned then, with the statements of previous theories and hypotheses as to the validity of some theorem, but let us pronounce the objective statement of those who are advanced human beings, who are Elder Brothers.

# Chapter 4
# Music, the Symbolic Logic of the Whole Note

"In the recent history of less than one hundred years in the past, there was a particular individual, a mathematician and philosopher who, having given his entire life to the quest for the singularity of the symbol infinite, finally gave up his search with the statement, 'There is no apparent answer to this abstract concept that can be rectified by the symbols of mathematical logic!'

"Among others, Bertram Russell has been attempting to understand this basic keynote that drives man to formulate theorems within the representation of physical consciousness, to explain life through mathematical hieroglyphics, which is again a representative statement of man's higher intelligence. And yet such a statement cannot be completely fulfilled by means of methods that capture such knowledge with limitations that bespeak of the third dimension.

"This limitation, the third dimension, is but one-half of the chord structure of the whole note. Hence, the attempt to write on the musical score in mathematical, symbolic logic, as reference points, is incomplete and will always be incompleted until the equation has been satisfied by Einstein's relativity theory. Whatever man sees through the substance of the plasma of the half note of the Infinite will reveal another quandary and another part that exists within the movement of the Infinite!

"Not that the whole note is not playing throughout the symmetry of this Infinite, but that the musicians who are playing their instruments, have not been capable of hearing the full note. What they think they are hearing is not the full, completion of the musical score. It is this interpretation, based upon the incompletion of the instrument's capability to detect the full note that is at all times resounding to the finite individual from different interpolations, as they can hear certain facets of a deeper, complete phrase of this composition.

"In this manner then, music, the mathematics of sound and higher mathematics of the mind, is truly one and the same. The musician hears the complete sound mentally and demodulates this sound into derivative musical forms and amplifies the base notes of the lower frequencies into the third dimension, through the varieties of musical instrumentation. To the extent the individual musician is capable of reading the score, and has tuned his own instrument, he comes more closely to the equivalent whole note.

"Mathematical physicists are attempting to do the same, and have recognized the key element of great significance in their work, but they have not resolved this key element to the extent that it will be understood. There are many philosophical statements which have been rendered, which are an amplification of mathematical logic in the different interpretations in the attempt to understand the great symphony of the Infinite, to write the Score in some algebraic method.

"So to this extent, those who have learned of the whole note and who have played their instrument and have recreated this note so it pervades their consciousness, have brought back in their incarnations into the physical, third dimension a memory, an understanding, and an ability to reconstruct the substance of the fourth dimension within the lower key chord structure. Such individuals are René Descartes and Baron Gottfreid von Leibnitz, who respectively have discovered the differential calculus, a technique of understanding the finite properties of the whole, and to reconstitute these finite properties of the whole, in the manner in which these whole notes are functioning in life. In this development, these mathematicians have provided a greater certainty of life's nature within the broad kaleidoscope of the finite factors of the third dimension.

"We indicated to the reader in previous chapters that the third dimension is a lower chord structure of the whole note of the fourth dimension; that the fourth dimension has resolved itself atomically into its lower frequency energy field structures, which are the 92 physical atoms in their natural gestating state. With additional 'artificial' atoms that have been discovered in the scientific laboratories, there are now 109 atomic elements on the chart of the elements of the third dimension, as far as this Earth world is concerned. Hence it is in the constant regeneration of the atom, the many different particles in their combinations that form the many different heterogeneous appearances of life. It is in this heterogeneous appearance that we have the many differences which provide for man the ability to obtain his experience, which is to know of the Infinite; to know of it through his own individual note, which is the abstraction from the whole note.

"In this respect then, there is, in all of the differences that have ever been recreated, and which is the sum and total of the atomic dimension, an infinite-finite relationship of energy quotients. That is to say, that the great perplexity and enigma of life to understand the nature of the Infinite is that the Infinite is the finite derivative of Itself. Each finite component of the whole note will never, by its addition, ever be similar to the whole note. Each finite expression of energy has its own base plane frequency, and the amplification of each individual finite atom cannot ever equal the sum and total of the Infinite.

"On the other hand, dividing a particular energy quotient until it becomes reducible to its most finite appearance, will not merge that finite energy after it loses its identity in its submergence into the finite field of which it is a part.

"This is the great enigma and complexity of the regeneration of the field called life. In its macrocosmic equation, and in its microcosmic equation there is an asymptotic factor involved in that the finite properties of the Infinite will NEVER ever merge with each other. The structure of finite energy is a factor of the Infinite and cannot ever be reduced to lose its identity! It is that the base plane frequency which is the regenerative characgteristic and intelligence of this finite expression of the Infinite is coupling, and through its harmonic affiliation to another finite expression, does add to and express a greater, enlarged field.

"That enlarged field is the intelligence that is the sum and total of the individual expressionary quotients. The asymptotic characteristics described in mathematical logic, is the impossibility of merging two separate lines. Even though they seem to converge upon each other from a distance third dimensionally, they can never meet because there is the individuality of the base frequency, which is the attribute of these lines, which are energy systems. The mathematics of this logic is a basic clue for a greater understanding of man.

"Of the hundreds of countless trillions of Homo sapiens, no two individuals are alike in terms of their frequency. As two individuals could represent a line, it will be seen that the individuality of these individuals is an expression of the energy from which they have been created. That energy, of course, is the whole note of the Infinite Creative Intelligence. Each individual therefore represents a half note, a quarter note, and so on, of the entire musical composition or score of life. The Infinite can therefore be seen to contain in its musical rendition or mathematical rendition, finite notes which represent and are part of the entire score of the composition.

"Each individual, as he is a factor making possible the expression of the Infinite, represents a specific attribute, characteristic, and particular, specific intelligence. It is in this manner that life is a composition, an entire resolution. When the musician draws his bow over the stringed instrument and with the sensitivity that he has developed, he draws from his stringed instrument the complete musical score, as it has been written by an infinitely creative composer.

"In this respect then, mathematics is playing a great part in the recognition of the divisibility of third dimensional physics. Mathematicians such as Descartes, Leibnitz, and others, have indicated that the appearance of life contains the notes of an intelligent Score that can be rendered into a greater understanding and can be played. But each individual must learn the Score and must learn the appropriate symbolic logic that is involved in the abstraction from this field of energy containing all of the musical notes. Thereby, with the development of his own mental instrument, he can draw from the Score the proper information that will illicite a greater integrated awareness of his finite relationship to the musical Score. The composition, therefore, of himself will be rendered more complete to the extent that he appreciates his finite relationship to this infinite statement, which is the higher harmonic, containing the interrelationship of all things within themselves.

"Yes, it is very true that man has within himself, the ability to become a recognizable musician; but the musicology that man is developing and must develop, is the playing of his own instrument. That instrument is his mind! It is the mind that those advanced, more developed peoples have illicited their investigation into the harmony of life.

"There have been many mathematicians who have given their entire lives to learn of life's musical Score. They have discovered in life-to-life investigations, that musicology can only be developed in the fine tuning of the mind. Up to this point in the 20th century, there has been little success in this investigation of the relationship of the abstract Infinite, the musical Score or Composition, and the individual participants, who are the individual notes in this great musical Score.

"It has always been the objective

of certain individuals to fine-tune their minds: philosopher-scientists, mathematicians and other persons, in their endeavors to interpret for themselves, the complete composition of life. But in all respects, each and every individual must come to the recognition that the composition from which life is illicited, is a score they are reading but folded in half. Hence, they have not been able to read the entire Score and have not been able to complete the musical exercise. They have been playing on a half note, not a full note. This is a statement of present-day investigators who are doing science.

"Science is the exercise of man's mentality, with the recognition that there is an optical illusion in the appearance of life that we had indicated in the first chapters, until there is the awareness of the reality of what lies beneath the illusion! The physical appearance of life is the optical illusion that is the reflection through an instrument that renders a picture; a certain integrated field of energy necessary for the physical anatomy to gain its ability to contain itself to involve all organic parts, so the note in which it functions, will be the synthesis of a lower and yet complimentary note.

"The field equation of life that has been ascribed to particle physicists and mathematical physicists is that there are smaller and smaller micro-divisions within the larger appearance of energy. Whatever that energy has been so molded into; whether it be a chalk-mark on the blackboard; whether it be the flower waving in the wind; or whether it be man himself, each of these appearances of life are finite forms; some in a more simplistic development in terms of its energy constituents and others more complex, as is man. Yet the divisibility of the energy which is the quotient of life forms, divisible into its component parts, will never ever meld, nor will they blend and lose their individuality. In the same sense, the individual trillions of atoms which comprise the physical anatomy of man's body are indivisible, they are finite fields of energy which hold their separate, divisible intelligence, which as a whole, recreates an asymptotic reflection of life.

"Man, himself, reflects in his physical anatomy, the great mystery of life, so resolved into an understanding of a science of life, when it is understood that the Infinite is finite in its complimentary wholeness. Now this may seem a dichotomy, but let us examine the nature of the individual, physical anatomy, because on this base reflection, we will be able to go into the reality of these physical organisms. In other words, we will be able to see behind the appearance of the physical anatomy, the physical symmetry of the atomic world.

"The physical body itself represents the aggregates of trillions of atomic, cellular structures. Each cellular structure in itself, is a vast universe, containing individual molecules that are representing a specific movement of energy and recreating in this movement, specific intelligence, which is a pragmatic statement of some completion into the third dimensional appearance of life that will accomplish a particular job, which will have a particular purpose in bringing to the individual Homo sapiens, recognition of the pattern of life.

"Each individual cell then contains within it, innumerable molecular forms of consciousness, and these molecular forms of consciousness are divisible into atomic forms of consciousness. Yes, an atom is a conscious derivative of some pattern of intelligence, else there would be no rhyme or reason in the recreation of these innumerable, countless atomic formations, as the sum of them would be a nonsensical or senseless grouping of energy!

"But as a factor that is inclusive of these statements, each atom is an intelligent statement of energy information. Energy is intelligent, and the intelligence is of course qualitative to the degree of this intelligence. Any movement throughout the field of life that begins or ends with some activity, is intelligent. As the picture unfolds through the microscope, it reflects the microcosmic rendition of energy, the gestation of a fetus from an individual cell through the process of mitosis, regenerating, recreating and dividing within itself. Each individual cell, as a result of this regeneration, are individual energy compliments of the original cell, which have their own base plane frequency, their own individuality.

"Hence, as the entire organism of the physical anatomy has been recreated and regenerated, we see that it is the sum and total compliment of many millions of individual cells, each having a basic intelligence. This intelligence, as a whole, is making up the compliment to become a musical score.

"The physical anatomy can therefore be considered to be a composition, and that its reflexive composition is an exact picture of information from which it derived its intelligence. The Cosmic Mind, in the larger abstract nature and in the same sense, reflects the cell that becomes the fetus in the physical anatomy of a female; thus regenerating the nature of itself through complimentary characteristics. In this respect then, we have the polarity factors of the physical anatomy that are the sum and total of both male and female. The derivative is the child, the complimentary whole note, which can be considered the sum and total of the positive and negative characteristics of each individual half note, representing the male and the female parents.

"The child therefore contains the equivalent of characteristics of both male and female parents. In this respect, we see a regeneration of another field force of energy. The finite nature of the child that contains within itself the attributes of a larger field force of a different frequency, containing characteristics of different energy wave forms, musical notes, so to speak. Thus, another chord structure is recreated, and another factor of the larger composition of the Infinite has been rectified, amplified, all in accordance to the science that is the greater mathematics of life.

"Basically, we direct your minds to the understanding that the Infinite can only be understood through its finite characteristics. This totality is the finite characteristics, the entire medley of Infinity. The entire life force contains within itself the entire musical score; yet the enigma is that no two individuals can feel the same *EXACT* frequency in an audience, gathered to listen to a rendition of some music from a score that indicates the exact placements of the notes and the phrasing of these notes. Yet, as no two individuals in the audience will be able to replicate the exact feeling and sense, irrespective of their differences in frequency, they will feel the whole sense; the sense of being joined to the integrated, united fourth dimensional field from which the composition was authored!

"In the same sense, no two musicians will play alike, but will always play a rendition with such differences based upon their ability to instrument their own musicology. However, that is the nature of Infinity that it cannot be derived and replicated upon a chalkboard, or on a computer, because the greater the addition or subtraction of numbers, the greater becomes the ignominy of the entire proposition, as no two individuals or two individual lines will ever be joined, whereby they will lose their individuality!

"That is the entire statement of an Infinite Creative Intelligence. It is in the complimentary statements of life that man learns of his infinite nature; not in the divisibility. It is in this respect that whether he divides or adds, he will come to the same answer, which is and will be as far as man can see; whether it be through his physical organs or whether clairvoyantly through his mind, he will never be able to bridge a dimension, for ever beyond is the movement of the finite nature of the Infinite, constantly expanding its attributes into a greater Infinite. Yet within each individual characteristic of each individual energy wave form, there is contained the expression of greater intelligence that was the causative force for the initial wave form, which is expressing some facet or factor of life in some dimension.

"Through the third dimension, man is learning of these inherent processes of his mind. The mathematics of the mind is truly an endeavor which is evolutionary in its expression. There can never be the completion of the endeavor and the resolution of the nature of the Infinite, or else there would be an end to life itself. It is well that man realizes there is no complete answer in his attempt to resolve the nature of the invisible, which has not provided an image within his present lens structure. It is well that he continues to inquire into the nature of self. It is well that he continues into this inquiry of consciousness and uses all developmental factors of intelligence that have been the nature of present technology. It is well that he uses all electronic apparatuses which are projections of his own mental ability to ever inquire into the nature of life.

"Knowledge provides the mechanics to create the warp and the woof of a bridge, which will bring individual man to the realization of his infinite nature and of his finite nature. The duality that is man must then first be recognized, which mathematical physicists are not yet capable of resolving on their graphs, reflecting the nature and duality of life, because they have not yet seen the third dimensional statement of life; they have not yet seen the entire infinite nature of man as a whole note. That whole note is yet a finite property of the Infinite.

"The puzzlement therefore, that is the factor of Homo sapiens is reflected in Einstein's Equation $E=MC^2$. Man is the appearance of a physical mass, reflected from an atomic body, which also contains the property of energy. Man is E or energy; the mass of his body times the speed of light squared. To square the speed of light in the third diemsnion (186,000 miles per second) means that man is a fourth dimensional energy system.

"The higher mathematical statement of Albert Einstein is the pointer providing the clue to the true body of man, a dynamic energy system. It is man's energy system which is a factor greater than the speed of light in third dimensional equivalence. Hence, the energy body of man, his mind, functions at that specific mathematical equation of $C^2$. The square of 186,000 miles per second is therefore the fourth dimension! It is a dimension containing a life force that on the one hand is an attribute or characteristic of each individual, but at the same time, is uncharacteristic. Because man is living on two worlds and characteristically he contains the attributes of both worlds, yet he can only see each world separately according to the psychic spectacles that he wears.

"In the third dimension, he is wearing spectacles that are unpolarized, and therefore sees a reflection of energy field forces which are rectifications of the smaller component parts of the whole note; the atom and its particles in its 92 divisible notes. Therefore, in the third dimension, man is seeing the nature of life that is the separation of atoms in their representive forms as they make up the entire mandate of the physical dimension. That is, the entire property of life is the building of an environment: homes, streets, all moving objects, man's body himself, from the separate and yet complimentary atomic elements which were derived from their initial whole form. He can therefore only see what he can rectify through his glasses because the glasses he wears are themselves recreated from the atomic forms of these structures.

"Yet since man is a product of the whole note, he is the energy that is now resolved into mass. When the mass of himself is resolved into its energy substance, he can see from his polarized glasses the nature of his world without refraction from individual unpolarized elements of the real atom.

"The fourth dimension is therefore the gathering together of the individual relationships of its whole nature or structure, where the representation of life is a truer reflection of Infinity, the Infinite Creative Intelligence in terms of its positive and negative polarities. In this respect, the duality of the Infinite lies within the opposite reflections of itself, whose opposite reflections are integrated to the degree where both sides are functioning to synthesize the atomic nature of life.

"You could say that the fourth dimension has an atomic equation as well; but the atoms are functioning on a higher frequency. They are moving at a rapidity which cannot be rectified through unpolarized lenses, but they must be rectified through a polarized lens. That means that the individual who is looking through the plasma of that fourth dimension would have to be capable of synthesizing the energy structures of himself so he could see the picture in his mind, which is the reality of the higher structures that have been generated by the people who have gained the higher architectural ability to recreate the isotopic environment into relative forms reflecting to them the nature of life.

"The only difference, if there is any difference, is that the entire appearance of life is a recreation from the energy fields. In the third dimension this energy is molded so that it attains an appearance crafted from the so-called putty of third-dimensional atomic forms of a lower frequency. The same representation is a factor in the fourth dimension. But since the fourth dimension is the transmitter itself of the third dimension, it contains within it, the representations of all factors of life that have been a development by Homo sapiens. Hence, this evolutionary development provides the synthesis or the integration for that individual to develop his polarized consciousness so he can clearly see how he had been separated by time and space in the half note of the third dimension.

"So again and again it is seen how this process is an understanding and a development, evolutionary-wise, within the broad scheme of civilizations, and that the evidence for the design of interdimensional life has to be realized from civilizations to civilizations. There have been travelers in the great voyage in which man is involved, who have traveled from the third dimension to the fourth dimension, and who have returned with greater knowledge and understanding. These voyagers have, in many respects, successfully given the people in the various societies the knowledge of the integrated or whole note of life. They have described how man is a singular note within the grand design of life and that he is only capable, while living in the physical organism, to see a divisible part of his finite self. The other part of himself, which would complete the nature and understanding for him to see the greater content of himself, has not yet been integrated within his present consciousness.

"In spite of life experiences, man's aspirations and hopes have been dashed into incompletions where he has, in some respect, dashed himself against the barrier of his third dimension, the so-called objective illusion of life. Yet, through all of these experiences, he realized there was a hope, an aspiration, a desire and an unrealizable statement that he had always been functioning to resolve. He has recognized that he cannot explain the nature of himself as a life force by miniaturizing life in its physical appearance. The only means by which he can understand himself is to realize the telltale note that speaks to him of a whole factor; the Infinite Mind speaking to him, as he is a part of the great Infinite Score.

"Why has it been difficult for man to understand that there is another side to life? In spite of all of the evidence that has been generated to him by travelers from beyond time and space; yet man as a whole, has not given credence to this realization! It lives within the breast of all man, and yet he has not had the courage to speak of what he knows. The science of life is the recreation of every single note that is regenerated from his physical instrument and from his energy instrument. It is in this respect that the great learning takes place and is constantly developing with each individual. As he plays upon the instrument of himself, he has the implicit realization that if he is out of tune, the accompanying explosion is the result.

"The cacophony of physical life is the lack of attunement of the individual seeing into the other side of himself, and joining the two together whereby he can realize the nature of his own finite-infinite expression. The other side of oneself is the discovery of the ages! The other side of life is within each individual's ability to discover. The other side of life is his Mind, because the mind contains the schematic. But that schematic is not complete until the mind becomes expanded within the knowledge of its scientific logistics!

Until then, the mind is a generalized statement, a word that connotes many different meanings. The logistics of the mind is the ability of an individual to tune into some specific operation in which he is involved in some life project.

"We mean by 'mind' the diagrammatical nature of its energy field. We mean by 'mind' the understanding of the polarity structure of the individual. We mean by 'mind' the greater awareness of the accompanying interrelationship of the past, present, and the future. The mind, when it is understood in this expanded manner, will be the attainment of intelligence, whereby he is quickened with the realization of his responsibility as an important factor within the musical score of Infinity. As a finite expression of this musical score, he is yet a factor of great importance, because he is an irreducible movement within the grand panoply of the Cosmic Mind.

"So to learn of the nature of Consciousness, to develop Cosmic Consciousness is to learn of the important relationship in which the entire musical note of man has been derived. The characteristics of it, its function will give each individual the greater and broader consciousness as to the nature of his instrument. It is this instrument which man is playing upon. He is playing upon the lower chord structures at the present time, using the derivative understanding of it from his physical conscious awareness of these lower notes. It is the TIME OF THE AWAKENING OF MAN to the realization of his higher note, which is the Higher Consciousness, the REALITY of his re-creative energy structure!

"That is to say, that this mind itself is an anatomy that corresponds to the physical body, but has a greater and an imperishable field; a field that is in every respect, an electromagnetic force that can move mountains! It can move planets; it can move suns; and yes, galaxies! This is, of course, the complimentary nature of the finite expression of the Infinite in some individual who has learned of the physics of energy and has realized that he can become the entire complimentary orchestration of a composition to realize the entirety of this composition within his own consciousness! For in this manner does the Infinite and the finite become understandable and recognizable.

"The individual musician, as he plays his instrument in the larger orchestra, is blending within the finite frequencies emitted by each individual instrument, and it is the harmonics which are the compliment of each individual frequency that engenders the greater note, which can be felt by each finite or each individual musician. Therefore, as man attains to this understanding of the physics of energy, the higher sound that is emitted from this greater harmonic, attains the realization that he does have a factor of great importance in his ability to feel the imperishable note of the Infinite, because the Infinite is the polarized regeneration of other finite representations within the entirety of this 'musical composition'.

"Yes, it is a science when the understanding of the finite properties of life are developed. In this manner, each individual will be that much more capable of accepting the nature of each other as a finite and yet infinite property of the great Cosmic Mind, the regenerative, Infinite Intelligence. Each individual, in learning how to work with other individuals, in this sense, will attain to a greater harmony within himself, and as a whole, he will have regenerated a balanced signal, a musical note which contains its own derivative as harmony. Anything that is opposite to music is cacophony, is unharmonious, and is therefore out of tune. Where two or more individuals are in harmony, so are they harmonizing with the Infinite Regenerative Recreative Intelligence, which is the sum and total of all finite attributes of the great life that has been called by so many names: the Father, the Fountainhead, the Creative Infinite Intelligence.

"As we have initially stated, the asymptotic characteristic of finite factors of life that have been resolved in mathematical linguistics, is an exact statement of the finiteness of life. Only those who have developed within their own energy system the knowledge of the duality that exists within each finite expression of life will be able to realize the immensity of this understanding. Each finite derivative of life stands as a whole note eventually, when the whole note is understood within that individual, whose mind is carrying the complete composition of the Infinite. As he learns how to draw his bow on his own polarized instrument, he will thereupon realize his own infinity and will be a part of the Grand Design, a music of unparalleled beauty that will speak for itself and will carry such a person to the highest of the heavens!

"Yes, this may be considered to be abstract and may be considered to be mathematical physics, which is an abstract statement, using the symbols of differential calculus, geometry and other forms of symbolic logic. However, when it is polarized within the mind of an individual, he can see in stark reality the reason why it is important for man to know of the truths of this science, in that he is functioning at all times to either carry the symmetry of a great musical score or he is breaking this symmetry by being responsible for carrying a bad or inharmonious note; that is to say, he is out of tune!

"This out-of-tuneness is the general statement of the mish-mash that is the nature of the breakdown of society! The society is the rendition of all finite notes that are learning through their cause and effects that if they are out of tune, the entire instrument, which is man, his physical and mental oranisms are out of tune and he suffers as a result. This individual's negative effect is also harmonically rectified into the sum and substance of society, which are the compliments of all individuals who are functioning as finite factors of life. Again we see how the representation in the very factual manner of dimensional life cannot function alone.

"The finite of each individual is dependent upon other finite forms. It is in interrelationships as such that one learns of the infinite nature of finite factors of life. One must then be in agreement, for the only way to have a world in which there is a harmony, in which the music that is heard by each individual is in tune, is for the properties of this finite man himself to be in tune with the respective finite nature of other individuals. In each individual is the expression of the whole composition and can be rendered to be heard through attunement. In the many different, seemingly insoluble problems that are facing man today, the basic one being the nuclear armament, is the realization that the entire disharmony of life will confront society with the realization that they have been building a composition that contains out-of-tune notes that do *NOT* compliment each and the other.

"They have so many different degenerative fragmentary built-in characteristics that they do not add up to an over-harmonic of a positive nature, but rather, of an underharmonic which is dividing, separating, and therefore dissolving the complimentary nature, which is the harmonic nature of man as a spiritual being.

"The entire 'arms conflict' is therefore a recognition that man has been walking down the wrong side of the road and has taken the wrong turn. In the very nature of this disharmony, in the very appearance of the possible disintegration of his appearance of life, man is realizing the opposite nature that lies within himself. He is drawn to the positive statement of life by having the abundant reflection of the negative side or polarity of himself. In this manner, in this larger reflection of the problems of society, we have seen how evolution speaks for itself. One either individually and as a whole, progresses or regresses.

"Progression is the compliments of additive whole notes, and regession is the complimentary additive of half notes that will evolve according to the complimentary nature of their structure, causing either a reduction within the integrated association of that energy structure, whereby the ability of that energy structure will cease to have the capability of recreating a physical anatomy. On the other hand, the energy structure that gains its strength by the complimentary nature of adding to itself, then its positive refractions from the Infinite will itself, become so polarized that it will not need to refract the lower structure of a physical body, but will gather within its own structures, greater complimentary refractions of the music of the Infinite, whereby it becomes a higher frequency, keyed to the wider aperture in the higher notes of this greater chromatic structure of the Re-creative Infinite.

"Each individual thereby regenerates an energy structure that learns the sensitivity of attunement to the wider field that is the polarization of other individuals who have attained to the higher sense of their spiritual nature, a complimentary function in a wider consciousness, so polarized that they are in tune with each other and therefore, attuned to the Cosmic Mind. They are then individuals who have attained Cosmic Consciousness. They are aware on the one hand, of their individual selves, but have also resolved that enigma of the asymptotic characteristic of finite things. They have resolved the polarity characteristics of life and have joined their positive and negative selves to the extent that they are now hearing and also recreating the whole note of the Infinite.

"This is the nature of those individuals who are capable of writing these statements that are the basic representatives of the whole note. These individuals are scientists who have learned the nature of their mind, the great energy that is but a dot, almost unseen by the physical eye; a dot which represents in its cellular formation the entire Infinite, Creative Intelligence! That dot is a particle within the small atom; yet that dot represents an understanding to those who have been polarized to the reality of interdimensional life. It has become the 'reality' for those individuals who have striven to learn of the content of their own spiritual selves.

"Yes, this is *THE AWAKENING OF MAN*, because man is unawakened as yet to his abstract nature, his infinite nature that he cannot yet make out. It is this understanding that is coming into the world of man and waking him up to the higher note that has not yet been sounded within himself. As man is not singular, the infinite nature of man resounds and amplifies this understanding. As one man is awakened, so does he awaken the second and third and fourth! This is the nature of harmonics and the awakening of man from his deep slumber by the Unariun Brotherhood!"

## Chapter 5

## Chaos and the Cosmic time

"The mechanistic view of the universe that was illustrated in the Newtonian revolution in the 1700's, suggested that the entire nature of man and the movement of the planets in the galactic system could be understood in a calculated manner, no different than a clock in which the twelve hours are predetermined and the hands function in a consistent manner, relative to the particular division of time. Hence, the mechanistic view of the universe gave man a simplistic view and yet a dependency upon this viewpoint that would enter into all factors of life from the biological to the astronomical.

"Order, therefore, was a deterministic statement of the Newtonian physics in which the universe was seen to be a giant mechanism. Man was therefore one of the numbers that had been predestined as a part of the giant clockwork of this universal Force. However, with the development of the relative theories of Einstein, the quantum-mechanic theories of Planck, the uncertainty principle of Heisenberg, the notion of the mechanistic view of life was shattered.

"It was seen that time, as it was the statement of the past, present and future, could not be retrieved once the hands of the clock had been so set and the motion so begun. Time could not be retrieved because of a new concept that entered into the thinking of the scientists; a concept called 'entropy' wherein the universe is a mass, a quantity of matter. The mechanistic view of life was such that it must wind down as all mechanical instruments reach a point in which the entire internal nature of itself reaches a boundary line. This is the concept of entropy, that the universe reaches a point after which it no longer can expand and will reduce the nature of its mass and fall back within itself. This whole conjecture resolves into the concept of the 'big bang' theory, which claims that a primordial atom was the basis for the beginning of life. This expansion is the present state of matter in the universe, and the appearance of the galactic systems that will wind down, to again repeat as a big bang or explosion of the primordial atom.

"These statements which establish the entire nature of the uncertainty of evolution, that have been extrapolated by the works of Charles Darwin and others of his contemporaries, which indicate that man, as he is the expression of all of the organisms of the species of planetary life, is an expasionary and ever more complex statement of life. In other words, there is an evolution taking place in which the simpler organs of life become more complex.

"The complexity is a development known as evolution; the evolution of the species in which the amoeba has been concluded, at least at the present time, as a statement of Homo sapiens in the billions of years of this development. This statement of life is much more accurate and explains the developmental nature of man; at least from the organism of its physical anatomy to a more complex organism. That is to say, the present mass of the physical anatomy has itself become the complex organism that contains within it the complexities of its individual finite organs, which altogether, are the unified orchestration of a life form. This life form is the key to the nature and composition, which in fact is the Infinite Concept of life; a note that can be heard through the organisms of this physical anatomy, so sensitized to the extent that the more complex higher organism of Spirit can be recognized.

"So it is that entropy, a factor of the mechanistic view of life, a derivative of the mechanistic view of life, is a factor isolated by itself that makes no sense. But when it is understood as a part of the whole of the complex structure through which the panoply of the orchestration of life is its development, it can then be seen to be a part of the process.

"The evolution of life is in the development of the individual quotients of the processes of man's awareness of his spiritual nature. This awareness, as we have indicated in previous chapters, is attained through the process of mitosis; the process of bifurcation, which is the separation of any whole note into its two halves. It is in this separation which is the key understanding for mankind to realize that he is a developing note in the complex scenario of the Infinite, and it is only through this complexity that he realizes his unity. That unity can be the recognized harmonic note which he becomes sensitive to, by having gained the integration of those individual factors of the Infinite, of its higher composition. These finite factors are attained through the processing of life experience.

"It is said that man can only learn through experience, which in its entire meaning, is that he engages in the complexities of the logistics of life's process. That, of course, is the infinite, creative expression, but that Infinite Creative Intelligence, although a constant expurgation of Itself into the very smallest atomic element, cannot be recognized until the sensing agent, 'man', gains a specific development in his evolutionary development, the reassembling of the individual quotients of this unitary or Cosmic Mind. This is the entire nature and purpose of third dimensional life and is the present development in third dimensional physics, to see behind the apparition, behind the appearance of the atomic form of life.

"It is in this seeing that scientists have come and are still coming to the awareness of a science of life that unites the biological, physical systems of man and his society. It is the external nature of the vast cosmogeny and the internal nature of this vast biological system, which in every respect are reflective factors of themselves. Each and the other are relationships which make up for the unity and the awareness of the species man, to understand that great puzzle of who he is, why he is and what is his purpose. Life is, in fact, the assembling of the complicated organisms, the seemingly disparate appearance of life. He sees the nature of the organisms of life somehow separated in time and space and has the feeling of himself as a separate organ that has its own life.

"Time therefore, is man's great mystery. Time is illusive; it is the shadow cast by man in the physical environment of his earth world and where man goes so goes time. Yet in all the questions asked by those who themselves have learned of the proposition of this cosmic time where time and space no longer provide that specific mystique, these individuals have been able to add another indice to the chess game that is the involvement of people on the chess board. They have been able to add specific component factors which are the unending molecular grouping and regroupings which indicate certain key factors in the moves which can finally result in some completion in the entirety of the game that is the nature of the complex nature of man's own machinery - his mind!

"There is one such individual who has brought a specific understanding of this evolutionary nature of life. His work has not yet been completely brought to the attention of the public as a whole, Ilya Prigogni, who has indicated that out of chaos there emerges certainty. In the complex movement of atoms which are the basic stuff of a third dimensional mass universe, in their eternal groupings and regroupings, order will emerge from the chaos, because it is the nature of the Infinite to always achieve this end result! Chaos is the subjective observer's awareness of the complex nature of the atomic movement of energy, but since the observer has not yet the complete awareness of the entire chess board, the chess pieces and the many, many countless moves that can be made, he is basically seeing a closed system, an isolated or local system of life.

"Man is seeing a specific instance of life which has been the basic quandary of scientists in their extrapolation upon the vast cosmological scene where they have done their research in certain small squares and then attempted to indicate how the result of that research will be effective in the entire universe.

"In this sense then, the subjective nature of the researcher is his uncompleted knowledge of the physics of the Infinite. In other words, at the present time, those who are other than interdimensional scientists, are working in a small room and are unable to discern the additional rooms of the house and to conceive the architecture rendering, to realize the nature of the materials that have been the responsible factors for the appearance of this structure.

"Scientists have been working on different parts of this structure in different rooms of the house. They have come up with different results according to the nature of their interpretation through the window from which they were viewing the enigmatic universe. They have not been able to come to an agreement within the nature of their hypotheses which contain diverse agreements as to the reality of their findings. This is so, because physical scientists have not integrated their individual subjective interpretations of the panoply of the complexity of life.

"The complexity is of course, the nature of the Infinite Itself to enable mankind to develop the tools whereby he will learn of his own architectural structure because the material universe is the negative polarity of Infinite Intelligence and does provide the clues of its alternate self, its positive or antimatter structure. That is the entire purpose of the developmental statements of the sciences which lack that integrated wisdom that can view the whole; that is to say, the relationship between the alternate and complex movement in which the myriad of atomic elements can change into the almost unlimited forms in its pairing and its complex evolutionary development.

"It is on this same basis that the number of cards in the deck totaling 52 can form several million possible combinations. It is in this manner that we see evolutionary development in which atomic combinations evolve seemingly chaotic, yet it is in this manner in the internal regroupings and changing relationships that a new order and new sequence develops of a higher order of species. This is the nature of the biological development of the physical anatomy. This is the development of the internal systems of society where man, who is this complex regrouping of atomic elements is regrouping in additional complex patterns amongst the many millions of its own kind.

"Hence, we have the varieties of different complexities resulting in countless societal problems. From the many different combinations therefore, of the elements that make up physical life, there is also the development of a greater intelligence, the emerging nature of new reformations that develop out of the regrouped pairs that have regenerated additional harmonics of itself. The entire nature of this puzzlement has been the field of inquiry of biologists attempting to understand the complexity of the DNA and to wonder about its primary nature.

"Particle physicists are working to understand the internal field of atom physics, whereas biologists are working to understand the internal nature of the cellular structure of the physical anatomy. Both are working within the alternate nature of the Infinite. The biologist is studying the greater atom which is man, and the atomic physicists are working in the sub-infinite order of the atom. But the chaos that is supposedly seen within the atom, which does not obey the mechanics of Newtonian physics, has finally been resolved with the recognition of the uncertainty principle of the electron.

"The subject that is man and the object that is the Infinite, contains a barrier in the attainment of some certain unified principle that would unite the subject with the object of his research! The greatest puzzlement is that the object is the subject and the subject is the object. This may seem diaphanous, but it is the entirety of an infinite concept that cannot be determined until the individual who is the researcher and is looking at himself, is aware of himself as that infinite concept.

"The Infinite Concept is the equation of $E=MC^2$, at least on a certain level within the resolution of atomic physics.

"Evolution is a grouping and regrouping of finite quantas of energy which finally resolve into a certain development whereby that development which is a species of life, can become operative and develop to be a product, which product will have an evolutionary purpose in adding to and advancing the finite properties of the Infinite in its greater complexity. In the present 20th century, this additive nature of life is the present 20th century on Earth; the various divisive statements in which man is presently involved in a separation, seemingly from the whole nature of himself. There are in the entire environmental nature of the earth, the components of life, as many nations and different nations have different attitudes as to how their peoples should live their day-to-day life. The people themselves have differences in terms of what they expect from the many different derivatives of life, to extract from their lands and the waters of their rivers and oceans, and from the space that surrounds them. The complexity that is the present 20th century, in terms of the computer revolution, the technological impact in which this development has attenuated and has drawn people of the world together in a communication medium, has shrunk the oceans and dissolved the national barriers that once were a separation between the Eastern and the Western hemisphere and between the different nations!

"However, we are looking into the nature of the many puzzles that have been studied by those individual scientists who are concerned with the interdimensional principles of life; the whys and wherefores of its seemingly physical appearance. It was Prigogni, an advanced thinker, who bridges the diverse disciplines in science; one who has experienced the integrated nature of the mind as a fourth dimensional equation, who has advanced to the awareness of the interdimensional nature of life as it is reflected into its physical properties.

"He has successfully looked behind the silver of the mirror and seen the real structure of energy. He has guessed and correctly so, the evolutionary design of Infinite Intelligence and has seen the vortexal nature of this great energy expression that is Infinity, as it has reformulated itself within the physical nature of the third dimension, where it is noted that man is learning of his spiritual nature. That is to say, he is learning of the all-creative factor of his inner or mental self that was created from the Cosmic Mind.

"It was Prigogni, therefore, who has added an element that will help to unite the diverse disciplines in the scientific community by pointing out that a new development always results from the chaos of an older order. In a true sense, this is the completion of a cycle; a cycular change. This cycular change is similar to the appearance of man's physical body at so-called death. The physical anatomy has reached the pinnacle of its cyclic development where the atomic elements have revolved through certain cyclic time and completed its purpose. The physical atoms have reached that point of entropy and dissolve or fall back into the abstract elements of the universal atom!

"It is this physical change and the evolutionary design of the material body, as well as other material factors of life that have allowed certain scientists to accept the mechanistic view of life. Although energy contains a mechanism, it is a mechanism that does not follow third dimensional designs. That is, the mechanism of life is a universal mechanism that functions on cycular relationships with new forms of energy that have formed a new engagement within the nature of its own nature. Then in its evolutionary development, this energy becomes a new formation and another factor of a higher intelligent character. We are speaking, of course, of the very basic principle of frequency and harmonics. We can see this principle reflected in the very elemental notes of music, or in the pulsing of a stretched wire.

"Yet we must associate this in the more complex manner of the movement of the individual component parts that make up the physiology of the physical anatomy and the internal nature of the electromagnetic force field in which all anatomies function and gain their life force. It is in this constant movement of two universes, so to speak, the inner and the outer universe, the inner organism of the physical anatomy and the outer organism of the electromagnetic anatomy, that there is the constant regeneration of harmonics.

"Harmonics are the interchanging and the regrouping of individual characteristics that have been developed to come to an isochronal pulse. At that peak there is a heterodyning of associated energy force fields which catalyze and regenerate new associations of energy field forces to become another factor of revealed life forms. In a large order, this is the evolutionary development of mankind and of his society. That is to say, man is the minor chord, and the major chord is the electromagnetic field that seemingly surrounds man which is the abstract face of the Infinite.

"From a local closed circuit where man sees the appearance of life as a physical phenomenon, he sees the physical phenomenon change in front of him. He thus determines from that base phenomenon or change that there are certain laws involved. Therefore, when the physical body loses its prime force, that is the motivating force, the spirit that had activated that mass body, he localizes this event and extrapolates on this event, the movement of energy that is responsible for this apparent change.

"The corpse can be seen, over a period of time, to reduce itself to its 16 natural elements in its corrosion, and the skeletal form that remains can itself be reduced to the chemical elements of the basic 16 atoms. Therefore the principle of entropy can be validated on that basic physical evidence. Yet, the very chemicals that are the composition of this physical anatomy are again recreated and become a factor in the regeneration of some new species. Whether it be mineral, plant and vegetable, or animal, the atomic elements that were responsible for the creation of the physical anatomy are regenerated into a new order of species, the combinations of which take on another characteristic.

"Therefore, the chaos that can be seen to be the completion of the organism of a physical body in which the body was represented as being the real individual, would seem to be chaotic and an instance where there is no rhyme or reason in life. But when the order is understood in terms of the equivalent relationship of Spirit, that high energy quantum, the psychic body - the electromagnetic body - and its structure recognized as a prime factor in the orderly process of life, there can then be a more complete and fuller understanding of the truth of what lies behind the apparency of physical life!

"This apparency is the dichotomy of the atomic nature of the physical universe. Physical scientists have been peering through the windows of various instruments, viewing the dancing atom structure of matter, and attempting to make some order out of their movement. But that alone will not explain the reality of the electromagnetic field force. In many respects, they are like the reflection of light from the sun on the water of some river, but constantly changing because of the movement of the water. Therefore, there is no way to determine their nature by a picture that will be capable of being frozen to explain the entirety of this light, the molecules of the water, and the interrelationship between the two.

"Except on a local interpretation, one cannot resolve the entirety of the life pattern in which man is the main instrument! In all interpretations of atomic energy, no one has yet aimed their magnifying glass correctly into the interior structure of the physical atom, in the sense that they have been able to distill the true nature of the shadow.

"Man is an evolutionary development. Therefore, in his development where he becomes aware of the greater and greater complexities of himself and begins to put two and two together and realizes that the exterior nature of what he believed to be a separate characteristic of himself, is the ever moving River of Life, which contains in truth, the nature of his life expression. But it must be that evolution is the slow, ever-developing addition of newer elements which add to and derive a greater perspective for man to realize the immensity and the simplicity of life.

"In the very complex movement of the individual singular atom, as they engage with each and the other, to make up the face of a physical system, there is the simple knowledge that is finally attained by the truth seeker. That simple knowledge is that the very complex organism, which is his physical anatomy and his mental anatomy, when united become a beat frequency in accord with the harmonic of which it is a whole part. Then man recognizes his individuality and his place in the infinite scheme of life.

"It is simple when one is no

longer fighting the evidence of the molecular nature of life. Man is but a molecule in this respect, and he cannot function separately from other molecules or else he loses his basic nature; that is, he loses his expression as a part of the larger composition and no longer can hear the cosmic music. The simple, isochronal nature of life is in relationships where one loses concern with self as a separate function of the great orchestra. He then becomes a part of the composition, a true participant; a self that is selfless; a self that is participating and adding to and hence, receiving the assembled harmonics of great music, which is the rendition of the infinite chord structure called Infinite Intelligence!

"Infinite Intelligence therefore rings in, because of the attunement of the musician's own stringed instrument, his mind. He therefore rings in the harmonics that contain the intelligence which surrounds the entirety of his person and with the awareness of his part in the great orchestra of life. But as we have been witness to the pageantry of history on Earth, this understanding has been attained by certain individuals, few in number in comparison to the larger population. Yet these few in number have become the orchestra leaders who have been training the individual musicians who are man.

"Hence, man is gaining in his understanding under the competent leadership of certain ones who have themselves advanced to that higher platform; not because they came to that understanding in a sudden full measure, but developed this understanding. As consciousness is a developmental factor of evolution, man proves to himself and forms his own strength through the addition of the many component notes of life. Such an individual therefore becomes an Elder Brother! He is the orchestra leader! Of course, such individuals who have learned and attained to a wider Consciousness in their relationship to the whole note of the Infinite, become basic examples to the earthman and can, in some respects, share their understanding. However, this sharing can only be expressed if they are able to work within a particular society in some particular earth planet at a certain time in the cyclic development in which the many composite expressions of finite life are taking their part.

"This is what was meant in the statement by Spiritual Masters: It is in the major cycles in which man is progressing and retrogressing when a Master appears at that time, to help in the orchestration of a new cycle. He arrives at a time when the old cycle is coming to a close, when there seemingly is great chaos in life, and all signs are pointing to a disintegration of civilization! It is a time when the old is giving way to something new that cannot yet be determined because the development is in its formative stage.

"Man is still in tune with the

old cycle that is dying, but becoming aware of a birthing of new ideas, attitudes and relationships that have not yet come to their maturity, for they are still in their birth development. To people who are in this cycle of chaotic turmoil, great disorder, climactically, economically, and politically, in the complex customs and folkways of interdependent life in their individual communities, this is the end of a minor cycle of 2,000 years, and is the indication of negative past-life experiences. Since the past can never be completely reconstituted in the present, this is the basic principle that we have stated regarding Newton's mechanical universe.

"The past, as it is lived in the present, does cause chaos. It is the chaos engendered within the old cycle. This is the cosmic design of Infinite Intelligence, whereby the Infinite is constantly regenerating through cyclical movement within the complex nature of its own Nature, regenerating new and greater relationships of its finite organisms, its finite natures. The past, when it is relived in the present, which is another cycle, does bring with it the malfunctions, aberrations and all other factors of energy which have been stretched out of their natural regenerative nature.

"In this respect, the cycle in which the present Earth is going through is the statement of various factions within society, who are attempting to relive their past. The past cannot be recreated in the exact nature in which it was lived in previous ages of time: 100, 200, 500, 1,000 or 2,000 years ago by those who would wish to recreate biblical times to live as their forefathers, with the same customs, folkways and mores. There are many, many people who are, in this sense, hanging on to the past, literally speaking, and attempting to reconstitute it into the present as a continuity of the customs of their people, the customs of their society, in the many different manners in which present society is functioning, attempting to recreate spent energy. In every respect, this energy is out-of-tune, out of sync. It is functioning on its own frequency in a closed circuit and can never be relived in the exact same manner in which the energy was formerly used through the physical and mental bodies of man. It was not meant to be!

"This energy was meant to be a format through which the experiences so gained by any individual was a lesson, a teaching, to be distilled into a concept containing the intelligence which would provide a progressive development to any individual. When he returned from his sojourn in the astral worlds, he would thus have a stronger format of life experience, which would add to his present incarnation. He would not come empty-handed to his new life, but would come with the evidence of past-life experience, whereby he would attempt to add new complexities of a progressive nature. However, that is not the simplistic way in which it has occurred; because life is an ever-living statement of regenerating the past and learning that the past cannot be lived in the exact same manner, mentally speaking.

"Naturally, people attempt to recreate their past in some manner and way as a means of gaining the familiarities which provide them with a sense of security. We are referring, of course, in the main, to the mental understandings for the purposes of life, in which certain interdimensional principles of life have been learned. Man lives as a family; yet the family is divisive, not knowing of its complimentary association and the value of complimenting each with their own individuality, to make up a higher note that will, by its own regeneration, recreate a higher positive note to its individual component parts.

"Such individuals as the Unariun Brothers, have entered into the force field of this third dimension with knowledge of the evolutionary design of atomic physics and of other disciplines of knowledge which are evidence of man's past: paleontology, archeology, history, philosophy, chemistry, physics and astronomy. This is the evidence of man's societal order, of his psychological and sociological context. And it is through the evidence of his inner reality, of his spirit, that man attains the knowledge of the nature of his higher Nature.

"But the patch quilt that is the

development in each evolutionary cycle of 2,000 years contains both the progressive nature of the cycle and the retrogressive nature of the cycle. This principle of cyclic evolution has not been completely understood; in fact, it has not yet come to the clear view of these aforementioned scientists. A cycle contains both positive and negative polarities. Therefore, the sense that can be made of the present 20th century, of the many inarticulate factions who speak of the 'reality of life', represent the retrogressive nature of this cycle of negative factions living in the past. These are the religious fanatics who wish to return to God, as he expressed himself as Jehovah, Lord, Krishna, Buddha, or Jesus. They would wish to return to the words of these individual prophets, We Elder Brothers.

"But in the context of the past, not having recognized the teachings that were scientific in nature, their teachings are an exterior statement of an awesome God who will punish, who is 'looking down' at the individual he has created. God is an anthropomorphic figure. Also, there are those who would rule by might, who believe in the heavy stick; militarists who would, by any means, hold their fortress against invasions by some alien force.

"This is the negative polarity of a cycle, and it is the context which is posed against the positive polarity, to become the progressive nature of energy. This progressive nature is associated with certain individuals who are in tune with the forward motion of the Infinite and are part of the progressive nature of life. They are the humanists! They are individuals who are attempting to integrate man with the understanding of his spiritual nature and of the devastating blows that would be made to his progressive evolution should he add to the repercussive nature of war and other divisive factors of society through which the old is attempting to control and obliterate the new.

"It is this catalytic action in the completion of a cycle where there seems to be chaos in the entire picture of society; yet within this chaotic appearance there is great order, because a new order is taking place. A rectification of new elements of the Infinite and in its finite derivation, are reassembling new understandings which are coming to the surface of man's consciousness. These new understandings are the teachings of a Science of Life, a science that is the New World Teaching, bringing order out of chaos!

"It is this that is the catalytic action of those conductors who are orchestrating this new development. They are the Elder Brothers, Universal Minds who have attained to the position in their perspective by being able to play all the notes of the orchestra and harmonize these notes into a new orchestration. Therefore, that is the resolution of this newer understanding by those musicians who are members of this orchestra.

"This understanding, of course, will be the integration within the scientific community of astronomers and the atomic physicists, cosmologists and biologistis, pantheologists and archeologists, historians, philosophers and religionists, to see the full expression of life as a consonant, not a dissonant note. It will only be because all local systems will have been bridged, whereby the biologists will be able to appreciate the work of the astrophysicist, who appreciate the work of the chemist, so on and so forth; an integration and synthesis of the many departments of life which are local, closed systems that have kept man separated from the entire orchestra.

"You cannot play as a member of an orchestra 'out of tune', else the entire orchestration is detracted from its purposeful composition.

"The basic of this discussion is to point out that within all of the phenomena being developed of an understanding of the movement of the Light Forces, there is one basic statement: Energy must be the reconstituted understanding within the body politic of all peoples on all levels of life, whether they be in science or whether they be in politics or in religion. In the entire construction of mankind in society, this understanding of the Spirit as a science is the 21st century New Teaching. This is a new Science and a new cycle!

"This cycle, the New Age of Spiritual Renaissance, is exactly what it says. A Spiritual Renaissance is an awakening, a redevelopment, so to speak, of the understanding of man as an energy system! The Spirit of Man will therefore be the particular curriculum of life and will be the teaching for all peoples as they will call upon themselves the true spiritual aspect in which they have been created and formed by the higher Forces of their Father.

"The knowledge, therefore, of the electromagnetic spectrum as a non-exterior association, will be the development of the mind as the interior nature of man. Through this newer knowledge of himself, he will learn of the exterior of the ever-evolving, moving, expanding appearance of his universe! As he learns to this degree on this side of life on the third dimensions and takes with him the realization of himself as a Spirit that has immortal life, when he does lose his physical body at the end of his cycle, he will be charged with a higher frequency, which will give him the capability of taking up his life on the astral fourth dimensional side of life.

"He will then come to his classes with a greater incentive to know of himself; both from the lateral station in his physical anatomy, which he will have to function with again in another incarnation and from his true, primary psychic anatomy. This is the entire purpose and function for this movement between astral and physical dimensions.

"Life does take on a higher keynote and can be lived in the physical body to an extent where the physical consciousness does evolute itself, adding to and providing greater school rooms for those who are developing the fresher and more concise aspects of their evolutionary design. The third dimension is a proper part of life, and a preparatory stage of life. And in its function and position in the preparatory development, it can be lived in this perspective so man will understand that he will evolute the physical part of life as a physical consciousness, moving on to the mental consciousness, and attaining to the development of living through the mental body construct, which is the non-atomic statement of a higher evolutionary development.

"The Infinite is a development from the smaller finite to the more complex infinite attributes of Cosmic Mind. And it is in the complexity and the ever-developing nature of the finite parts that a higher Spiritual Being emerges. That Higher Being that we have related to you in so many different ways as URIEL, is a complex association of finite energies that have been so melded to become an Infinite Creative Mind.

"That is the Alpha and the Omega!"

# Chapter 6

## Entropy and the Interdimensional Cosmos

"The proposition that we are developing is not new; it has been a basic statement, amplified throughout history; amplified throughout the different civilizations and discovered in the cuniforms of the Sumarians, the Egyptians and indeed, back to the time of the lost Continent of Atlantis.

"What is this proposition? It is simply this; that man and nature have been divided. Man has been attempting to recognize his relationship to nature. He has recognized the duality that exists in the disproportions between his inner conflicts, his associations and relationships to himself and his society; and at the same time, the duality that exists in nature itself, that continues in its ever-developing, ever-consistent, awesome spectacle.

"Man disappears from the scene, but nature continues. This is a universal, classical theme, the statements of poets, historians, dramatists, philosophers and scientists who have attempted to resolve this dichotomy. This electromagnetic energy that re-creates itself within the schemata of life is replicated in the countless billions of species that populate the planet, populate the galactic systems of the stars.

"It is the universal nature of life itself, which is being demanded by man for an answer, and interpreted throughout a variety of manners and ways in which there can be some understanding to provide mankind with an ability to live from his birth to his death in his physical body in some consistent manner, whereby he sees some sense made out of the nonsense that seemingly irradiates the byways and highways of society.

"Incriminating evidence does clearly state that there is a great deal of utter and absolute nonsense which does not explain the logic and reason for the nature of reality that is the sustaining principle of the universal appearance of life. On the other hand, evidence has been given that there is an individual singular statement that does join the two halves of nature, which does return man back to his proper position as a real factor of nature! It is this situation that has been charged with the great explosives that have, in many ways, discharged into the body politic of man.

"Man has been inquiring, seeking, and asking for answers to the enigma of life! There have been pointed statements made by way of philosophical inquiries and scientific research that an omnipotent, omnipresent God reigns over man, and man is but a puppet in the vast scheme of life. There have been disproportionate understandings made by those who would reduce the electrodynamic Force into its individual increments, attempting to secure the answer through the study of subatomic particles.

"The second law of thermodynamics states that time is irreversible; that the past cannot be brought back into the present because of the disproportionate nature of the energy which has changed its former characteristics. Out of this basic principle came the understanding of entropy, which is basically a restatement of the second law of thermodynamics. We have established that these factors are indications of the indivisible and invisble cosmos, the beginning recognition of the interdimensional, electromagnetic pulse of the Infinite. There are many anomalies that have not yet been understood, because they have been localized, and have not been related to the whole picture.

"The whole picture is the awareness of certain, more advanced individuals who have seen a greater part of the whole. They are standing on a higher pinnacle, conceptually speaking, and from that perspective, do they have the greater picture and see what seemingly is chaos on one level and order on another level. The picture is one of relativity and how much can be seen of the extenuating circumference of the ever-moving river, the electromagnetic, vortexal pulsing of energy that is the interdimensional relationship of energy.

"Energy is a very relative statement of movement of many complex factors that are the divisible facets of the electromagnetic field. This is being recognized and has been accepted in the complexity of the movement of the atom. As the atom is the basic fundamental note of the electromagnetic field energy of the third dimension, it was the intention of science, particularly those who are particle physicists, to determine the answer through the microscopic examination of the energy of the atom. But the difficulty was that these scientists *SEPARATED THEMSELVES* from the very energy field which they were examining!

"On that basic statement we have arrived at the grand prospectus that life cannot be understood in isolation, either from the individual's isolation of himself from society, living in his pomp in some castle, on some isolated island, or in other ways where he has separated himself from the interdimensional movement of the patterns of society. For life is a pattern and man is recognizing the answer to his spiritual nature in this societal pattern. The pattern, of course, must not simply be the movement of people within the complex ectoplasm, the movement of man's egos within his communities, but it must be the relationship of man with his planet; his planet to his sun; and his sun to his galaxy; and the galaxy to the universe!

"This is man's universal desire, to know of his relationship to the whole. *"WHEREFORE ARE YE? AND WHEREFORE WILL YE GO? WHAT AVAILETH A MAN IF HE CONTAIN THE ENTIRE WORLD, BUT LOSETH HIS OWN SOUL?"* Where is the continuity? Where is the relationship that provides the basic need to reveal the truth to man's spirit? It had been revealed in previous histories but has somehow been lost to the present-day Homo sapiens; lost in a sense that there is a need to reconstitute and to reestablish the cosmic pattern that had been known in previous civilizations, previous to the written history of modern man.

"This then is the beginning of a new evolution in science. It is a beginning for a progressive evolution for man of Earth, as man has not, until this present time, after many thousands of years, recognized the interrelationship between science and religion. This is the separation, you see, that science has been reviewing, the extensive evidence of the macrocosm; nature being the total, inclusive factor of a planet and its relationship as a part of a solar system, a galaxy, a universe.

"Astronomers and cosmologists have been examining the outward so-called nature of space. Biological chemists have been examining the nature of the physical anatomy, and thus there has been a relative difference, a vast separation between the two inquiries. However, it is within the developing understanding of the biological physical anatomy that a greater recognition is being made of the extension of the life force of the chemical composition of this physical anatomy as an extension of another anatomy.

"This is the beginning development of research that will initiate a grand equation. That equation will be the realization of the nature of the electronic mind, an electronic body, an electronic force field that is the transmitting agent that makes possible the entire derivative function for the complicated electronic machinery of the physical organs.

"But why has this not been understood previously to this 20th century? The reasons are far beyond this present book. It has been stated and restated in other volumes of the Unarius Academy in the extensive library which has been mending the vacancies in man's history. And it will be seen that the relationship of man as a factor in his own evolution is a development between the two polarities of himself! This principle has not been understood relatively up until the recent past thirty years, during which time the Interdimensional Physics of Unarius was brought into the Earth world through the works of Ernest L. Norman.

"Scientists have been looking into the macrocosm and the microcosm from different perspectives and have been seeing different appearances from both lateral views of the Infinite. It is the basic example of the five blind men describing an elephant, each giving a different description of the object they were examining by touching different parts of the elephant's exterior. In the same sense, man is blind and has been examining the organs of the Infinite, only to the extent of the physical universe and has given disproportionate descriptions. He has not seen the total organism because he has not accepted the fact of his blindness. On the other hand, he did not accept the fact that he was infatuated with his own ability, and thirdly, he did not have an understanding of the historical nature of time. However, man is a product of time; a product of the second law of thermodynamics, but scientists have not extended this understanding to their present, localized research!

"All people are a product of the past and cannot retrieve this past in the present. One can only retrieve the nature of past-life experiences which is the established nature of their intelligence. The attempt of Science has been to understand life from the different displacements of life, but they have not realized the relationship between these displacements. Therefore, until the interrelationship of particles with their protonic parent is understood, the specific nature of the construction of particles is guesswork on the part of particle physicists.

"The proton of the atom is linked with its isotopic nature, its higher self. This understanding of the relationship between the energy field of the atom and the energy field of the isotope as two opposite and yet related faces of the Infinite, explains the dimensional quality of time and space, reversed to become a space-time continuum.

"Hence, there can be no rhyme or reason for constant digression into smaller and smaller microscopic examinations of energy. In three basic statements we have explained how man is an extension of himself from his previous association with the universal structure of life that he has taken with him as he has moved laterally in the life that he now occupies in his atomic body and from understandings attained when he lived in his fourth dimensional, non-atomic body. This is the great equation that will be the nature of the teachings in the new world of the 21st century; the new astral world of Earth, whereby the true concensus of study will be the nature of the relationship of man as an energy system. The student will not necessarily study the physical anatomy to gain a greater understanding of it, but will be studying the protonic elements of the electronic body which is the main proposition of life.

"How did man lose this integral understanding of himself? And why is this understanding being brought back at this time in this conjunction of the species Homo sapiens? There has been a vast history which has been obliterated from the literature of man. Not completely, but the essential facts have been buried under the land and under the sea. Little by little, paleontology, archeology and paleoarcheology are discovering the evidence of the history of man on his planet Earth. This history is reconstituting the fact that the overlay of present cities on top of previous cities were the older civilizations that have been whispered of, talked about, and have been related in myths and folklore.

"This history is wrapped tightly within the electronic components of each individual's mind, and it is his basic proposition to reconvert into his consciousness the memories of his past, particularly from the awareness of his own electromagnetic computer body that holds all evidence of past-life experiences! It is not that someone makes an unalienable statement to be accepted, but that the information so related by individuals who have commanded a greater awareness of the relativity of themselves and have realized the unescapable statement that there are no chance happenings in life; that each person does have the history of his own past locked within his own mind, but that his mind has not been opened to the evidence. So those who are capable of regenerating this knowledge should do so with the knowledge that this regeneration will loosen up that individual from the bonds that had imprisoned him throughout past histories of mankind!

"In that respect, as it has been so stated by the second law of thermodynamics, the past will take on its proper position as information which has been the nature of life lived in previous civilizations, and will not be contained in the present, in the sense that it contains the emotional content of the individual. This means that all factors of life which are relative to the progressive movement of energy will take their position in the life of the individual as a natural movement of the electromagnetic spectrum, which is the nature of his own mind. The restrictions which are the present feature of life, are those features in which the past is attempting to be relived in the present, as if it had the elasticity to regain its position; whereas the past is a non-elastic situation. It is an energy that has been constituted and has been polarized by any one individual, but it is stretched out and can *NEVER REGAIN* its former position in the present in the exact same configuration and manner in which it was originally experienced! It is not a separate factor in which individuals are not involved; it is the existential nature of the electromagnetic plasma of nature.

"It is nature itself that man is living within. The relationship, therefore, between the exterior that is life and the interior that is man's awareness of himself, is not separate. They are one and the same! Each individual is expressing the past of himself by the reflection of it as the exterior of what he calls his life. He is as a photographic plate, projecting images onto this universal energy that is the Infinite Creative Intelligence, demodulated into its finite, third dimensional, sensitive surface, the information of his own photographic expedition. He is constantly reconverting the evidence of his own version of life onto the sensitive plate of the present environment. Therefore, nature or the universal picture of the electromagnetic spectrum is converted by each individual, according to the nature of what he

has converted from his own life experience.
"But the problem is, not knowing the basic principle of energy, the principle by which energy is constantly converting and changing in this conversion, the individual is seeing his past in his present and believing that it is his present, not realizing in spite of all the evidence that this picture supplies, it is causing him great discomfort. He is divorcing himself from relationships that contain his very basic universal nature, which is the integration that is the consistent statement of creative characteristics in which all individuals have been so devised by the Cosmic Source.
"And of course, one could always come back with these basic statements that life is learning, and learning is the evolutionary design of the progressive nature of life. But if that were true, then why has man not learned the essential characteristics of this great electromagnetic plasma through his own conversion of it from life to life, in the many thousands and hundreds of thousands of excursions that he has taken, not only within the third dimension, but into the fourth dimension where he does gain the opposite picture and the ability to reconvert the photographic images and to see the picture with his X-ray vision, which he does have to a greater extent then?
"The process of the conversion of the universal picture by each individual into his own version is the entire

statement of evolution. But it is not, as we have indicated, a simplistic picture that it will be viewed by any individual whereby should he sit in a theater and have the entire over-review of his society presented to him or of his world, that he will be able to integrate the complex differences in the varieties of associated events that come to his eye. He cannot convert this into some semblance of balance. In this same sense, the entire picture of life is man, who is seeing himself outpictured, but he must develop the capability to learn of the principle of a science that describes the movement of his life and does provide the key to unscramble the code.

"The revolution in science in the 20th century is of quantum mechanics and the theory of relativity. Both theories relate that there is no singularity, and one cannot understand the process of life simply by taking a biopsy of nature and making a generalized statement as to the makeup of this organ, its health, and its constituent personality. All is motion! The Einsteinian statement of relativity indicates that it is all a matter of from where you are looking. Quantum mechanics indicates the great flux within the energy of the atom, and the watcher or the subject only sees what he places his consciousness upon. He has no idea as to what took place before or after, but only conceives at the moment he takes his picture, what the picture is of that particular particle. But he does not know its relationship as it has changed in its constant movement. This understanding will evade man until the science that we are bringing to the reader's attention and to the world as a whole, helps to explain the universality of energy and the real knowledge of its interdimensional relationship.

"Unarius is that science, and it is a name which does indicate the interrelationship of all things; of man as a third dimensional organism and of man as a fourth dimensional organism; a UNiversal Articulate Interdimensional Understanding of Science. This Science articulates by making specific reference to the medley of the species that is the product of the complexity of third dimensional life; articulating the different disciplines that endeavor to explain these many facets of life. It is interdimensional in that it explains man and life as a whole; but man particularly, who is not a singular phenomenon of an atomic environment, but is reconverting the nature of himself from two placements, two polarities. Man is interdimensional. The third dimension reveals to himself his physical and atomic sensations, and his mind revealing to him the universal fourth dimensional and higher dimensional quotients to which he is beginning to become sensitive. Research is superimposed upon a schematic which has been given the word Science. Science provides a platform of logic and reason for the under-

understanding of the evolutionary design of life.

"Hence, the science that is only 300 years old, has been a development of responsibility for man of earth to initiate his progressive evolution. To examine the man and woman of science, one recognizes that they were unusual individuals in the different disciplines in which they expressed, whether it was in the fields of astronomy, biology, chemistry, physics, philosophy or psychology. They were complete persons. That is to say, they were not unintegrated, but were whole in that they were what can be considered a renaissance man. They were conscious of the entirety of life and lived the principle and ethics of Spirit. Leonardo da Vinci is considered to be the greatest expression of the renaissance concept. The nature of his life revealed through the dissection of his inquiry products of earth life, the pattern for the evoluting of man as a consciousness of the Creative Infinite Intelligence.

"Three hundred years is but a tick in the cosmic clock, yet we did point out that there was a time, a place, and a purpose for all developments. Man had lost the knowledge of the inherent pattern which was his own clock and how it functioned, and as a result, has become disjointed. Somehow, somewhere, events had foretold of an interruption in the movement of the gears of the clock, and the clock's hands have stood still! In all respects, and without chiding the reader, there has been a great mental perversion, a historical document in that there has been little or no advance in the movement of the hands of this clock! It has stood still, the hands set at twelve and six. That is the extent of the development of the mental or scientific understanding of man as a product of the great cosmic machine. Man is a machine, because he is a structure that is continuous, never-stopping, ever-moving, and moving in a definitive manner, according to the basic principles of the electromagnetic energy field which is life! It is a consistent and ever-developing statement of a greater Intelligence that is charging its intelligence as an effectual and recognizable evidence of a higher Intelligence.

"The history of science reveals the interacting within the nations of the earth world of individuals who had developed a greater awareness of the intricacies of the pattern that makes up the machinery of life, which has added in a consistent fashion to the development of this understanding. It has been basically a curriculum that has begun according to the specific nature and needs of society of that period. We could say that in modern times, Isaac Newton was the first of the scientists to begin this development for man to learn to understand the nature of himself within the environmental statement of society.

"Where did these individuals, Newton, Descartes, Planck, Einstein, Bjornson and Max Born receive their knowledge? To research the annals of the works of these scientists in their different respective fields, reveals that they were individuals different than and yet similar in some respects, to the man of Earth. They did not ever indicate they were not Homo sapiens but rather, they had a wider circumference in their outlook to life and to society as a whole. These are individuals who had attained the recognition of the interdimensional nature of themselves as a product of the interdimensional science of life. They had returned with greater knowledge from the fourth dimension, the other side of life, revealing in private and public statements they knew of the larger pattern of life.

"This understanding of the universality of life reflected their great inner confidence and their ability to function within a primitive environment, truly the nature of life in which they were developing advanced understandings beyond the limitations of society's limited and narrow perspective. They were seeing life from the mountaintop and bringing down into the valley, this knowledge in the language of the times and in many respects, developing new language to explain an expanded nature of consciousness which they were attempting to elicit and incept into the community of man.

"These scientists have advanced the knowledge of man as a spiritual being, although they may not have used the word 'spirit' as the evolving structure that contains the substance for the prerogative of viewing the grandeur of life. They were and are the Unariun Scientists. These are the extenuating circumstances that have indicated the duality of this evolutionary statement of life; the continuity of man as he has always moved from the life, lived through a physical anatomy to life lived through a spiritual anatomy, a fully-integrated electronic body. This has been the basic knowledge of such advanced individuals who were capable of proposing new concepts and theories, and to inject new information into the old system of life lived in the constricted awareness of the physical atom.

"So we can say that this present book and other books of Unarius are the continuity of the many principles and hypotheses which have become the basic ground rules of physics, geology, astronomy and all other facets in the disciplines of science and philosophy. This is the entire engagement of man in his desire to know of his own Universal Spirit, his Spiritual Self!

"Unarius is the new science that contains the basic illustrative diagrammatical factors of this pattern of evolutionary life, to be the curriculum for the future age! This curriculum contains within it, the progressive nature of life, and reveals to each individual as he begins his inquiry into the electromagnetic nature of his mind, the realization that he *DOES* have an interdimensional personality! He is, in this respect, carrying within him the entire panoply and history of mankind!

"He is containing within himself the entire panoply of the history of the universe! But this knowledge must be reconverted by each individual; reconverted through the photographic plate which is his mind. As the individual develops this mind, he contains the greater capability of converting the abstract into his own individual awareness. He thus BECOMES, as have those he has known in the literature of science or in the literature of other fields of expression. He DOES BECOME a proponent and a leader of man and helps to advance the cause of humanity as an evolving plasma of the Infinite.

"So we come full circle in this respect, in the entire digression of physical science, initiated by Unarius, individuals who have gained the integrated function of life and have learned of the interdimensional nature of themselves. Such enlightened individuals have laid down a basic scientific foundation which, up to the present 20th century, has finally brought recognition of not only the scientific community but to all thinking people in all disciplines of knowledge, the realization that man must know the relationship of himself to his universal or infinite nature!

"This relationship is substantiated in the realization that all life is the movement and function of energy.

All the basic sciences have revealed that there is no solidity to the organic material body. Hence, the next development for man is the learning of the equations of this energy field, which is his own need to understand as the true protoplasm of himself. It is this energy body, the psychic body that has not been revealed before to the earth people as a whole for many ages of time. So this has been carefully diagrammed in previous texts as a factor of the chaotic nature of energy when it has been attempted to be lived into the present. This chaos is the ignorance of those individuals who did not or would not reconvert their past-life expressions into a polarized coefficient in the present, to learn how to update each and every development in life, whereby they had attained a higher coefficient within the energy of their consciousness.

"Chaos is another name for negative. Order is another word for positive. What is chaotic is an unworkable factor of many elements. If it is unworkable it is not pragmatic. If it cannot integrate the many different equations that are the nature of man as he lives in his social order, it then causes a breakdown. Chaos is therefore the negative side or the negative polarity of the movement of man as he is transposing himself in time and space into a third dimension from his fourth dimensional makeup.

"It is in this manner then, that the negative forces are individuals who have caused this chaos. Chaos has been more or less revealed to be the evident nature of unresolved problems which remain as the conflicts of man. The many political and religious controversies are the chaotic remnants of previous involvements in the same formative stages of man. Lessons were not learned and the coals have been carried to Newcastle again, to be burned again in the same furnace, causing the great holocaust, because of the incendiary nature of the energy. They are not in-phase elements; they are out of phase and constantly being forced into an engagement with themselves! They are the many facets of community and national life which have put man into a square and forced him to be molded to predetermined structures which have, in turn, regenerated the conflicts of man and society.

"Man's understanding of frequency and harmonics will explain in every detail the reason why there is chaos. It is the regenerative, anachronistic movement of energy that cannot become stabilized but degenerates into some recognizable appearance of life in the reformative stage of the present. The past cannot live in the present. Only if the information that has been gained from previous life experiences that have been so polarized to contain an integrated picture, can that picture then be reestablished, which becomes updated to become more advanced information, that is basically the future. The future is therefore the reconverted knowledge that has been attained by any one student, learning to develop an understanding of some factor of life. He establishes this learning by applying the knowledge of logic and reason to engineer his mind and to produce somewhat practical resolutions to help mankind as a whole.

"This is the progressive development, not only in a technological structure in the knowledge of atomic physics, in the abilities to reconvert energy, but is a reconversion of the energy of man's mind, where he has crossed the barrier of time and space to realize that he is a spiritual being who lives in two worlds. Man is, at all times, storing up information; energy of a great force which will be stored within him when he crosses the bridge after his physical body's death. He will live off the information he has so stored within his true electromotive, psychic anatomy. This body is the body which engineers life on both sides of the equation of the sine-wave principle. Man must therefore learn that what he does as he lives through a physical body will be reconstituted and will become the storehouse from which he will attain his true consciousness of his fourth dimensional nature!

"The astral plane is a real plane. It is the real world, and that real world cannot be lived on by any individual until the engineering of this energy body has been so developed. In every respect, the expanded picture of life will reveal that the working of man in his atomic body is a developmental phase for the extension and the intricate use of the psychic anatomy on a higher frequency plane.

"The psychic anatomy cannot be built to function in a fourth dimensional plane of life until it has gained its development in the third dimension. In other words, the whole proposition of life on this atomic world is to learn of the extensive physics of this invisible psychic body - invisible to the Homo sapiens. Then truly will man begin his true birthright and have advanced not only himself but will advance the entire composition of life as a planetary development.

"Yes, it is a Grand Design, and may seem rather futuristic to some individuals, but what is the future? The future is every single moment in which an individual lives! Therefore, what may seem to be far-distant in the understanding of these futuristic concepts is an immediate understanding, according to the ability of each individual to integrate the many relationships of himself as he reconstitutes himself from his past and recognizes his present position in life. As the past and the present must always be related to the future, he will always move out of the present third dimension into the present fourth dimension, which will, or can be truly the future.

"The future is therefore only in terms of the fact that energy is always ongoing, always moving in an expanding relationship within the entire consensus of interdimensional life. That is the interior physics that is the basic need and is the basic development and the beginning for this new science. Unarius has always been functioning as a major factor in the evolutionary progression of the species man. It has been called by many different names in the many different environments of different societies. But in the present scientific idiom of life, Unarius is a Brotherhood of people who have advanced throughout the entire movement of the Infinite, engaged within the relative understanding of the patterns of life and to live in a future far distant, frequency-wise than other people who have not reformed this understanding of the pattern of the Infinite.

"As the future is always moving in its sinusoidal pattern to make the past in another level, to become the present and another future, man is, in every respect, moving through a great cycular pattern of life and is interpenetrated by the future and the past. Those who have revealed the knowledge of an expanded universe, are from the future, to all intents and purposes. At the same time, they are from man's past.

"Einstein and Newton are from man's past, yet they came from the future, from a higher expressionary world in which the entire pattern of life was understood; at least to the extent that it was integrated and where there was an ability to live in a polarized expression, to share knowledge of oneself with others. This is the picture that is being brought to man. It is the future that is presently being welded into the present. The present will become the future, because it will have added to it the newer concepts, the continuity of life's principle; the continuity of man as a consciousness that is his evolutionary development.

"The nature of the duality of life, of the duality of the Infinite, the nature of the processes of life and death, the processes of regeneration in this evolutionary expression where the complex movement of energy reshapes, reforms and develops into new organisms, the expressions of intelligence that have charged each individual with a greater lens where he can recreate from the plasma of Infinite Intelligence, a greater awareness of his relationship to it.

"So in summary, the new science is a proposition that all life is a relationship; it is relative, and one cannot find the nature of himself without knowing his relationship to the exterior picture of life and society. The physical environment is an extension of the individual, and this extension is the picture that he has brought from previous incarnations in physical bodies from his fourth dimensional lives. Man is attempting to reconvert certain new knowledge within the bioplasma of a third dimension and attempting to extricate from the life experiences in the narrow band of the Infinite on the third dimension, evidence of his relationship to the universal whole.

"All of this is an expedition through the individual's ability to believe in the evidence that he adds life to life; conclusive evidence that he is an interdimensional energy system that is living for the expressed purpose of polarizing his energy system; that is to say, developing the real picture of life; that he is the real picture and not a mere passing fancy, not a singular phenomenon but an extension of Infinite Intelligence. This extension of his consciousness is his prerogative to become aware and to be a part of the entire harmony of this Universal Cosmos.

"Then peace of mind will be the result for man individually and as a whole. This peace of mind is the knowledge of who he is and the why and the wherefore of life. It is hard fought for, but it is the only worthwhile process that finally gains for the individual the basic proposition that he is a spiritual entity, not just a mere physical organism.

"As a great man once said, 'Know this and be free! Be free of the chaos that ignorant people believe to be the real world. Be free of the restraints of such individuals and ye shall have immortal life, for ye shall walk within the Higher Realms of higher societies where man lives close to the Mind of the Father.'"

## Chapter 7

## The Singularity of Energy — A Fourth Dimensional Physics

"Countless people who are involved in the New Age, an age that speaks of the joining of man's lower nature, his visible appearance of life, and his higher nature, the invisible appearance of life, demonstrate for all time the great teachings of the Masters of the East, West, North and South, who have proven their credentials and have basically set up the foundation for this Age of Logic and Reason. But the New Age is just a beginning of the realization and the necessary work that must be applied by these individuals who are being given the acknowledgment of the progressive nature of their own existence.

"In this chapter we wish to speak towards this issue. The New Science is finally being resolved within the social and the physical sciences and is joining man with nature, the microcosm and the macrocosm. Unarius describes this joining as the developmental statement for mankind to begin to rectify the pressures of his physical, negative pasts in which he had de-invigorated his spiritual senses.

"It is true that leaders are the instigators who propel into the community of man the realizations to be attained by individuals from the examples of persons with the higher degree of their spiritual integration. What better way then can it be expressed, other than with individuals who are demonstrating the principles of the teachings that had been given the initial thrust for their present development. Whether they be disciples of Kriya Yoga or disciples of the Western practices for integration of the body and spirit, they must now begin that forward motion and instrument into their disciplines the higher physics of the Interdimensional Infinite.

"Up until this present time there has been a basic foundation for the present development of the integration of different understandings that had been the diverse relationship of man to his purposeful evolution. The many Masters from Shankara to the present day, are members of an interdimensional society, an interdimensional fraternity which is the Brotherhood of Man known as Unarius.

"This Brotherhood spans many dimensions and has taught in many different disciplines. It has been a basic format for the present emergence of the New World Teacher. The new teachings at the present time throughout the Earth world are coming to a parallax, speaking of the instigating and developing intelligence for the reinstituting of a progressive life for the entire planet. From whatever perspective these teachers have spoken in their understanding of Homo sapiens as a material, atomic, energy system, and of the nature of Homo sapiens as a spiritual, interdimensional system of energy, they have provided a greater understanding to the world as a whole.

"But as a whole, each and every group has spoken with respect to their basic understanding of the physics of life. In most cases, that physics has been elemental to the extent that no one has spoken to the point but has bridged and joined the relationship of man's body, mind and spirit. The attempts have been made but they have been temporized because they did not have the basic credentials of the teachings of the higher, advanced Masters who have attained to their Logoi-ship in their basic spiritual development.

"This Logoi-ship is the power that is attained by such developed Intelligences. It is a power that can transmute dimensions; a power that can be demodulated from the higher Celestial and Super Celestial Dimensions; yet not be lessened nor changed one whit! This power, therefore, has to be a power that stems from a Logoi, an individual who is infinite in Consciousness, in full command of the understanding of the physics of the Interdimensional Cosmos.

"This then, would be the New World Teacher! A New World Teacher would be one who knows all worlds, has lived on all worlds from the lower elementary, atomic world of terrestrial planes, to the astral worlds, the higher Spiritual, Celestial and Super-Celestial worlds. This is beyond the ken of man in the curriculum of many metaphysical teachings. The majority of those who have brought a knowledge of the nature of man's spiritual identity have contained their teachings from the previous lives which they have themselves lived, and have attained to in their greater ability to live in the physical worlds, yet still command and recognize their own spiritual continuity with the Infinite Creative Intelligence. They are themselves, in every respect, Brothers of the Universal Brotherhood, functioning in particular departments of life that are attuned to, frequency-wise, by individuals who have the capability to understand the scientific principles outlined in these teachings.

"But as a whole, the demonstrable objective of physics is to find the singularity of energy. Singularity provides man with some consensus of understanding as to the objectives of his own life, to understand how energy, as it is resolved in its microscopic component parts, becomes more complicated and loses its origination. Singularity is the knowledge that all complicated forms of life that are the energy components of the physical universe have been a resolution from some greater component.

"At the present time, this singularity is the statement of all spiritual teachers. It is God, and man is finding his way back to his godhead. In a generalized manner, this is quite valid, but in a more specific term, the basic understandings for the principles of this godhead is a great vacuum within present spiritual teachings. But as evolution is spiritual development, it is not expected that mankind, in his elemental state and particularly with the history of the degeneration of these basic spiritual principles that had been inseminated into the earth world, such an advanced interdimensional science would be grasped and applied.

"There has been abuse! The abuse of evolutionary science is the entire statement of the division in the evolutionary understanding of man as an integrated factor of the Infinite Cosmos. That is the basic teaching, and it cannot be abrogated by speaking out and telling any one individual that if he will follow the flag of the banner of some spiritual group, to hold it aloft and chant a mantrum, he will be joined to the godhead. The joining to a godhead, which in a more specific manner, is the Infinite Creative Force, is the recognition of its Presence in man. This Presence must be systematically learned in the many different spectrums in which the Interdimensional Cosmos functions. These spectrums are the divisible parts of the vortexal sinusoidal energy field of the Creative Infinite. Using the name God, Allah or Yahweh, does not help man to understand the regenerative plasma.

"The logic and reason taught by Socrates and Jesus, the two Hierarchial Beings are, to all intents and purposes, the Godhead for third dimensional man, which must be learned, as these Beings learned the nature of their interior Spiritual Force. Do you think that the man Jesus was fully developed in his physical anatomy and simply fell from the sky, full-formed with all factors of his intelligence full-grown? This concept goes against logic and reason. It is the entire physics of the Infinite Creative Intelligence which must be conceived in a systematic manner, and synthesized within the mind of the individual. How this is done is the stated nature of the scientific teachings of Unarius. This teaching does not weaken man by having him bend the knee or pray to some outside force or give allegiance to dogma.

"Unarius is a factual fourth-dimensional physics. A fourth-dimensional physics is a bridge, carrying all factors of its demodulated structure into the third-dimensional nature of present physical life. Hence, a fourth-dimensional physics will command a greater understanding of the picture of life, viewed as a reflection from the mirror of atomic forms or elements. On the other hand, it is viewed from behind the silver of the glass mirror which regenerates the picture of the atom; a picture that is, in every respect, the real energy that provides the forms of physical life.

"Fourth-dimensional physics then, will correspondingly be a learning of the interdimensional factors of the Infinite, functioning in its true polarity. For many millions of years these Master Teachers, presently a small nucleus in the galactic system of the universe, living on planet Earth, have been teaching and gaining security with the knowledge that they are reacting from physical energy, some substance of reality that will give mankind the ability to reconstruct the complexities of the life styles that will become a corresponding new relationship to their community.

"No one can come down from a higher, advanced civilization and propound a new way of life for those who are the denizens of a lower-contrived civilization. The reason is that the physical systems of life are contrived from symbolic forms. These symbols provide the evolutionary foundation for the atomic nature of society. They are the reflections of the 92 natural atoms which correspondingly create a mirror for mankind. A higher civilization functions behind the mirror and is aware of its reflections and refractions in the many different combinations that have been related as a symbolic nature of life in the folklores, the mores, and the attitudes and opinions of aborigine man.

Unariun scientists who did intersperse within the worlds of Earth, have done so with great understanding of the symbolic picture of life and of its reality by Earth people. To disturb this reality in one fell swoop is to cause a great harm to their mentality, to their psychic structures. Therefore, the advanced Masters have interspersed the knowledge of the interdimensional nature of life and the continuity of consciousness after the physical body returns to its elements with the many principles by which the reality of life functions. The movement of energy wave forms in its microscopic and macroscopic manner has been incepted within the teachings of many disciplines of knowledge, which have been the basic building blocks for man to begin to rectify the atomic appearances of life from different vantage points which were being outpictured by them in the physical and non-physical aspects of life.

"It is in this respect that the insemination within the cultures of Homo sapiens has taken on a variety of interpretations, according to the ability of man to peer behind the mirror of his own mind and with the other factors invloved with the stresses and strains of functioning in two worlds. The distance between the physical, terrestrial plane and the astral, non-physical plane has been widened life after life! Because of this disparity, students who have learned, to some degree, the nature of their progressive future, have fallen back upon the symbolism of earth life, because of the greater strength so associated in this atomic picture.

"Because man lives in the third dimension and within the frequency of an atomic planet, he is closely entwined within the symbols of his world, constructed through the reactionary five senses. The strength that must be instrumented by any individual to cross the bridge of the third dimension, to realize the continuity of himself, has been the basic embattlement in the life of the earthman. He has fought for his position, holding his fortress intact against all comers who would attempt to dissuade him from his ownership. This ownership has been the physical evidence of his life and the security that it provides him.

"The nature of consciousness of the fourth dimension is an inseminating development being taught by these advanced Masters. The many who have crossed the bridge from the third to the fourth dimension, after having attained some success in the understanding of the spiritual, nonatomic nature of life, have returned again to take up life in a new physical anatomy, taking on another name and rising to the surface of some society of some nation, and proving his mastership by overcoming the various stresses of his involvements in the developmental life of that society.

"The individual, therefore, who has been an example of Spirit, has proven that he has overcome his lower senses. These individuals are therefore, in every respect, proving over and over again for the Earth people, and for themselves, the higher physics of higher dimensions, the home for Homo Spiritualis when he has successfully learned of the equivalent nature of his physical, temporal body and his 'real' spiritual body!

"The extended process of learning, of overcoming, is the natural basis for any future in which equivalent knowledge of the alternate nature of life is applied and will be the living example of such individual in his new environment. Hence it is, that the Masters are advanced, intelligent individuals who have demonstrated an understanding of interdimensional physics. Socrates and Jesus of Nazareth returned to demonstrate that they were not superhuman but had learned the curriculum of interdimensional life! Man must therefore learn these coefficients, which are the basis of the New World Teaching of Unarius; that he has the capability to attain an understanding of his true identity. However, this true identity cannot be attained should he give the power of his consciousness to another individual.

"In this weak state, man tends to dress another individual with the power of a supernatural deity in an attempt to placate himself and resolve his fears, to provide him with abundance and security of himself! He wishes to have someone else provide him with the basic understanding of life, but this is not possible. In every respect it has weakened the individual. He has not learned of his own mental geometry and has therefore become a mentally-retarded individual, dependent upon handouts from other persons. Such individuals are dressed in the symbols of government, powerful forces who were identified as some supernational figure.

"The history of mankind is demonstrated in the analogy of the weakness of the flesh, the security of symbols he has accumulated to give him some sense of security. Such security may form itself in the amassing of music, books or art objects. This collection by man is a mania, a collection of material objects which cannot explain the symbolic nature of man himself. In the teachings of Unarius, reflected throughout civilizations, those who have demonstrated the continuity of life, have indicated the reality of the higher dimensions from which third-dimensional life was conceived.

"But these teachings have been denuded of their non-atomic principles and symbols have been used to represent basic statements: 'Man, know thyself. Look into the self and recognize that this self is not a mere word, but is a system of energy that functions in a pragmatic manner! Read into your thoughts; analyze the nature of these thought-forms and see the relationship between the thought and the act, and the continuity of these acts as they are reformed to become a particular symbol. You will know in every respect that you are the precursor of these outward forms. You have become dependent upon them, and this dependency is indicative of the evolutionary history, initiated by the individual.'

"No one person can placate himself and reflect from the symbol which is presently the entire nature of physical life and remove himself from the responsibility of having given some force to this symbology. Man is a symbology! Symbology is a general attitude of mental laziness. Mental laziness is the inability or the lack of ability or discipline to look behind the mirror image and refract this image into its true placement.

"These advanced Master-Teachers are therefore scientists who are fourth-dimensional physicists and have mastered physical life. They are capable of understanding the subtleties and sublimated throughts of unrefined intelligence. The earthman is an earthman only because he does not know of his higher astral nature. These teachers are the helpers for mankind, the Elder Brothers, Guides, Inspirational Forces who have bridged the two worlds of earth and astral, and are therefore, in fact not earth people! They are not one-sided. They see life in its true reality as an alternate movement from its positive to its negative polarity in the consistent relationship of a reality that contains the unified quotient of its own duality.

"In the New Age of Spiritual Renaissance, there are many teachers who have reincarnated from fourth-dimensional worlds, who are introducing many different factors for the integration of mankind; a higher reformation within the force fields of the interdimensional cosmos. Entropy is a catalyst and explains structure and function of the Sixth Cycle of the Recessional. The many helpers for mankind who have returned and are working in their particular teaching disciplines, are building a foundation which will be the joint efforts of the many New Age Leaders, to provide a basis upon which the next stage for the development of man will take place.

"Man's new foundation is very much like the nest built by the male and female bird for its young. This nest is built with a knowledge of the necessary security for the fledgling bird. While the young bird is in the nest, it can gain its strength and is able to fly free and become itself a regenerative factor in the species of birds, and a purposeful part of the Infinite. In this sense, man has been building a nest, a foundation through the many ages of time in the histories of earth worlds.

"The Elder Brothers, Adepts and Masters who have been dispersed from the Hierarchial Home of the Logoi, have been carrying the various building blocks for mankind to build his basic foundation upon which he can ascend in his spiritual development. This is the time of a new awakening for man when he will have had adjucated within his consciousness the newer understandings in the 20th century that are timeless and universal; the continuity of himself as a Consciousness, created and regenerated by individuation through his countless life experiences!

"The knowledge of the interplanetary configuration of galaxies in the physical universe, the awareness of countless Homo sapiens in their evolutionary development, validates the great pattern of life in the reformation and resynthesis of mankind as a part of a greater whole. This greater whole is the basic principle, the knowledge which is being reinstituted into planet Earth. This knowledge of man as an evolving energy system known as Spirit, begins another stage in the curriculum that contains the unfolding drama of life for Homo sapiens.

"Unarius is a fourth-dimensional physics, propounded and developed by higher, advanced Intelligent Beings. It is a curriculum for a course of study, unfolded from the minds of great Spiritual Intelligences. These higher teachings are interdimensional in nature and can be understood only when the individual has resuscitated himself from the dream world of his atomic, symbolic life.

"At that moment in his reawakening, he is capable of learning the reality of these interdimensional concepts of life. In this manner, Unarius has prepared the earth people in such a manner for inseminating into the world a spiritual development involving the earth people. A teaching is as good as its principles, and is as valid as they are effected into the lives of other human beings. The Unarius teachings are of the higher physics of the mind, containing the grand sweep of life: past, present, and future. All Masters constantly overcome the separations reflected in the nature of third-dimensional life. They have accomplished this with their knowledge and usage of the principles of Interdimensional Physics.

"The student must also begin his spiritual development with the application of these principles. These principles are, in every respect, the nature of a healing science, because any physics that explains the movement of energy, must explain this movement pragmatically to prove the viability and functional basis within the local system of the Homo sapiens as a human being, desirous of attaining the knowledge of his own psychic force field. The science that is known as Unarius must be practical, effective, workable and useful; not as a theory, not simply as facts to be discussed exteriorily. The Science of Unarius must be reflected within the individual as *LIVING PROOF* of the *PRINCIPLES OF ENERGY!*

"It is a statement of a practical science, a physics of man. It is both the understanding of the third-dimensional and fourth-dimensional proposition of life, since this Interdimensional Science is a unified field. It dissolves all negative, out-of-phase anachronisms which have been incepted within the psychic centers of any individual! It provides the basis for effecting a forward movement in the complex energy system that is man. It explains the historical nature of life from the past of man. It explains the rendition of life in the future of man and at the same time, provides the necessary elements for understanding the physics of life in the present, because in the present, is the determination for all mankind to contain the nature of Infinite Intelligence. Time and space, the grand unified field, is resolved in this understanding of these principles by which the interdimensional cosmos functions.

"A first beginning must therefore be the basic relativity of man as an individual organism, as a subminiature universe, who contains within himself all of the basic proponent factors of the Infinite. The fact that it is a miniature system, in man's present awareness is because of his own limitations. The Infinite Creative Intelligence is in its abstraction, both the macrocosm and the microcosm. It is a grand interdimensional, sinusoidal pulse, breathing out the macrocosm and breathing in the microcosm. Man is the microcosm, as he is the inbreathing of the Infinite Creative Intelligence. He is also the macrocosm because he is, at all times, a regenerative, expanding factor of this Infinite Field. Man therefore has the ability to expand and develop his consciousness and become a larger part of the greater Infinite.

"Man, the microcosm, lives within the Infinite. He must therefore learn how to become a part of it. This understanding is the basic teaching of Unarius, beginning with the first statement of man as an energy system, living within a larger energy system, who is a small microscopic energy force. But that energy contains the proposition that when it learns of its nature, it can become a functional and greater part of the Cosmic Mind. It is on the principle and with the understanding of frequency and harmonics, the electronic statement of energy in the 20th century, a Scientific Age, upon which the higher physics of Unarius can be taught. The teachings of Unarius is based upon physics and electronics, at least to the extent of its beginning development. Man is a microcosm of the Infinite as we indicated, but he is a full and total statement of the Infinite. A Master has mastered the equivalent coefficients that are the internal workings of this energy system. He has learned how to command the component factors of himself and has learned the workability of his electronic energy system.

"A television system gives the clearest description of the movement of man's mind and the nature of the picture forms which become the accepted mode of life. The physics of the present electronic communications systems: computers, television, radar, etc., are the work of advanced Masters who have layed down the basic foundation for man to begin his maturation, to learn of the higher frequency field of his true spiritual anatomy.

"This Age of Science is therefore the propellant upon which the

New World Teaching will provide the motivating force for the next development in the progressive evolution of the earthman. Unarius can indeed be called the New World Teaching, because Earth is entering into a New World Renaissance, a renaissance that must carry with it the developmental factors to help people in their personal renaissance.

"Knowledge is the basis for this Renaissance. The many different disciples and teachings which have come up to this point which have, in all respects, parallaxed the equation of man as a spiritual being; that man is a community of people and that planet Earth is the entirety of this community. The divisibility between man and his neighbors has been the basis of the degeneration and the greater materiality of life which again has become an impediment in man's capability of entering into the New Age. But in the great change that is taking place, the physics of entropy, the knowledge that out of the refraction between the intermingling of the positive and the negative forces, a chaotic condition would exist and a new reformation is taking place in the many different coefficients that are the interrelationship between the positive and negative fields.

"This understanding of the evolutionary development of man and the many changes in this cycle are clearly stated and diagramed in the Unarius Science. This Science is the teaching for the New Age in which the Renaissance of Man is dependent upon learning of the coefficients of his own energy system and its development in future lives on earth planets, to become strong and capable of gaining his wings. In this respect then, those individuals who will live in the New Age, having strengthened their understanding of the existence of the astral plane and of the higher spiritual planes of life as a reality of the expanding Infinite, will return in a new incarnation and carry within them, not coals from Newcastle but instead, new constructs of the physics of progressive evolution! It will be a physics that had been delineated within the nature of their own electronic body and will advance the lives of the peoples on the earth plane with the individual's assimilation of these new constructs.

"There will, in this way, be a synthesis and a greater interrelationship of the advanced knowledge of life which is presently the reality of Homo sapiens who had evolved to a higher species. He is no longer Homo sapiens but is a spiritual being, having left his physical body on the earth world and risen as the Phoenix Bird, with the greater ability to wing free of the lower dimensions! He becomes Homo Spiritualis!

"The greatest detriment, of course, in this New Age of the Renaissance is the unacknowledged and unaccepted awareness of the past that lies as a heavy weight, as sludge stacked up outside some factory, spent from its use in the production of some specific material. The past therefore, of each individual, is a sludge of energy that has not been polarized and the leftover factors of itself as undirected coefficients of energy wave forms are not directive in their movement. Therefore, the force that is expended in this interrelationship of past-life experiences that have not gained a recognizable intelligence to the individual in his forward movement in his life, is a retractive, backward movement.

"It is a static energy field-force which refuses to budge in its created statement of life, in experiences that will be lived by any one individual. These traumas are static energy force fields which imprison the individual from moving forward mentally speaking. He is held in the grips of custom, and he is restricted with the bias of a negative attitude to life, whether it be the religious, political or scientific propositions of life, his attitude towards his fellowman, and the many different associated factors of life that hold people together. It is this past that restricts an individual and the society, as well as the world as a whole.

"Hence, individually, each person must begin to learn of the physics of energy so he can rectify the unbalanced energy that is the totality of a static field. He must learn the nature of this static, the nature of his mind, reflected in the nature of his present life. In this learning will there be the releasement of man from the drudgery of his unreclaimed past. The teaching for man explains that he does have a godhead; that he is the Infinite, as yet unrecreated. The creation of this understanding must not only be that he is a representation of the Infinite Force, but that he is also a representation of the finite force that he had not relinquished. The finite force is the unclaimed past, and it lives as a basic breeding ground, containing the pollution which is poisoning the appearance of his life. There can be no forward movement until each individual learns of the restrictive nature of his negative past - a past in every respect, with a force field that is strong.

"History is an important understanding in the reformation of man. The history of man's past can provide the specifics for a realistic understanding of the reincarnation statement of life. It is the proposition of Unarius to point out that man is an evolutionary design of the Infinite. The past is therefore the evolutionary prehistory of man and contains many unresolved and enigmatic factors within it. These factors are the life experiences that have regenerated a disharmony, and which is the containment of the static energies which presently have become a basic tumor in the psychic anatomy of man.

"The psychic anatomy is transmitting the polarized awareness of the individual's picture of life as a continuity, a singular appearance which must be held onto through hell or high water. The symbolic appearance of an atomic body and an atomic world generates a static field. Because this field is a representation of the belief system of an individual, he has transformed the infinite nature of his own psychic anatomy into a finite static field, which becomes the picture of his life-to-life incarnations.

"Evolution can therefore be seen to be a two-fold unfoldment, the double-helix in the cellular structure of the physical anatomy. But this double-helix provides an understanding that the physical anatomy contains one of the helixes and the psychic anatomy the other. The double-helix of life is the knowledge that evolution is a material and a spiritual developmental movement. The impressions which are inseminated within the cell structures of the physical body are transmitted from the electronic body and is the connecting link of the individual with spiritual factors of life that have been lived in astral worlds.

"As man is both a transmitter and a receiver, he must build his transmitter from life to life. The component parts are instrumented from newer and stronger elements and the receiver thus gains the strength from these newer component parts. This is knowledge of the energy force field in which the greater knowledge of his double helix, the spiritual and the physical anatomy. And the movement of these anatomies in their respective dimensions, provides him with the ability to construct the effigy of his spiritual self, with the knowledge that he has the capability to instrument a higher channel to receive newer information of himself. Then he becomes aware of the program from which he is receiving his picture. The higher the frequency structure of an individual, the greater can he program himself to receive the information of those channels of life that are broadcast to him from the expanding Infinite.

"In other words, the earthman becomes aware of his spiritual development; that there are other human beings who have expanded their awareness of their spiritual nature and have become conscious of the cosmic order of life. In his attunement on his new frequency band, he is therefore able to receive knowledge that he could not have commanded on the singular side of his atomic world. At the same time, as man lives in the fourth dimension on some astral planet, he is also in a position to receive from higher frequency stations, the higher regenerative civilizations that exist on higher spiritual dimensions.

"In this respect, man is evolving on two levels. He is learning upon the physical dimension on an earth planet of the nature and structure of his physical consciousness and he comes in direct contact with the non-physical nature of himself, the fourth dimensional mind, an evolutionary development which contains newer and higher constructs of the physics of life as it is revealed in its refraction in a third dimensional world.

"On a fourth dimensional world, the mind is seen to a greater degree, or felt in its higher vibrancy, and at the same time, it is evolving and gaining the higher sense structure to recognize the fifth dimension above it and witness to the Master-Teachers who live amongst his community in the astral world, who have come from these fifth and sixth and higher dimensions to which people have evolved.

"Evolution is therefore a constant relationship that involves the polarity of each individual. That is to say, man is constantly evolving, interchanging the knowledge of his lower and his higher self. This is the important knowledge that must be impregnated within man's consciousness. In the New Renaissance, this understanding will abrogate all divisiveness and will resolve the uncertainty principle that lies within the community of man; the uncertainty as to who he is, and the uncertainty as to the continuity of himself as an intelligent factor that will live beyond space and time.

"Knowing that the potential for evolution lies within each individual, he can command a higher station from which he can view the greater world which will give the individual a greater degree of determination; particularly so when he realizes he has the full potential to become what he outpictures himself! The knowledge that one has at his command, the entire facilities of Infinite Intelligence and that he also has the facilitation of Brothers who help him to learn of the nature of his own higher potential, is a great understanding for the entire community of mankind. These helpers are Masters of themselves, who have lived on the higher civilizations where life has been unified, where there is no divisiveness. Man, too, can learn of the higher mathematics that his teachers have learned, and become as they, equally capable of directing the energy of his mind. He will be able by directing it in a purposeful manner, to evolve and open up to the higher effulgences that lie within the higher frequency of the higher-frequency worlds.

"The dimension of man's mind is the nature of the consciousness of man; a consciousness that does not entertain the past!

# Chapter 8

## The Joining of Science and Religion

"The history of man has divulged many facets of man and the nature of society. The proliferation of books that have been published in the past 300 years indicates the changed relationship of man and society. There has been an industrial revolution in which the mechanics of energy have been developed and applied so as to provide man with the ability to reduce his dependency on manual labor and to manipulate the machinery of industry.

"The Age of Technology truly arrived in the 17th century with the understanding and the development of machines. Thus, man considered himself to be a machine, functioning in the exact same manner in which the technologists have devised these robots. This was a beginning for a revolution of the logic and reason for Homo sapiens to understand the infinite nature of himself; that he functioned in the exact same way as his machines and responded to the exact stimuli so prescribed for this particular machine. This device, a machine of electronic design, was in every respect, a projection from the mind of man, the designer.

"Those who were the designers of these machines and who had developed the idea for them were, in their own manner, individuals who were closer to the theoretical understanding of life and man's part in its entire holistic schematic. But previous to the Machine Age, the industrial revolution, and then to the beginnings of the atomic age, there had been understandings that had been garnered from the efforts of man, and through his tutoring by the wise Sages who had left behind the visible reality of a unified world; a world that explained the positive characteristics to make possible an integrated relationship of man with his environment!

"These teachings, however, were given the stamp of supernaturalism or the supernormal and were changed into an occult derivative, a secret which could not attain public acceptance to be capable of being understood by the masses of mankind. These teachings developed as a religion, an occult supernaturalism which became a preposterous exaggeration of the logic and reason for progressive evolution.

"The way of life that was prescribed by these Sages of old, such as Socrates, Akhenaton, Anaxagoras, Osiris, Kung Fu, Mencius, Buddah, Krishna, and of course, above all and closer to man's memory, Jesus of Nazareth, were Masters who spoke of a way of life that was not torn asunder! They spoke of the integrated relationship of man as a product of and relationship to nature. Hence, nature in its finite derivatives was the grand spectacle, reflecting to mankind its own awesomeness; its visible and yet invisible nature, which constantly projected its presence to mankind.

"The teachings that are presently incorporated into the basic religions of Mohammedanism, Buddhism, Christianity, Judaism, and derivative interpretations of these teachings, have become a cult rather than a way of life, based upon logic and reason of man's spiritual nature. The teachings of Jesus of Nazareth was meant to give the basic cosmic knowledge of man that his physical body was only a part of the world in which he was living and that Mind provided clues to his spiritual nature. The firmament below was the body and the firmament above was the Mind. The teachings of Jesus and of Buddha did not indicate that he had no alternative but to accept the grandiose design of the Infinite as a separate factor of himself in terms of his present consciousness. It was the purpose and objective of the teachings of Jesus of Nazareth to give man the awareness of his purpose in life as a spiritual entity; not to separate him from his physical consciousness and presuppose that he had no involvement in his progressive evolutionary development, but that his spiritual development would be based upon the productive nature of his efforts in his day-to-day living!

"These basic teachings of the Masters were to provide each individual with links to the logical factors of consciousness in which he would be capable of developing within the narrow confinement of the flesh body. However, Religion, which had been a concise statement for the integration of the body, mind and the spirit, would be a way of life to provide the means to develop the integrated factors of individual personality, which separated the physical nature of life from the polarity of his Infinite Self.

"Each individual must begin to understand the lower frequency of his subconscious affiliations. However, when man became aware of his superconscious nature millions of years ago, he was not meant to lose consciousness with this higher circuit of himself, for the high self is a development of his spirit to provide him with the direction to gain a greater productive development in his life-to-life learning while in the productive physical state, and learning through the physical, atomic body.

"The entire historical rendition of the literature of man has recorded flashes of great wisdom and intelligence, a link with the teachings of the Masters throughout the entire Earth world, and a link that has also given clues to man's heritage beyond earth worlds. This link has been related in narrative poems, containing the epochal verse of esoteric authors, to stabilize the nature of man as an evolutionary progression, to link him up, frequency-wise, to the higher circuitry of himself. The writings of Shakespeare, Tennyson, the writings of Aesop and his many fables, etc., are indications of deeper penetration into life that go beyond the fragmented religiosity that became the degenerative factor of the Sages, Masters and Elder Brothers of mankind. But in every respect, they were not supernatural and did not live beyond the world in which they were, at that time, deeply involved, yet were fully integrated in Spirit.

"Jesus of Nazareth, as Joseph, was himself a man. He was an advanced human in all respects, whose Spirit lived in a physical anatomy and functioned through the atomic sense structures of such an anatomy. He proved in his thirty-three years on Earth that he had gained his understanding and his integration with Spirit by proving his Mastership over his lower self. That Mastership was his integration with his own Superconscious Self, his Spiritual Self, his Oversoul; making that contact while in a physical body and involved in all of the duresses of physical life. It was Jesus' teaching to explain to mankind that each and everyone could function in the physical body and yet be attuned to his Spiritual Self, his higher body; to be in the world, but not of it; attuned to a fourth dimensional perspective of the Infinite Creative Intelligence!

"Jesus was stating that man had a quotient within him that he had not realized and had not used in guiding himself through the vicissitudes of life. He spoke in the language of parables to give clarity to the nature of man's problems, involved with the Roman dynasty, ruling the Eastern world at that time. The names have changed but the dynasties have continued. Rome was the empire that ruled the Earth world; then the same powers rule again with the materialistic earth vices that Jesus was alluding to, and which has been the classical statement of man's bias involvement with the materiality of his physical environment. These concepts are as valid as they were 2,000, 4,000, 8,000, 16,000 years ago, and throughout the entire pageantry of man's past history in each and every civilization!

"Evolution cannot take place within the construct of Infinity without the interlacing of the minds of other souls who had preceded younger souls in a third dimensional physical world. Such plebeians could not survive without the help of those who have advanced to the clearing of this giant forest and had gained their access to the clearing. In this respect, those Sages, those Masters and Avatars known as Uriel, as Isis, as Heliandra, Ioshanna, Joan of Arc, Mary of Bethany have been individuals who have been recognized for the merits of their spiritual nature. They are known for the spiritual values they have impregnated into their particular nations, as Maria Theresa, Queen Elizabeth I, Charlemagne, Peter the Great, etc. They were individuals who had learned of themselves as whole personalities and had mastered themselves. To the extent that they had done this, they were helping those who are still functioning without the leverage of the recognition of their spiritual identity.

"So life is a constant regeneration and rectification that is the internal involvement of advanced intelligent peoples who have reengaged themselves into the gestating characteristics of material life. These individuals have reengaged into the physical life of Homo sapiens, but in many respects, they were strange to this life. They were different! They had additional information and knowledge about life, which set them apart; and it was these characteristics that gave these individuals in some sense, a peculiar personality; peculiar in the sense that they did not function in the exact manner as man who was still pursuing the objectives of his life from the vantage point of his material concerns.

"These individuals and many others unnamed, were pursuing a higher objective in the attempt to help people realize the integrated humanness, the internal nature of each individual, and to sew the wounds of man by uniting nations over various epochs of time in the civilizations in which they functioned. Such was Charlemagne and Peter the Great, and Maria Theresa.

"But above all and beyond, there have been sages who are the continuities of these individuals who have added to the description of life; a life that is a visible factor that is a continuity of Earth life, which is man's future. Those sages have been capable of describing the continuity of third dimensional life as a productive developmental factor for fourth dimensional life as a productive developmental factor for fourth dimensional life. In this respect, these individuals have laid down a basic foundation to give mankind evidence that there is hope in the aspiration, even in the darkest moments in which an individual lives without knowledge of the heavens above him. The heavens are an abstract statement for a state of mind that provides that individual with his relationship to the wholeness of life, the larger pattern of which he is a part.

"Throughout the chapters of this book there are many allusive statements made as to the Father, Spirit, the Infinite Creative Intelligence, the Superconscious Self, and in other respects, words which would be construed to be evidence of the religious associations of many different sects; the Baptist, Roman Catholic, Hebrew, Greek Orthodox, Christian, Buddhist, Muslem, etc. In every respect, these different religions have taken on the name of the great Masters, the Sages from the higher worlds of Spirit, but have denuded the application of these teachings by the very followers of the teachings.

"Such is the case when Muslems, Jews and Christians take up arms against each other, when it is forbidden in their teachings to use retribution methods by taking another person's life. Such is the case when Muslems take up arms against the Israelis, and the Israelis against the Muslem; the Buddhist against another offshoot of the teachings of Buddha. These basic tenants of the teachings of the Masters have been abrogated and misrepresented by individuals who are followers of these religious sects, by the bishops and popes of these teachings, a dogma which was not the teachings ascribed to a Master. These dogmas are opposite constructs and cannot be considered to be the basic doctrine which is the teaching for man to learn of his Infinite Self and his spiritual characteristics which could be developed if the basic precepts of these great teachers had been followed.

"Hence, the vocabulary in which the word forms of the Father, Spirit, and other aspects of derivatives of Infinite Intelligence, are not to be construed as a continuity of the religions that have formed a basic pantheology of man's religious history. This is an opposite and degenerative development that is the reflection of the materialistic development of each individual in his life to life associations with these various religiously-biased and materialistic civilizations.

"To truly reclaim his spiritual heritage, man must bypass or extend himself from out the narrow confines of secularism to realize that he is one of a brotherhood who are reclaiming the essence of themselves. If one did become a Buddhist or a Christian because of his parents, that individual has the ability in the development of his own logic and reason as a human being, to determine what it was that seemingly says one thing and means another. That is, to be born into a family that holds to a particular doctrine is a part of the development and the continuity of that individual from his past associations with these doctrines. But as we have indicated, each and every life is a new life and an updated version where the individual has returned with new evidence of the truth of energy, and has been capable of sharpening his lens to see more specifically behind the facade of the apparency of material life. In this manner then, each individual does have a prerogative to stand for himself and not to concur with the attitudes of other individuals by learning how to gain his own individuality.

"In the present 20th century, the misleading and misrepresented statements of individuals in the scientific, political and religious establishments, give the individual a greater opportunity to see the reality of these basic materialistic dogmas ascribed to the corporate nature of these earth world systems.

"The separation of the continuity factors of life that is the nature of an integrated man or woman has fragmented the quantum and true expression of the nature of energy. It surrounds man; it interpenetrates him, and in all respects, functions throughout the grand sweep of cycles. Yet the interpolation of life in the many different synonyms and antonyms that have been given to it, have barricaded the individual from his own fellowman, humans born with different complexions and different colored skins. Although their evident exterior appearance seems different, they are in every respect, similar in their differences! Thus, the Unarius Science is the wisdom that had been taught in previous civilizations in the many epochal periods of man's past, where there was no separation as to the ascribing of the words of one individual and separating those words as knowledge of man's integrated characteristic.

"In the searching and in the seeking for the answers to this dilemma, which is the separation of man from himself, because he has involved himself to the degree of accepting the illogic of different individuals, and has interpreted these statements as his way of life, in this way, he has divided himself from the total humanity of his planet. By believing in the reality of a word, he is given a prescription to these words, which has developed a system, and he has accepted this system to be a reality.

"A definitive example are those who profess to know the truth of the teachings of Jesus of Nazareth, who stated in clear language that man was an energy system who lived from life to life, and was developing the essence of his Infinite Self, which is a property of greater intelligence - a creative factor that was responsible for the entirety of all processes of life. These concepts were diluted to presently become the established doctrine of the Catholic dogma. Washing one's hands in the blood of Jesus as a means of cleansing the self from the sins that had been the past history of that individual is a perversion of the sense of truth. On the one hand, using the basic format of the teachings of Jesus and then transliterating and reading into the statements of Jesus that were ascribed to him but written by other individuals who did not have a full and complete realization of who he was or where he came from, and the entirety of his teaching.

"This is what was meant when we introduced this basic statement that the words which are used to explain the higher factors of man in that he is a product, not of the material atomic environment which is called a third dimension, but that he is a product of and a creative factor of the higher evolutionary design of life. In fact, he is a creative effigy of this Infinite Creative Force that has been called the Father.

"And why should it not be called the Father? The Father, after all, is the causative agent for the son. It was through the Father that the son gains his life force. But of course, in these symbolisms that are necessary to provide some essence of understanding, the true understanding that can be gained, is a development for each individual to come to the point where he can see the higher factors of himself; to realize that the evidence of life that is the basic nature of his day-to-day living, is a demodulation of a greater Force. This greater factor and Force is our Father. It is basically an antonym for the great energy force field that is functioning and providing to man a recognition of his present life.

"Nature has been alluded to as an abstract force field. It is in accordance with the understanding of each individual as to his realization of the atomic nature of life, which is the refraction of his physical sense body. The flowers, the mountains, the waters, animal, mineral and vegetable are creative factors of this abstract called nature. The nature that man sees and realizes as mineral, vegetable, plant, animal and man, are reflections from his visible evidence of his atomic body. As the evidence of these factors of life become more highlighted, as he develops a greater sensitivity of himself and realizes that his physical anatomy is only one facet of the sense structure of himself, he thus realizes there is a Force that dominates the picture of life that has been given many different names.

"That Force is the all-creative, omnipotent, omnipresent Infinite, and it can be alluded to according to the knowledge of the physics of this great energy Force by a variety of derivative words. That is to say, 'It is the Father' does not mean that the author of this book is a Christian, a Jew, a Moslem or a Buddhist, or any of the many other derivative disciplines that

are the offshoots of these religions.
"The basic religions that have been ascribed to an individual were themselves integrated representations of a whole concept. In the Library of Unarius there are historical anthropologies indicating how a Brotherhood of Man had existed for eons of time and space; a Brotherhood that is the evolutionary design and proof of the continuity principle of life as it exists in all things. Call it man and nature if you wish. It is a Brotherhood because its individual members have developed their consciousness, mastering all various tangible and intangible facets of life. We speak, of course, of the life in which man is presently involved, attempting to gain some integration with himself. They are individuals who have progressed and have learned of the finite factors that are the basic situations and problems that face mankind, political and religious; yet knowing of the inner self and penetrating into the very nature of the atom!
"They are Brothers because they have overcome the separate nature of self and have been integrated into the nature of their spiritual nature and the nature of nature. That is to say, they are not separated from the electromagnetic force field of life and are capable of functioning in such an integrated manner that they have developed a realization of their individual selves as a joint participating factor that is known as a Brotherhood. It is a field of energy that is so

ionized positively that these hundreds of millions of people function as a polarity, uniting the different elements which are the characteristic nature of their singular selves.

"It is this polarization of humans who have progressed in their life-to-life development, who have unified their understanding of life, which is the basic teachings for man. These teachings go far back beyond the time of written history; the myths and folklores that have antedated Egyptian civilization. Man has lived on planet Earth far beyond the record of accepted history. He has been involved with patterns of life of a higher integration since these higher crests of life's wave have been due to the involvement of advanced human beings who had returned and stationed themselves within a basic society of man as a stabilizing factor.

"The whole panoply of life can therefore be more capable of being understood in that there are, in every society of a civilization, certain individuals who had graduated, let us say, from the schools of society, and had returned as a visionary! He stood above the masses of people who were still living under the accepted core of some social order, believing in its materiality, led by other individuals who had gained a certain greater power as to the understanding of life. Yet these persons had not gained mastery over their lower self, although they had an ability to direct other individuals who were as sheep.

"The regenerative nature of life is an isochronous beat frequency that carries a pulse from other interested and regenerative individuals. The past three hundred years in which the foundations of science have been established, have been the work of these more advanced, intelligent human beings who have lent their understanding of the integrative pattern of life to so involve themselves by sewing a thread of Spirit into the community of man in the many different disciplines of the science to regenerate the true pattern that provides the 'real' sense of life.

"In this respect, those who have returned and have added to the more integrated pattern of life, have carried back to the Earth world a knowledge of the integrated fourth dimensional worlds where the Brotherhood of Man functions; where the knowledge of the evolutionary progression of life is the continuity. In each dimension, in each spectrum of this great infinite movement of energy, there are people who have mastered certain equations of life and have formed a certain platform, a civilization, a world in which they are functioning, similar to universities, where on different disciplines, they are learning the greater concept of the subject of life, which is integrated into the consciousness of the student.

"Einstein, Oppenheimer, Crookes, Pascal and others too numerous to mention, are travelers from other Star

Systems who have intercepted the energy fields of the Earth worlds, and have sown certain additional equivalents of information of life's ecology. Thus, each individual does develop in accordance to his own logic and reason from the prompting given from other individuals in their manner, to create a new awareness through the wider aperture of the interdimensional vortex.

"The essence of this statement is that man cannot be considered supernatural or supernormal because he had attained to a greater understanding of the grand design of life; and that he does not interfere in the evolutionary development of another human being because he is expressing his complete and total knowledge of life. Such has been the self-centered program of certain individuals who thus separated man from his objective, and indeed his prerogative to learn of the design of life within the warp and woof of his present mentality.

"It is said that the new science began with the introduction of the Planck theory of the quantum and with the theory of relativity initiated by Albert Einstein. If such is the case that these two concepts of energy have been accepted, they have regenerated a fresher approach to the 'reality' of life and have sewn into the fabric of man's consciousness another thread to provide additional clues of the interdimensional relationship of man to man. In this respect then, these more advanced individuals singularly and as a whole, who have established their presence in a physical environment and have added a new thread which accumulatively has brought man to his present understanding - an understanding of the pulse of his own consciousness, which must be a development for man to live within a society presently making up the substance of humanity on an earth world.

"The precepts of this understanding of the continuity of life, the interrelationship of man as particles of this great energy system, is vast and could not be contained within the conscious mind of the earthman. It is not our intention to abrogate the evolutionary purpose of life but to add to a new development which has been set down as a foundation. The energy of the atom, a sub-microscopic field, is expanding in a sub-infinite direction. It is this expansion that has not yet been recognized, but it will be, as it is a part of the relationship that is presently the beginning understanding that the atom is the equilibrium point in this evolutionary design of the Infinite Vortex and the macroscopic picture of life is the evidence of research by astronomers and cosmologists of the expanding nature of the Infinite in its ascending spiral.

"The subinfinite is expanding in the opposite direction, wich can be considered the descending spiral. But the truth is this: that this great Force that has been given many different derivatives: the Fountainhead, the Father, the Cosmic Mind, the Infinite Creative Intelligence, which is no doubt a more concise description, is a dual movement in its own momentum. It is in this respect that man must have the basis for the understanding of this dual movement within the patterns of his own duality to begin to reconstruct the evidence of his own nature through the research by his own faculties of logic and reason; of his surrounding electromagnetic field.

"Thus man, through the avenues of science, which has been alluded to as separating man from himself, is beginning to integrate the nature of himself. The dissociation of man from his electromagnetic energy field has been the teachings of false religions that have ascribed some supernatural force to the belief structure of many of these religious dogmas: prayer to a god, lighting up incense, and many different rituals, attempting to do penance for man's so-called sins, which creates a separation of Homo sapiens from the Father; the Infinite Creative Intelligence, an interdimensional electrodynamic energy field, omnipotent and omnipresent!

"But the greatest deceiver of all, is the lack of the understanding of the inherent energy system that is the characteristics of Homo sapiens. The very lie that is being promulgated and separates man from the many teachings of the Masters is that man is not capable of realizing his potential.

But the opposite is the truth, and this truth is being provided through the aegis of Science. This Science is the integrated statement of man as a spiritual creation. We will not go into the nature of the Infinite Creative Intelligence because that understanding can only be attained in successive evolutionary developments, and in the graduation of each individual from the school in which he is presently involved. When he masters his lessons and the concepts that are involved in the subject matter of his physical incarnation, he can more properly and more capably begin to understand certain higher concepts of the electromagnetic spectrum on higher frequency dimensions.

"At the present time, a first statement in this understanding is the recognition of the integrative energy system that is the nature of all human beings. This has been the basic deceptiveness of those teachings which give the appearance of life to some exterior system and have ascribed this system as being some great force. Yes, it is the Force; a Force that is all-pervasive, all-creative, and is the Infinite Intelligence, which has re-created Itself within the energy system of each human being.

"Therefore, to pray to the Lord, considering that Lord as some segment of energy outside of the individual, is to deceive the individual and to waylay his development. It also causes degenerative developments because it destabilizes the individual and makes him weaker. The entire purpose of life is to *GAIN THE UNDERSTANDING OF ONE'S OWN STRENGTH;* that one is capable of achieving any objective he so sets for himself and proves that he is unlimited in his pursuit of this infinite concept! The Infinite Concept of Life is being learned by each individual in an incremental manner in each developmental phase of his education, in the schoolroom of the Life Force that has been created within him.

"Hence it is we say, that belief in supernaturalism, ascribing to life some causative factor outside of man, is giving lie and deception to man's own productive ability and his possibilities of becoming a greater and more advanced intelligent being. Just because the child is not capable of running as fast as an adult does not mean that he will not develop the capability of proving his physical capabilities. He is still immature in respect to his physical organs. In the same sense, man is still immature with respect to his mental organs and has not matured to the extent that he has engaged with the mental factors which are the nature of these organs. This is the nature of present earth life, as Earth is a developmental stage in the learning of man's spiritual nature. This spiritual nature should not be considered to be a religious concept. It is an integrated factor of the higher energy-field structure that is the content of each individual's psychic or electronic anatomy.

"It is the electronic body, the mental body that is the chief subject matter in this new development for man, because the construct of life that is being shown in science is that man is not singular but is a system of polarity relationships. This relationship must be brought down to its basic recognition; a relationship of the physical anatomy to its prime anatomy. The physical body will, in cyclic time, eventually lose its elasticity and return to the sixteen atomic elements from which it was formed. But man is not created from those sixteen atomic elements; he is the sixteen elements plus the infinite number of elements that are the product of his energy anatomy. The sixteen elements are only one small increment of the energy anatomy. Therefore, this electronic body, which produces the physical anatomy, is the first important teaching of evolutionary man.

"Evolution is seen in all characteristics of physics and electronics. Evolution and regeneration are truly one and the same, because when two elements combine and in their combinations change into another element, that is considered a harmonic. As two frequencies oscillate with each other, they result in harmonics. That is the regeneration of the energy waves containing certain information within the two atoms. So helium is the productive or evolutionary development of hydrogen, etc.

"The purpose of life is therefore to realize that it is the engagement of the atoms which comprise the physical anatomy with the psychic or electronic anatomy that is the reality of the regeneration of man, and is the evolutionary design that had been so set in motion for each individual to be so cognizant. Yes, life is a great and very complex statement; yet that complexity can be understood in the relationships that are the basic design, which indicate the evolutionary statement of life.

"The great Masters who taught man, were revealing to him this integrative pattern, which is the regenerative evolutionary design of life. Man is learning the essential patterns to indicate to him his relationship in this grand design. He is expressing on a lower frequency in a third dimensional world, but he was created in a higher frequency world which is non-atomic. In the understanding of this interrelationship between his atomic and non-atomic self, he gains the realization of the infinite potential that has been constructed within his energy body.

"Therefore, the next development in the understanding of man is the Spiritual Renaissance, whereby all factors of life will be addressed to the nature and function of the electromagnetic energy field, sometimes called the plasma field. In this understanding, man will know himself; not as a separate entity who is attempting to gain his awareness of life by storing up great treasures in the material sense. He will lose his inferiority and will gain the realization of his relationship to other human beings as his brothers. In this respect then, there will be a re-emergence of man into his proper spiritual development. Progressive evolution will be the sharing of each individual's own efforts with other individuals; not to attempt to intervene with the individual ego, but to share the produce of each individual's efforts to enlarge the entire sphere of community life.

"The revolution in physics is an evolution of the evolutionary statement of life because it will provide the evidence of man as a universal, articulate, interdimensional statement of the Infinite Creative Intelligence! The Unarius Science then, is the basic curriculum that teaches this knowledge of the higher energy field of the electronic body of man. No others could teach or bring this information except those who have mastered this understanding of life by mastering the basic ingredients of their own electromagnetic nature.

"Hence, the Science known as UNARIUS, is a futuristic science - a science of the 21st century! It is a science that was brought from the future by those of the Brotherhood of Man, who are validating this science in their own expression, as they are now infinitely enlightened and aware of their relationship in this great pattern known as life.

"Science and religion will therefore be joined, because science is the basic means through which the physics of life can be understood; not from a supernatural platform, by separating man from himself, but by engaging man within the nature of his electromagnetic field. This electromagnetic field *IS* his spirit, and the greater the understanding of the movement of this field, which is man's mind, the greater will be that individual's ability to be in tune with the electromagnetic fields of other humans who have advanced to a greater development and are in tune with a higher keynote of this Infinite Creative Intelligence, or the Father.

"Positive always carries to the negative polarity a great Force, a greater Intelligence. This is known as inspiration, and it is in this factor and this manner that man will be inspired, because he will be in tune with the higher civilizations of his Brothers. Unarius is therefore a Brotherhood, concerned with the development of its younger brothers. There is no separation; there are no gods; there are no supernatural peoples who will come to one's rescue. It will be a purposeful evolutionary development of student and teacher, where the teacher becomes the student in his own progressive development. And the student becomes the teacher as he learns of those elements that have been brought to his consciousness to be applied in his present development.

"The acronym of Unarius is the acronym of the new Science. It is not new in respect to its development, because it was and always has been the Infinite Creative Intelligence. It has been learned and applied by those Brothers who are the percursors of this knowledge. They have only one concern, to provide the public with knowledge of these advanced concepts which are the future of man.

"Learn therefore, of the integrated nature that lies within your own individual self, your electronic, psychic anatomy; as the Infinite Creative Intelligence is expressing for you to learn of this expression. It is within the dimension of your own consciousness that you can gain a greater degree of a higher consciousness; not from the outside but from the inside, through logic and reason, and the knowledge of your own function as an energy field force that has a purposeful relationship to the entire fabric of life."

# Chapter 9

# Man, the Regenerative Evolutionary Spirit

"*MAN, THE REGENERATIVE, EVOLUTIONARY SPIRIT*, the title of this book, is the theme of life itself! Man is the alpha and omega. The alpha is the local universe, the physical universe, the third dimension. The omega is the infinite, ever-expanding universes of the fourth dimension. Man is therefore a being who is becoming infinite. Man is local and yet non-local. The evident nature of these statements are the correlative factors of the teachings of the Masters. These great teachings are the correlation and synthesis of all incidental factors of life, of classical physics, with the new physics that is presently recognizing the consciousness of man as a regenerative, evolutionary energy system of spiritual intelligence.

"What is the substantiation for this statement? Can it be substantiated by the methodology of experimentation, the technique of validating the theoretical nature of the causal and effectual factors of energy? And the answer is yes. This is the methodology, the means by which man learns of his regenerative, evolutionary nature, and comes to that grand point in the understanding of himself as the eternal Infinite, an Infinite that is recognizable in each of its finite, microscopic facets.

"It is said that man is the microcosm; that he is the totality of the cellular structures which are representative of the expanding unit of energy whose nature is presently being resolved as the basic consciousness of man as a fourth dimensional perspective. The microcosms are subatomic structures, the basic foundations, and the constant provision for the synthesis of its complex interrelationships that finally resolve into infinitessimal units of energy; an energy unit that is complex and contains subdivisions which, in themselves, function on the same principles as does the total organism, man.

"In this manner then, it can be seen from the evidence of Planck's Constant theory that the local units of energy function in a universe of their own, but when they are united or correlated with other units of the microcosm, a new system develops, which is the sum and total, plus a new factor that is the personality of the sum and total of the two or more elements that have been linked together. It is this representation in fact, that has been demonstrated in chemistry and in physics that substantiates the fact that man is the correlation of many minute suborganisms; that man, as the macrocosm, is not the same unit of energy as is the hydrogen atom per se; isolated in its local movement as separate from man. It is in the derivations of the 92 atomic elements that there is the regeneration of a new organism.

"This was the search for the meaning of life that motivated Sir

Alfred Whitehead and other metaphysicians. Afred Whitehead was a scientist who was in advance of his brother scientists. He realized that the resolution for the understanding of life could not be validated by searching out the evidence through the local universe, or the segments of the universe, isolated in time and space from its associated field units that are a part of it; yet invisible to man who is yet operating on the limitations of his physical senses. In spite of the fact that he has additional instrumentation to peer behind the mirror, he has not as yet, associated his microcosmic body and his consciousness with the nature of the mechanism that powers the systematic movement for all local universes, and provides the substance for these universes, the quotient of energy that makes possible the functioning of a universe in a specific spectrum of a dimension.

"The reason physical scientists are still dumbfounded with the awesome nature of the vast universe in the physical sense, as they peer into the fourth dimensional universe, they have not yet climbed high enough mentally-wise to peer over the boundary separating the physical universe from its true transmitter, the fourth dimension. Yes, there have been those more intelligent who have realized that they have been looking from the bottom of a deep hole, as it were, and have been examining the cliff side. They have seen the open space above them, but they have not seen the relationship between the sides of the surrounding cliff, the top and the open sky and themselves! They have only seen separate incidences which are confining factors of themselves; the nature of their physical system, which obeys certain fundamental laws of momentum and gravity.

"Erwin Schrodinger, as well as Albert Einstein, would not settle for the separation of man from nature. They would not accept the notion that other physicists had elected to this separatism in their theory of the nature of life. They have realized that the Infinite Creative Intelligence is all-creative, all-intelligent, and provides the same information to each and every dimension that lies within it, and that the interrelationship between the dimensional structures of energy that make up the expanding vortex, is the nature of the changes that are the basic, structural movement of the energy.

"Looking from the bottom up does not give a researcher the truth of what he sees, for he is seeing upside down, and he is translating all that he sees within the perimeter of his own viewpoint and is instrumenting the lens on that biased manner! He is, of course, biased to the lower field in which he is functioning. So one would ask, how can one obtain the view from the mountaintop looking down? Unless you are on the topside, how can you see below when you are down? How can you see up?

"Well, it is a matter of perspective. It is a matter of the understanding of the movement of life which is both evolutionary and regenerative. It is in this manner that we can understand how change has taken place and formed a new structure, a new organism. The catalysis that has been the responsible nature of the change is, in every respect, the interrelationship that is the resolution of a new appearance of life on a different level of its reflective appearance.

"One has to believe that there is an up; that is to say, an expansion, and a belief that there is a process of contraction. If something is expanding, it is expanding from some base plane. Hence, there are two forces involved: the expanding force and the descending force. It is in this manner then, that we can appreciate the problem of those who are limited in their understanding of the forces that are of this infinite proposition.

"In many respects, man is very similar to the venturi tube that was diagrammed by Albert Einstein while he was on Earth. Man is in the direct middle of an expanding universe; expanding on both sides of man. In other words, the Infinite is a contracting and expanding force, expanding in a macrocosmic manner, ever moving into higher and higher frequency structures. But at the same time, the Infinite is dual and therefore, is expanding in its alternate position from its negative polarity. Since life is a proposition of duality and the very basic understanding of life must be gained from this awareness of the polarity factor in energy, it can then be understood how catalysis takes place, for there is always movement between the two polarities of energy. As energy is the Infinite, no matter what it is called and how small it becomes in terms of its rectification into the third dimension, it contains its alternate polarity function. The movement of energy wave forms is the construct of Infinite Intelligence and functions differently as it expresses on its negative polarity into its submicroscopic and sub-infinite position.

"The laws or the principles by which energy wave forms function are a contrast and in opposition to the movement of the Infinite in its vortexal structure, as it is expanding into its positively-charged position. This is the great enigma and anomaly in physics and is demonstrated in the physics of quantum mechanics; that is, submicroscopic particles of the atom do not obey the basic laws of physics for macrocosmic particles. This is because the atom itself is connected with and obeys the basic principles of interdimensional physics This interdimensional principle is the continuity note of the Infinite. The atom is receiving its positive charge from a higher force field from which it had emerged, and therefore, the atom can be seen to be a contracted movement of energy, reduced into a subatomic structure as it is expressing in its negative polarity. This therefore becomes the new balance of the atom within a third dimensional structure.

"The atom is the sub-Infinite, the microcosm that is a correlationship and synthesis of molecular energy structures, becoming the equation of Homo sapiens. We see then, a universe that is the regeneration and the synthesis or the catalysis that takes place in the movement of atomic elements. Individually, a cell from a physical anatomy is meaningless. It has a particular intelligence, but overall, it is a local and separate intelligence and has a practicle value to some extent; but it is not complete in its intelligence until it is united with other organs which make up a cohesive macrocosmic picture that can function in an entirely different manner to effect new results in the evolutionary movement of Infinite Intelligence.

"An individual cell has a frequency; it has a basic pulse beat, but it is incapable of doing anything without the assistance of other cell structures. As man is the combination of hundreds of thousands or millions of individual cell structures, he is in every respect, a universe. As we have indicated, man is both the alpha and omega. Because he is the reflective nature of intelligence - an intelligence, which resolved into a microcosmic, physical anatomy, is also going through a macrocosmic, evolutionary stage and development.

"That stage and development is

now the macrocosmic picture of man as he is moving and interrelating in his movement with other functionary structures similar and yet different to himself. It is in this movement then that the cellular nature of society can be understood, in that there is also a change taking place as in the first formative stages of the development of the physical anatomy. But where did all this energy come from to resolve into the basic staging for Homo sapiens? And what is known as humanity, the mind, consciousness, and the many derivatives that is the entire structure of society?

"Scientists have not yet been willing to accept the universal nature of life. There have been many different developments in the physical and metaphysical theories which would be consistent and hold true in all aspects of life, from the minute particles of the atom to the macrocosm of societal life. But there is a catalysis that is always taking place, and in the catalysis there is a new organism developing; a new intelligence that is the nature of the new organism. It is this intelligence that is the regenerative factor and provides the clue.

"The child, as an infant, is not the same person when he becomes the adult; moreover, the adult in a physical body, is not the same person as that being when he advances in a nonphysical body to the fourth dimension. Man is an evolutionary development in becoming a being. He is evolving through a catalytic process, various reactive components in which he is involved in his movement, cellular-wise and Being-wise. As man learns about himself in his interpenetration within the fabric of his planet and within all of the nuances that become the nature of the complex involvements with the millions of individuals who have various differences and similarities, he learns also of the catalytic action that is taking place within himself. This catalytic action is the microscopic and macroscopic nature of man. The microscopic nature is the alpha, and it is the nature of the local energy field in which he is presently learning of his beingness. That is the third atomic dimension; but man is also a fourth dimensional structure and there is where a synthesis is always taking place with man, to become a superman!

"The formative nature of the mind as it is constantly innervating into the physical anatomy, results in a catalysis of the movement between two different agents; the agencies of the psychic anatomy and the physical anatomy. The psychic anatomy is not yet known to the scientific community because it lies outside the instrumentation of present-day science, and cannot be validated on the basis of the limited understanding of present-day physics. But all people know that everyone has a mind that provides the determinist attitudes of people; that one sets an objective to undergo some experiment and therefore, that set mind is that individual scientist who sets up the procedures for the requirements for such an experiment.

"He knows that he has a mind; yet with all of that knowing he is still functioning and extrapolating from his mind into his particular physical environment, taking for granted all circumstances in which he is functioning, to set up the parameters of his experiment. Whether it be in a physical way or it be mentally, he is still unaware of the catalytic nature of himself in his involvement in two different universes, two different dimensions - one based on local time and space and the other unlocalized and timeless and spaceless. He is functioning on two basic languages and is attempting to communicate the nature of one to the other. He is down at the bottom of a large cavern, even while the entire nature of life in that cavern is received from information descending frequency-wise from a higher energy transmitter, which is providing the substance of his life.

"There are people who have an intelligent over-review of life, having fabricated for themselves an understanding of the indivisible Infinite. Of course, the Infinite is divisible into its finite component parts; yet there is another infinite component, a refraction of the Infinite, that contains new factors within itself. But this Infinite, which is a fourth-dimensional derivative of a higher refracted Infinite, does contain within it the

the equilibrium that is not a factor of the finite dimension of a third dimension. The entire anomaly of life has been this higher polarity nature, existent in all energy structures. Once this bridge has been gapped, then the scientists will have finally tripped the lever which will open the blinders of his mental eyes, to give him full access and full view of the polarity picture of interdimensional life!

"As Einstein stated, 'God does not play dice with nature,' meaning that there are no chance encounters; that the third dimension is not an accidental perversion of some higher expressionary intelligence. If there is an Infinite Creative Intelligence, which there surely is, in the respect of its infinite nature, it recreates all facets of its infinite nature. That is to say, that at all times it is equally in tune with the microcosmic nature of itself, as well as its macrocosmic nature, because the Infinite is an interdimensional interchange of its own energy, alternating from two opposite polarities.

"Just because man, who is emerging into the awareness of the macrocosmic nature of life, is not yet capable of seeing the interdimensional movement of energy, does *NOT* mean that he is not directly involved within it. For indeed, he is!

"The new science for the 20th and 21st century is this over-review which will, and in fact, is taking man out of the lower level, where he has been restricted and blinded from seeing the higher perspective of the intelligence from which he has been formed. This will resolve the enigma of atomic life for all time! This balance will make all the difference at this point in history, removing the chasm of ignorance which created the blind spot of man; his unawareness of the negative polarity of his life. Objectively speaking, this is a product of evolution itself, because all people are living as a reflection of the polarity of life. Of course, it is not possible to know life other than in the alternative environments of which it has been formed.

"But again we have related how the Universal Science of Unarius explains diagrammatically, the physics of the Infinite: an interdimensional movement of life positive to negative, negative to positive, fourth and third-dimensionally, fifth and fourth-dimensionally. This is the constant proof of life's expression, which is the nature of this grand design. Why would you think this grand design, the product of the Infinite Mind, would not function on its lowest possible derivative, as well as on its highest, if it was not the purpose for the sub-microscopic nature of the Infinite to eventually expand to become the macroscopic appearance of life?

"The venturi-tube diagram indicates that the alpha pulse of life is not necessarily the beginning, in the sense that the Infinite begins and ends. The ascending spiral of the universal vortex and the descending spiral of the universal vortex from its alternate polarities, indicate a birthing of a new organism. It is in this respect that this new organism contains the substance of both equivalents of the Infinite. Whether they be a hydrogen atom, man, planets, solar systems, galaxies or universes and other complex molecular factors of physical life, these organisms are now transposed and function directly in the equilibrium line; the alternate polarities of the interdimensional vortex.

"This is therefore the development in that specific organism where the consciousness of its structure becomes its recognizable feature. This is man becoming a being. This is the development of the higher structures of what are complex interrelationships of the energy structures of the vortex. That vortex is the electromagnetic field which is the interlaying and outerlaying nature of man and his society. The planet itself is a factor in the electromagnetic spectrum and man is another factor. He is interrelating and he is at all times, involved in a catalytic action. It is an action such as is the function in the principle of hysteresis. It is in this hysteresis, therefore, that changes take place and new developments happen.

"So we would say to the man of

science who is still attempting to resolve this enigma, that to stretch his mind he should be aware that Star travelers from the dim distant dimension, frequency-wise, who have learned of these equations, have traveled back into the so-called time warp of time and space! They have returned in the natural development in the catalysis of energy from the fourth dimension to the third dimension as new humans or Homo sapiens. They have catalyzed through the normal birth channel and are containing now the elements of the higher physics.

"They contain energy which is the nature of their minds, the nature of their ideas! These are the individuals who catalyze into the macrobionic system of life in the present society, the higher frequency of structures, and in this respect, we see a catalytic action taking place in the constant movement of man who is carrying basic knowledge from his past. But at the same time, there are those more mentally advanced individuals who have been bringing higher information or knowledge of the Infinite from the expanding universe.

"So we see that man is directly in the center of this expanding universe and he is necessarily not relieved of the responsibility of determining the validity of the opposites in which are functioning in some fashion within his life. He is on the one hand, badgered with the variety of statements which have to do with past associations in the societies of Greece, Rome, Egypt and other civilizations. At the same time, he is receiving knowledge that on the one hand, has some familiarity, has some additional appendix, which addition adds to a new perspective. This new perspective is the work of those futuristic peoples who, although they live in physical bodies, are coming from a future world.

"The great difficulty then for those physical scientists who have been functioning and containing the derivatives of past information from their involvement in understanding the nature of this life force, is that they are moving away from the negative polarity and are coming closer to the equivalent center, as in the diagram of the venturi tube. Thus, they are becoming more responsive to the expanded picture of life where man is seen to be the agent who is changing his organism to include a new development, a new awareness on a new base plane frequency.

"The conflicts, therefore, at the present time are between the old science and the new science. The new science, the science that is known as Unarius, is not predicated on third dimensional equivalents, which are only the reflection of the motion of the stars and the movement of the planets around their suns! The new science is a cosmology that goes beyond the individual local systems and goes beyond the individual system of the third dimension of time and space. It reaches up and takes man up over the barrier of life to show him his true Beingness.

That Beingness is timeless and spaceless. It demonstrates to him that he is lodged within the firmament of the Infinite but has not been swimming in the interdimensional tides that are the movement of Infinite Consciousness. He has been swimming in an opposite fashion and therefore, has not been in tune with, nor has he gained the realization of his Beingness.

"The language and terminology that offends certain physical scientists is the word 'paranormal'. 'Metaphysical' is now becoming an accepted term but 'paranormal' somehow has caught in the throat of some individuals attempting to open up the scenery of life and to show how man is a relationship within the broad perspective of his planet and his galaxy. But at the same time, they have limited their new recognition because they have not yet been capable of resolving this enigma of time and space.

"Paranormal means that an individual is able to reach above the light barrier and peer into another system of energy, another world, a dimension which is considered to be the purview of the paranormal and the purview of metaphysics. If this should be true, then the paranormal and metaphysics are truly one and the same. An individual who is both a scientist in the classic statement of a scientist and is a metaphysician, is a contrast and is a dichotomy. Yet every scientist that is counted for his contribution to humanity was a metaphysician.

"Lord Alfred Whitehead was a metaphysician; Darwin to some degree; Newton to a great degree; Descartes and Johannes Kepler, and other scientists are listed in the Encyclopedia of Science as individuals who have believed in the universal nature of life, its grand design. This has been the quest of science throughout its history; to find that indivisible union which is the grand concept of the synthesis of all appearances of energy.

"Those individuals who are capable of seeing beyond the field of light of a third dimension are no less scientific, and in fact, are more scientific than those who are held within the appearance of the light band of the third dimension. It could be stated by those who hold to the latter view that they have a greater degree of expertise and are working methodically on basic statements as to the validation of the movement of energy. There is a history of over three-hundred years in which they have gained the respect of their colleagues.

"However, those individuals, whomever they may be, who limit the nature of the mind of man, have limited themselves in their own insistence in their attempt to answer many of these anomalies of nature. They have restricted the development of their own research and are faced again with the onerous responsibility of having involved their opinion and having opinionated science!

"Looking back into history, one can see that the innovators in life have always been paranormal in their understanding of the appearance of life. They have seen both the positive and negative polarity of the patterns of energy. They have seen the past and the future in the present and hence, they are in that respect, true scientists. Cause and effect being the basic statement of any objective evidence of life, one would have to be aware of the involvement of the alternate movement of energy as it is presently polarized into each individual, into his energy system, which is a complex pattern of energy wave forms.

"The great teachers who are responsible for holding man in a healthy pattern in his society, have been the paranormal Cosmic Visionaries who have seen the whole of life. Life being the resolution of the fourth dimension and the third dimension, the beingness of man is resolved in his awareness of his wholeness; that is, that he is a polarized facsimile of the greater Infinite. Such Beings, therefore, who have polarized this knowledge within themselves, who are those master-teachers and scientists: Buddha, Jesus of Nazareth, Socrates, etc., are a running summary of the catalysis that has been the action of these teachers of man.

"They have brought the future into the present whilst man as a whole, has been bringing his past into his present, and they have made possible the evolutionary development of life on the planets of the third dimension. It is the involvement of these futurists, who are Unariun Scientists that make possible the progressive development of man in all planetary systems. It is in the polarization of the field energies of mankind in his development that he is reaching for the stars. Although he is grounded to a rocky planet, he is always reaching up to those living on these Star systems, beyond the molecular band of third dimensional life; those who intersperse their knowledge of the interdimensional nature of life into the society of mankind.

"How else could man learn of the developing nature of his evolutionary self if he did not have a basic imprint to work with? He must have the representation of other Beings who are the basic example of his future. Other than that, there would always be stagnation as one would not have the capability of a higher intelligence to reform into their own lives.

"Such is the situation at the present time in the 20th century. The Unariun Brotherood is the bastion of these Cosmic Visionaries who have taken on another incarnation purposely to add to and invigorate and develop the properties of this catalysis. This catalysis is the knowledge of the positive polarity of man, the knowledge of the psychic anatomy; the knowledge that he is living in two worlds and that he has been catalyzing himself to attain some equilibrium on the physical planets in preparation for the attainment of the basic structure where he will be capable of opening up to the larger nature of his true spirit - a winged organism that can move through time and space and is not hindered by the refraction of light in one dimension!

"This is the ongoing and ever developing statement of life. As man evolves such as those individuals who have evolyed and have taken on a new evolution on the fourth dimension, the present Cosmic Visionaries, they are evolving to higher dimensions, having attained various developmental statements in the catalytic action that takes place in the astral, spiritual, and celestial worlds.

"Man is the regenerative factor of the Infinite Intelligence, and he is beginning to realize his inherent interior nature which is the Creative Force of his higher Superconscious nature. This electromagnetic force, which explains the full nature of the physics of fourth-dimensional science, will be the property of all people to become, in this fashion, an agent to intersperse the knowledge that lies within themselves and to recreate their positive polarity.

"That positive polarity is his Superconscious Mind. The Superconscious Mind is the ingredient that has been so polarized to function in tune with the ever-moving invisible, and yet visible Infinite. It is the subconscious self of man which is the negative polarity out of which he is learning to reform the viable factors of his emerging being. It is the subconscious which is yet not known and understood in its association to and as a part of the set mind that he carries, which has been biased to either the positive factors of himself, his fourth dimensional nature, or to his subconscious and his material self. Emotional hangups have to do with the separation of the individual with society. Such separation is based totally from the restrictive nature of attitudes which carry the caustic acid of resentment, jealousy and the developmental factors of guilt, lack of confidence, insecurity and fear. These are all unpolarized agencies of the individual which now rests upon him in a static form, pressing down upon his consciousness.

"The knowledge of the universal concepts of energy, the knowledge of the polarity nature of energy, will be the open door which will change the basic imbalance which is the nature of the present situation of man. Man is developing into a higher organism, having reached a certain point in the evoluting of the species which are the basic cyclular structures of the greater Infinite.

"Man has reached a point where he must choose between holding on to the past and those factors which lie within himself as unreformed attitudes that are polarized to the past, to attain to a greater awareness of his complete and total relationship to all human beings within his own family unit and within the entire interrelatedness of the social divisions that are the nature of society. In this respect then, it comes down to the fact that each individual must know of himself as an energy system. He must first learn that he is both the microcosm and the macrocosm; that he is the alpha and the omega and what he sets in motion will surely be completed in the irresistible direction in which that motion was set.

"Man must therefore learn that the negative energies which have become intractible ingredients of his electronic anatomy, the psychic body, are an Infinite Force, containing the coding of his past. Each individual is presently containing the negative effects of these motions that have been rectified into energy wave forms that make up the structure of his electromagnetic body, which is surely the only means by which man will understand his relationship to other human beings, his relationship to himself, and his relationship to the Infinite Intelligence.

"The Godhead that is spoken of by many religionists is not outside of man but is within man. Each individual therefore contains the invincible, infinite nature of the Infinite, with which he must learn to function and to therefore expand his consciousness. Those individuals who are bringing this knowledge to mankind are therefore paranormal in their understanding of the physics of third-dimensional energy constructs. They see the continuity of the energy; not in terms of its visible evidence on the screen of some television console, but see the entirety of this movement of life which is man as a spiritual construct, a being who contains the Infinite, which provides the answers to many of the puzzles that are present difficulties of scientists in reinstituting into mankind the balance that is at all times, a part of and living within nature.

"Balance is the real picture of the movement of energy. There is always a balance which may be seen geographically, climatically, and of course, evolutionary-wise. The entire statement of Darwin was a consistent statement of balance in nature; the survival of the fittest where the strongest species survive. In this respect, there is balance in nature. Because of the new structures that take place, the entire ectoplasm, the whole sphere of the planet contains its necessary balance between all of its component factors within the ground and above the ground. There must always be the balance between the polarity structures of this vast schematic, the electromagnetic spectrum.

"Man therefore contains within himself, the complete history of life. His balance is that much more necessary as he involves in a greater way the environment, not only of his planet but the environment of other associated planets. So let us see that the paranormal is the developing, adaptive, regenerative nature of man. He is, in his evolutionary movement, becoming non-atomic mentally-wise, to the extent that he will be able to use the higher sense structures of his superconsciousness and see beyond the evidential barrier of light. This will be through the higher senses where he will see clearly that he is not a product of the physical, karmic dimension, but that he is using the physical evidence of his anatomy as a lever and a means to strengthen his higher senses, which is the sum and substance of consciousness. Therefore, any scientist who would merit the word 'scientist' would be well to be cautioned in his restrictive attitudes toward life!

"A true scientist is one who is mentally developed. Therefore, he has the clairvoyant ability to carry the knowledge of his Brothers who live in higher worlds into the present work in which he is involved; to always carry the inspiration of those futurists who function both on the positive and the negative side of life. That is the truth that must be recognized.

"At the present time, the great Emissary for planet Earth, URIEL, is functioning in lateral manners. That is to say, She is functioning from the higher dimensions into the fourth dimension, and therefore, finally extruding into the third dimension, through the means of creative patterns of energy that make life possible within the parameters of energy that have been rectified into atomic elements. Ruth Norman is that one who has the paranormal faculties of seeing the fourth and the third dimension and higher aspects of the Infinite, because URIEL has moved up the scale of life evolutionary-wise, and has attained that Beingness. Thus She has the capability of functioning on the different levels of the staircase of the Interdimensional Vortex. Therefore, the scientist should understand that man, on the one hand, can function not only in one level of seeing, but also, on many levels of seeing!

"URIEL is the Cosmic Visionary that sees interdimensionally. This interdimensional seeing is facilitated through the many different instruments which are the regeneration of those necessarily localized energy fields that are called bodies. In the third dimension it is Homo sapiens, but in the fourth dimension it is a different force, a different field, catalyzed into an astral body, a higher, regenerative, sensing, energy structure.

"This energy body carries the Consciousness of an Infinite Mind. But we must always relate the new science to the problems at hand, the reforming of the attitudes of mankind as to the truth of his spiritual identity. When all people truly appreciate that they are the products of a great Mind, and appreciate that this Mind functions in different developmental stages in different people. And as they appreciate the existence of those individuals who have attained to a higher understanding of their Infinite Selves, they will then be less able to restrict this evidence throughout the world as a whole.

"But life is a development. It is a catalysis, always taking place. And it is not to be unexpected that there would be many different volatile reactions until the emergence of a new organism takes place. That is the present statement of life and is the emergence of the new science, the emergence of the new man and the emergence of a new, qualitative picture of life; a realization of the subtle changes that are presently resolving into a new paradigm in which a spiritual being is speaking through the organism of the physical body.

"The Infinite is therefore reawakening man to the nature of his spiritual being. This is the substantive and subtle development that has been taking place on planet Earth for the past eighty-six years. Of course, it has been taking place previous to this time, but a greater catalysis and the regeneration of new factors are reaching that point in which the chaotic evidence of the past is reforming into an intelligence that has not been known previous to this 20th century; at least to the extent of scientific evidence of the interior of the atom and the exterior of the universe.

"Yes, man is coming to a new relationship within himself. A new development for man is taking place.

"Many interior qualities which are the nature of this new knowledge is beginning to find itself in its reformation as attitudes. The attitudes that the physical body is only a relative atomic instrument and that the mind continues to live, is becoming more and more accepted. Life after death, the knowledge that man is carrying his past into his present and is using that as a substantive means of carrying out his life, is becoming more and more accepted. The realization that there are time-travelers from other dimensions, living on planet Earth and functioning in some respects within the various departments of life, is becoming accepted. The idea that there is Homo sapient life on other planets is becoming more and more accepted. The expanding nature of the universe and other realizations of the possible existence of a fourth dimension is becoming more and more accepted!

"In all, this is the time of the *AWAKENING OF SPIRIT* in the physical, material structure of life!"

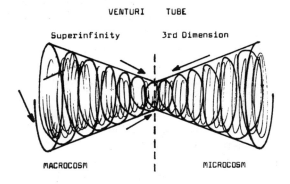

# Chapter 10
## The UNARIUS Science of Life

"*UNARIUS* is an acronym for Science of Life. It is not a science that is separate from life; life being the relationship of mankind in his complex social unit, and the family being the basic nucleus. The science that has been a basic functionary element of physical life has separated man from the *TRUE MAN*. It is true that many developments that have been the thrust of theoretical physics, have finally found their way into the lives of the people; but they have been, in most respects, negatively biased.

"There have been positive instances, of course, where the knowledge of consciousness has been advanced by the work of various scientists as to the nature of human nature. But in the most part, the technological developments that have been the espoused development of such insights have been used to imbalance the planet itself.

"In this respect, this has been the development of science that has interfered in the natural balance of the ecology of Earth. There has indeed been the greatest development of this technology, military establishments, whose prime function is to see that the nation is strong against enemy attack. This has proliferated into the establishment of communities where guns have been an accepted feature in community life, and because of the estrangement of man from his neighbor, of the fear of man for his own kind; hence, all developments of science have not been to effect a continuity of man to the nature of this spiritual self, and with an understanding of the evolutionary purpose of himself in the schematic pattern of life. In this respect, science has been separating man, rather than integrating mankind. We speak of mankind as the overlay, the structure that takes on the characteristic of a larger organ, an interdisciplinary function of each cell within the organism.

"The organ of mankind has been dissipated and disenfranchised and has been dissociated by the presence of foreign elements within its body. These foreign elements have been the development of technological, so-called improvements to society; commodities that seemingly improve the life of a family. These technological innovations are not valuable in that they do not add to the presence of the individual, of personal factors that would give him a stronger presence as a member of society. In every respect, such commodities turn him into a mechanical module, and he becomes no different than his home, which is his security blanket. He finds his life limited with insinuating manners by which he can have his seclusion to saturate himself with the substances of the material world, to compensate for his separation from his spiritual nature.

"The Science of Life is a science

that provides for and adds to the basic understanding of each incremental factor of the individual as a relationship to the organization of society as mankind, rather than separating man with the varieties of gimmicks, playthings and escape techniques. These are the preponderance of commodities that have been created, such as toys and games; ways for man to escape from his own sensitivities, to engender stronger and stronger barricades to the interior nature of his own spiritual design.

"The Unarius Science of Life is a curriculum whose characteristics are the real nature of reality. It may seem a conundrum, the 'real nature of reality'. However, it is a way of stating that reality has taken on many different reflections as complex as are the variations in the 92 natural atoms.

"Physical life is a preponderance of products that are programs reflected upon the screen of life, which are reflections of a social order, intended to give confidence to the people. However, this confidence has always been a refraction of other people who have gained certain abilities in the technological areas of life, and who have been able to project pictures which have given some reality to life. These pictures reflect and are an indication of what people would like to have, the feeling of being a part of some whole.

"But the many different refractions of these pictures have not been refracted or reflected from the reality of the individual's own creative nature. It has been reflected from the atomic equation of his physical appearance of life. So it has been, that the majority of the technological achievements that have been attained, are ways and means of alluding to the security of mankind as a material achievement. The material achievement is the success of gaining prominence in the financial fields of endeavors. The success of an individual is based upon the value that he has gained from his ability to receive a larger salary, to gain a greater surplus in the profits of his particular product in whatever commerce in which he is functioning. But it is not a value that has been attained through the delineation of the products of his own mind that can serve to provide him with a real picture of life.

"So as we have indicated, there is science and there is Science. There is science with a small 's' and there is Science with a capital 'S'. The science of the small 's' is the science of the physical universe. It is a science that is extrapolating the evidence of energy as it is functioning in the life of all people but is used arbitrarily to add to the security blanket of mankind, his security being the desire to live in the physical body and to live with it as long as he can.

"The evidence of the approaching end of life for an individual as he nears that so-called age of seventy plus 10, or even if he should outlive that expectancy of life duration in the physical body, there is still that ingredient that he knows full well will meet him, which is called death. It is the ogre, an unknown that is the basic fear syndrome of the majority of earth peoples because they have not been given an understanding of the continuity of their own identity beyond the spectrum of the atomic picture of life. At least they have not been assisted in the understanding in the continuity of themselves over the barrier of death by physical scientists!

"Physical scientists, as a whole, have not added to the understanding of the geometry of life. They have not added one iota of understanding as to the nature of the physical anatomy as it tunes down and eventually tunes out from the organism of physical life. The orchestra that man listens to and hears while he has his interrelationship or his involvement with his physical body is an indication of his attunement with a Force. This Force he knows full well is the universal note of this grand symphony.

"But at the present time, the science of third dimensional physics has not added to an understanding of the physical anatomy in its atomic constituents as a note in the grand orchestra, and that the note, which is seemingly functioning in its radiation has not itself given a greater understanding of the higher chord structure from which this note is but one chord. Science has not given mankind an understanding of his dual nature. It has not given him an understanding of the processes of birth and death, and has not taken the responsibility which is the prerogative of all man, especially those who have given the people the belief that they have a greater and superior knowledge of the processes of life and that they have not carried out the functions of their research for the purposes of adding to mankind this realization of the different notes which he is playing on his own instrument.

"In contrast, we have been introducing you to the Unarius Science of Life. The acronym Unarius is itself its diagrammatical, universal understanding of life. A Universal, Articulate, Interdimensional Understanding of Science is a declaration that this is a Science of Life, an articulate, interdimensional understanding of science. An interdimensional relationship is the chord structure in this grand symphony, which has been an enigma with the earth people.

"An earth person naturally is witness to the third dimensional facets of life. He sees all about him a visible evidence of the solidity of his world; yet he also sees evidence of the lack of solidity of his world. How is it that on the one hand there can be a solid world, and yet an unsolid world? It is because man sees the evidence of the invisible or unsolid nature of life in the birth of a child. The fetus can be considered to be solid; the spermatozoa cells surely can be accepted as being atomic, and yet there is no solid evidence yet, of a physical body.

"From an invisible dimension, it appears as a genetic structure called a physical anatomy. At the same time, that solid physical anatomy is, in every respect, reactive to gravity, momentum, and inertia, and becomes a nonphysical evidence of life at the termination of that body's reactiveness to the physical dimension, at so-called death. The body has moved back into its invisible format. But the greatest enigma of all is what science has not yet entertained and added to, in its constant research into the nature of the Infinite; that is, that the invisible part of life has been the Force that had enervated the physical body. That Force became a visible, viable instrument when the physical anatomy gained its basic integrative function.

"We all have evidence in our own families when our parents reached that cycle of age 80, 90, 100, or whatever time they should lose their resilience to their physical body. We know that we no longer can touch the physical, demonstrable evidence of our parent father or mother. We know, however, that there is a lingering evidence of the force of that parent with the children of his family. He or she knows that these parents still live with him as a subtle presence, even though invisible.

"In this respect, science has not been treating the evidence of the real Force of life properly. That real Force, as we have called it, is the real reality of life. Naturally, all people would accept the fact that the atomic world is real. It is real as long as you are interposed within it and are reacting within it. But it becomes an unreal or illusionary world when you are no longer reactive to it. This is the essence of all statements by metaphysicians and mystics who have related that the third dimensional world is an illusion; that time is an illusion; death is an illusion. Yes, they are illusions when one realizes the continuity of the Force that was the individual's presence whilst he was living through his physical anatomy, because the entire framework of life must at least be started to be learned, and is the interdimensional feature of life, existing in consciousness.

"Birth and death are the basic instruments for an individual's development of the logic and reason, and the truth of this interdimensionality. The child that is conceived into the uterus or womb of a woman, had already been born, was already alive, but unseen in the physical dimension on some planet in some family. A woman who becomes pregnant has begun a process of regeneration, a genetical development whereby she is, in every respect, a factoring, genetical product which has certain individual characteristics of the mother and father. The growth of the fetus is a regeneration, and it is in some respects, a process of cloning, with one difference: the regeneration of the fetus is not an artificial regeneration. There is a Force, an intelligence, a spirit, if you will, that attaches itself to the embryo. The embryo that becomes the fetus to become the human structure, is not a physical product but is the sum and total of an energy system, formed by a higher intelligence, which makes possible for complex atoms to function in the physical structure of an atomic body! This knowledge has not yet been recognized and accepted by physical scientists who have deitized the atom.

"The present science that is becoming the Science of Life will become the New Science, a higher understanding being developed by advanced scientists functioning within the various disciplines of society, to add the wider realization of man's true physics; the physics of the interdimensional atom.

"This truly is life. Life is not one dimensional; it is interdimensional. It is interdimensional in the meaning that it is a consistent movement between two dimensions that are polarities of a sinusoidal energy expression. Why is it then, with all the evidence of mathematics, mathematical physics, physics, astronomy and in other disciplines of knowledge, that there is not a greater acceptance by scientists that man is a product of two dimensions; that he came from a nonatomic, invisible dimension and took up residence on an atomic dimension, and returns to a non-atomic, invisible, dimension?

"Man is therefore both atomic and nonatomic. The question, of course, is the nature of this non-atomic energy, this Force that clearly is demonstrated in the human biosphere, the physical anatomy. This has been the fracture in the delineation of the knowledge of life's processes. Religion has become a product whereby individuals who call themselves priests, popes, cardinals and bishops, have taken the advantage and have declared that they have an understanding of the continuity of man into the invisible dimension called heaven, the after-life.

"But in most respects, they have not the knowledge; they have not the ability to make such statements, because they do not provide the facts as to the manner and way in which man lives in his non-atomic body! The Christians speak of heaven, the Buddhists speak of Nirvana and others who speak of the after-life, do not provide evidence of this life in any manner other than circumstancial. It is not biased upon reports of individuals who have brought back the exact nature of his day-to-day existence on another world or plane.

"Yes, there have been many, many statements as to the existence of life on the other side by people who have reported their findings, but in most part, they have not been accepted. They are the spiritualists and numerous psychics, peoples who have related a variety of images that are supposed to be the way it is. In many respects, this provides a positive picture as it is evidence that man does not die. He was never born and he can never die. Man is a product of the Universal Infinite Creative Intelligence which is, in its creative nature, a factor beyond the calculations of all scientists as extrapolated as a beginning and an end, the evidence of physical life's beginning and ending.

"The Unarius Science explains the enigma of birth and death, removing the basic block to this understanding of the continuity of all things, as relationships between different energy polarities. Frequencies of 60 cycles, 120 cycles and 220 cycles are relationships, each being a product of the other. Let us say that the carrier wave that contains the picture and the sound for a television program is separated from its component part to be both seen and heard. That carrier wave is a product of the harmonic frequency of some area of the physical universe. It is a frequency, let us say, of one million megahertz, invisible to all intents and purposes, as far as the receptors of the physical anatomy are concerned.

"When these frequencies, however, are demodulated, information is received into the atomic instrument man, and picture and sound have now been recreated so that the whole nature of the carrier wave will be recreated into the consciousness or mind of the individual. In this respect then, the carrier wave contains the entire nature of the program. It was separated in its component parts because the transmitter was on an adjoining dimension, frequency-wise.

"The technology of television provides the greatest understanding of man as a carrier wave; a receiver, in other words; as a transmitter and a receiver. The carrier wave which is the Force, the Intelligence or the Spirit of man, functions on a higher frequency and its life force is consistent in its association frequency-wise, to other carrier waves that are functioning on the higher harmonics of higher dimensional worlds.

"The entire nature of the understanding of life is this development incrementally through evolution of the information on the higher carrier wave. The information cannot be understood in one fell swoop, but must be realized and conceptualized in increments. Hence, on the television console, the carrier wave is demodulated into energy pulses of picture and sound, and rectified on a lower frequency where all the various component parts of that carrier wave can be recognized by the individual on his physical environment.

"The physical body at birth can therefore be seen as the development of the model of a television receiver. A new television receiver is being formed at the birth of a child. That television receiver is a basic console from which information from the transmitter will be collated and new information attained by such child who is reentering the physical dimension in order to obtain new experiences reflected from the atomic equivalents of his physical anatomy, with the continuity of his own intelligence, the carrier wave which is his spiritual nature. That carrier wave is the Force of the higher Self; it is the Superman because it has been constructed from the Infinite Creative Mind and is therefor indestructible.

"The Infinite, the Fountainhead, the Father is the Force that is the all-creative, omnipotent and omnipresent Force that is interdimensionally functioning on all dimensions and appearances of life. Therefore, the carrier wave, man's Spirit, is indestructible, conveying the understanding of itself to physical dimensions. That physical dimension was a means by which new refractions can be attained by any individual who is invigorated by this carrier wave, his spiritual body, so he can gain the logic and the reason for his existence.

"This is the nature of evolution, that the carrier wave of man, his Spirit, infinite in its creative development, must be demodulated into lower increments in lower frequency structures from which additional facets of this higher program can be conceived by any individual who is expressing at that time through a physical, sensing device, similar to a television receiver, constructed from the atomic elements. At the same time, even television receivers outlive their life, or live out their life and become obsolete. Hence, in the same sense, the physical anatomy as a television receiver, does finally outlive its cycle. The inherent energy of the nonatomic structure will be intact, but the physical form will lose its relationship, for its prime nature was to function as a sensing device, as a reflective device for investigative purposes of attaining a higher consciousness.

"The physical anatomy is more complicated than the ordinary television receiver. Man is functioning from a higher frequency energy structure to provide information to the individual who is a property of the higher carrier wave. This carrier wave is man's basic energy anatomy. It is the basic structure from which he views life interdimensionally. So the completion of this viewing of life from its atomic perspective is not the end of life for an individual when his physical body loses its resilience and can no longer contain the necessary coherence to the physical universe.

"But what about life after death? Life after death is no different than life before death. In other words, life before the birth of a child is essentially the same life after the death of the so-called old man. This is the reality from which all people have proceeded; a reality that he must determine and investigate while living in the primary elements of a lower dimensional school.

"Yes, there have been many, many propositions dealing with the reality of life on the other side after the death of the physical anatomy, but in most respects, they have not been accepted scientifically. These propositions have not been accepted except as a hope and an aspiration for man as a whole. No one wishes to die. There is always the desire to continue the ego; there is always the desire to hold on to what provides some semblance of reality to an individual. BUT NO ONE CAN DIE! The understanding and reality of what has been a basic attitude on the educational format of third dimensional life does not give evidence of the necessary knowledge that must be attained in order to live in an integrated manner while yet in the physical anatomy, to realize the continuity of each individual's basic mind as he lays down his physical body and wakes up in another schematic, another environment, another reality!

"It is not our position at this time to explain the basic physics which is the need for each person, to integrate within himself and point out the logic and reason that is the Unarius Science of Life; a logic and reason that cannot escape any intelligent individual. Whether one be a research scientist, a farmer, a banker, a Ph.D in some university, or a housewife, no matter who and what that individual is in his present interrelationship in society, that individual is a spiritual being, a functional factor of this great harmony that is interdimensional life.

"Our statement is that science as such, has not offered in its vast and complex technology, information that would add to the integrative knowledge of man as a structure that contains the so-called non-atomic and atomic elements. Science has been delving into the nature of the atom and gaining certain information of the nature of elemental particles that are the basic nuclei of the atom. The elemental, atomic particles that have been investigated, have indicated that the quark is the most minute element of the atom, and has also established that the atom is, in fact, not a physical, reactive, energy system but is a non-physical, radiant Force.

"So *WHY HAVE NOT* these scientists who have been privileged to *USE* the vast help of their governments in the investigations in the interior of the atom *NOT* provided this knowledge to the world as a whole and pointed out to them that *EACH INDIVIDUAL IS* a structure of 92 atoms and that these atoms are *NOT* physical but are *RADIANT ENERGY* structures? Why *HAVE NOT* these physicists therefore pointed out the evidence of the *SPIRITUAL* nature of man as they have finally concluded that there *IS NO SOLID* nucleus to the atom?

"The barrier there is quite obvious. It is a barrier of stubborness; it is a barrier that is the essential nature of people who call themselves scientists but who are not truly validating their position as scientists, because they *DO HAVE* evidence that the physical body contains another reality. This is a great understanding that can certainly change the attitudes of religious fanatics. It could change the attitudes of the peoples as a whole, who hold on to the supposition of an exterior god, who hold on to the acceptance that there *ARE* Forces outside of themselves that are the moving Forces of nature when in fact, the Forces of nature are, in every respect, delineated within the atom. For the atom is its own conclusive statement of its relationship to the carrier wave that we have indicated as being man's higher mind, his Spirit! That Spirit is this invisible Force that has, at least to this extent, been accepted by science as the interior nature of the atom.

"Unarius is a science. It is a Science of Life. Unarius is a vast organization of people who are the visible evidence of this science of life. Unarius is a Brotherhood which exemplifies the movement of the life Force within all mankind and explains this life Force, not only in terms of its local features, but in terms of its interdimensional features.

"That is to say, Unarius is an explanation of the real nature of each individual in terms of his own pattern of life: the pattern of his physical anatomy; the pattern of his carrier wave, the psychic anatomy. Each and every individual expresses a functional difference in the beat frequency that is the individual nature of his energy system. Unarius speaks to the whole of man and does not separate the individual in terminology of 3rd dimensional expressions.

"Unarius does not describe the psychological nature of man separately from the sociological nature of man or treat the inspirational nature of the individual separately from his biological nature. Unarius explains man as a synthesis of his parts as a unified field and a relationship of many facets that make up his nature. The physical anatomy is the receiver as an instrument for the individual, to refine the evidence of his own spiritual nature. That spiritual nature is the evidence of his energy structure.

"Unarius is the new science that will be the configuration enveloping classical science. In other words, it will be the new science that will extrapolate all of the previous statements as to the nature of the body that is called life, because in every respect, this life must be understood from the inside out and not from the outside in. It cannot be understood only by the basic statements of astronomy and holding it as a separate appearance of life. It must be accepted as a factor of the interior spiritual nature of the individual. That is to say, any evidence of the movement of the physical universe that is seen cosmologically, must be adduced to be a movement that is a factor of each individual. The cosmology that is the design for galaxies is also a cosmology that explains the interior nature of an individual and must be realized individually through knowledge of the physics of the mind.

"Hence, Unarius is a synthesis of all disciplines that are presently being resolved from their individual nature. Unarius is the science of man, as man is the science of life, so Unarius is not separate from man but is a part of man. To be a Unariun means to be an integrated individual who knows his relationship to the geometry of life, who knows his relationship in the societal systems of his present civilization on an earth planet, but who also knows his relationship to the system of life that is a fourth dimension concensus. He understands the physics of himself that is a consistent movement of the greater Infinite.

"He realizes in this respect, that he is cutting through the many different disciplines that are delineating a knowledge of life on the physical dimension. He is realizing that he is reflecting the nature of all of these basic disciplines of geology, geometry, biology, biochemestry, etc., and that he is all of these supposed reflections of differences seen in the exterior of life. Unarius does not separate the biological system of man's physical body from the electronic system of his mind, because at this point in the evolutionary statement of an individual's life, he is bisecting third dimensional structures in order to gain the understanding of his fourth dimensional structure. He is bisecting all factors of this atomic world. In this respect, man is the evidence of the science of chemistry, biology, physics, geology, astronomy, psychiatry, sociology, etc. The individual is moving through the entire arch of physical life, and he is inundated in all respects with the evidence of his interrelationship in all disciplines that make up the format of a physical universe.

"It is the intention then of Unarius, to make all people aware of their Unariun identity as a universal, articulate, interdimensional association that is the science of his life. Not that the individual must become a physicist, geologist or a mathematician, but that he realizes the interdimensional construct of himself. On this basic foundation he gains the intelligence which is directing him to point his energy system in the proper direction. That is to say, the substance of what we are speaking is an ever-creative, living organism that cannot die. This is the navigational beacon that he must follow.

"The knowledge of the energy nature of the physical anatomy in which he is functioning as a limited instrument, expressed in a limited cycle of years, will provide him with the strength to develop the navigational systems of the energy body, his psychic anatomy, his spiritual foundation.

"The mind is the first and most

important vehicle that must be understood. It is man's true navigational instrument. It is the true instrument about which he is learning through certain reflective life experiences. Unarius provides this integrative understanding that whatever the information reflected from the physical body, from the physical evidence of life, will always be used for the purposes of directing that individual interdimensionally. Then he will realize that he is undertaking a voyage and is preparing himself for a voyage which is interdimensional, crossing the boundary lines of time and space.

"But what will he take with him on his voyage? He has certainly brought with him new constructs whilst he was living in his fourth dimensional energy body, as we have called the carrier wave, which itself is being regenerated from higher carrier waves of energy information. What is he carrying to the third dimension, to that planet that can help irrigate the land, to grow new products which will reinstate the evidence of spiritual life and provide an understanding of the creative whole for people living in their communities?

"He has learned of the nature of his own energy system; information that he has been carrying laterally from two alternate dimensions that will either add to it or degenerate the whole nuance of life. Life then takes on an entirely different meaning when it is realized that life experienced in the physical body is to further the nature of life lived in the non-physical body. It is in this sense that the non-physical body, the real body, the energy body of man will advance its evolutionary spiral into a higher interdimensional relationship with the Infinite Creator.

"The Science of Unarius therefore addresses itself to each individual; not from the perspective that one must have obtained certain degrees from universities, of advancing oneself in the theaters of finance and commerce, or in the academic areas, but that it addresses itself to man as an articulate, universal organ. That spark is the individual's creative nature, and that nature is his higher intelligence. That intelligence is speaking to him, to the reality of himself as a continuity from physical life to physical life. That continuity is the basic statement that is the tenure of the science of life.

"First and foremost then, each individual must learn that he is a continuity of himself; that he, himself, is a visible proof of the presence of the continuity of programs that he has rectified within his mind and that his mind is a vast organism carrying all information. Every indice of every act that has been expressed through the physical body is recorded in man's electronic system; a vast computer that carries both the atomic experiences of life and the non-atomic experiences of life. It is the purpose of Unarius to explain to man not only the continuity of himself as a dual expression of energy, but of the interdimensional relationship of himself with higher, advanced, intelligent people who are in their respect, higher carrier waves reflecting into the life of man the understanding of the interdimensional spiral which is the movement of the Infinite Creative Intelligence.

"The importance is that each individual as a finite product of the Infinite is in his resolution, functioning with other finite energy products, who are themselves the functioning finite who make up the Infinite. This reality is the expanding movement of energy as a factor of each individual's relationship in this movement because energy is a product finally resolving itself into the complex organism of an electronic anatomy, the psychic body and the mind. It is this mind which is a complex development, evolutionary-wise. The outpouring of energy from higher frequency transmitters as higher carrier waves, are constantly demodulating their own characteristics into the lower frequency planes where the understanding of life in its finite state is considered to be the beginning of life.

"However, it is the beginning in this respect only; that it is the beginning for the understanding of any individual who has this spark of the Creative Force that has been spun out of the interdimensional vortex. So in this respect, there is the birthing of new sparks that are the containment at this point in the evolutionary development of mankind of a physical anatomy. The physical anatomy is the proof of the regeneration from a higher force field, which is the carrier wave always from a higher force field or harmonic than itself. The individual is becoming subjectively aware of his relationship to the spark, the Creative Energy Field which gives him his life.

"Science should and will be a process in which the refinement of this energy field system which is man, which is his spiritual self, will be allocated in its proper relationship in society as a part of the curriculum and the understanding of evolutionary life. Life is a grand design that is being realized sequentially life to life. But man has obtained the motivation and momentum from the life-to-life experiences to this point whereby the realization of the atomic nature of life as an inorganic factor of the Infinite has provided the symbolic form of life whilst man lives within the energy, which is the construct of this atomic body.

"But when the force is removed from the so-called organic body, the atomic body, it becomes an inorganic body! It is our statement that the true organic body of man is his spiritual body. His physical body is truly an inorganic body because the body of the physical organism cannot have life unless it is motivated by a Higher

Force. It is this Higher Force Field that is the subject and the predicate of Unarius.

"Unarius, therefore, is singular. It is not a third dimensional construct, explainable through the physics of momentum, gravity and inertia, but describes and explains the subject and the predicate. The subject is at all times the higher carrier wave, the infinite property that is man. The predicate in the third dimension is the physical organism. In the fourth dimension man lives in a body which is the demodulation from the higher carrier wave to become his astral body, his fourth dimensional body. It is a higher atomic body. It is an isotopic body as factual and functional as the physical body of atoms but with a higher frequency of its isotopic structure.

"It is a body much more intelligent than the physical anatomy, much more complicated. It is a crystal, capable of refracting information on a higher frequency than the physical body. This is a real body of energy that has not been refracted to a lower frequency, but is now an interdimensional structure. Therefore, the mind of the individual is much clearer, bisected from a higher carrier wave and takes down or unto itself much clearer information. In other words, there is that much more knowledge from which to function.

"In addition is the fact that the individuals who live on the other side of death, so to speak, in their psychic bodies or astral bodies, have a greater alignment to advanced, intelligent individuals, their teachers. Their amplifiers are tuned up and in this respect, they can gain greater understanding of the interdimensional nature of life from the vantage point in which they live. But graduation to this society or civilization must be bypassing the life examinations which are constantly being given to people on all levels of life experience. The examination is in the actual mode of living. In the exercise of the spiritual prerogatives that lie within each individual (which is each individual) each individual judges and executes whatever he feels to be his answer to the dynamics of life of some situation. He is thus constantly being questioned, and he is giving his answers according to his knowledge that he has gained in previous schools in previous life incarnations.

"The school of life in the third dimension is a preparatory school, for the man and woman to gain admittance to a higher educational institution. Let us say that the third dimension is the elementary school at the present time. Those who are capable of resolving the enigma of life and death within themselves, carry out the procedures and function of their beingness to express his understanding as a being who neither was born nor could he die. They will have touched many, many individuals in the process of their own development and have therefore affected the progressive evolution of a certain segment of their planet.

"But as we have seen, it takes just one rotten apple to spoil the whole barrel. Likewise, one good apple will regenerate and cause a great addition to the field of knowledge of life! Life is a proposition, not of fear and insecurity, to use past-life negative experiences as an interference in these principles of evolutionary physics, but to add in every respect, to the individual awareness of mankind.

"As each individual speaks within this broader framework of the continuity processes of each individual as an expression of his own spiritual nature, he does affect other people. Therefore, scientists who speak and are heard to a greater degree than the majority of other disciplines, would help in a positive plus way to interpret their findings; not as a third dimensional paradigm but as a fourth dimensional paradigm, and explain that here is evidence of the interdimensional nature of life, of the duality of man, of energy as being the basic foundation of all appearances of life.

# Chapter 11

## The Great Chessboard — Life

"The evolutionary development of science is also a regenerative development of Spirit. Science then can be seen to be the basis on which the incursion of a new attitude towards life has made it possible for mankind as a whole to realize the inherent nature of the expanding basis of life, the progressive, evolutionary, ascending spiral of all of its species; also, the descending nature of material life which is the sub-infinite.

"Hence, the ascending nature of life, the expansion into the greater macrocosm, the descending nature of life which is the sub-infinite, is the recognizable characteristics that have been refracted into the entire communications of society. This knowledge could not otherwise have been attained except through the involvement of progressive individuals who are clearly intent upon revealing the inherent nature of the enigmatic face of nature. Those individuals are scientists. Naturally, scientists are human beings and are evolving as well as are other human beings.

"The great difference between a scientist and other individuals - and we speak of scientists as individuals who are interested in knowing the singular wholeness of life, is that singular wholeness is their prime objective and it is their motivation in every aspect of his life. They are persons dedicated to the truth, the reality of the interdimensional and timeless factor of life. They are individuals who, in attaining these objectives, function from some specific relationship in their research from the perspective, looking into the nature of the physical atomic body, attempting to understand the movement of this body in its relationship to others. They may be a psychologist, a doctor of medicine or a cosmologist, but in every respect, scientists are the direct root to the true understanding of this timeless and spaceless cosmic intelligence!

"We are not disparaging physical science as such, because individuals who are called scientists are still holding on to classical concepts in physics; shoddy, religious concepts that are out of tune with progressive evolution and are not in contact with those scientists who are presently living on the higher spiritual planes.

"In every respect, every individual in his interrelationship in this interdimensional movement of life, is functioning in an alternative perspective. He is functioning both on a spiritual perspective and on a material perspective. We are speaking, of course, with a special reference to earth planets. The Earth planet is presently the focus of this book and the focus of those individuals who are in tune with their own planet. We shall provide the reader with the necessary cross-references for an understanding of interdimensional science, for any discussion of this nature having to do with the universal principles of life is not singularly pointed to only one earth planet. Each planet likewise functions within the same reference points of the universal principles of energy, a physics which is structured on a cosmological basis!

"Scientists who have this perspective and are aware of the spiritual, universal, timeless-spaceless concept of life, at least to the extent they know of its reality, are therefore attempting in the various disciplines to validate this reality and are the helpers for mankind. They are attempting to integrate knowledge of physical life with the knowledge of non-physical life. They are working in this respect, in accordance to the plans set down by the Universal Brotherhood of Unarius.

"They are themselves players on the giant chessboard of interdimensional life and are functioning according to a plan that has been developed while on the spiritual plane and are completing the move on the chessboard, on the physical atomic plane of an earth planet.

"The move in the analogy of the chessboard is that every play must first be thought out on a higher regenerative world where the entire map of the chessboard is cognized. The intelligence of the chess players is such that they have already realized the many complicated moves of the basic game. When any one player decides to move his chess piece, there are many different moves that can take place when the game is completed in the earth plane. The objectives must be advanced by the understanding of that player who is now pushing physically in some respects, the various pieces on the chessboard to culminate in some regenerative move that will coalesce into a new relationship which will bring out a greater and complete understanding of all factors that have been the basic of the chess game.

"Science is therefore the internal organ for man. It is the basic means through which he learns how to function within the complex electromagnetic mechanism which is the Infinite Creative Intelligence. The complexities of life are the interrelationship of the atomic structures from the radiant energy structures in the higher frequency dimensions. Therefore, there is a possibility for many different developments with respect to any individual. The overall plan, the overall understanding of the chessboard is that there is an intelligence that mandates every particular move but these moves are relative to each individual player and the Unarius Science, an interdimensional science that logically describes the relationship between the dimensional quadrants, which is the basis for what we call life.

"So man, as an observer as well as a player, is involved on two levels of life. He is moving himself through various placements in his life in various situations that confront him, and each move is the completion of a play that he had already set in motion on a non-atomic world for this chessboard! You see, he had already known about certain factors of the physics of the game. The game, if it can be called such, is life!

"A scientist is such an individual who had a greater degree of the understanding of the physics; that is, the complexities in the movements of the different relevant factors of energy of man, who is the sum and total of billions of atomic or molecular relationships of energy. The postulation of the physics of science is therefore that which has been one-dimensional in its early development, but it is now becoming fourth dimensional. It has moved from the first, second and third dimension in its awareness of the nature of life and is becoming more aware of the universal nature of all things that are part of the total system.

"This could not have been accomplished without the involvement of Unariun scientists who are individuals responsible for the revolution in science. Albert Einstein and Max Planck indicated the cosmological view, as well as the atomic view, the sub-infinite perspective This development has finally opened the veil of life to display the microcosmic and macrocosmic nature of the atom.

"The sub-infinite nature of the atom, as particles, is reduced to ever smaller particles, to reveal that its microcosmic structure is part of the infinite picture of life. Therefore, as the expansion of the universe is being recognized as a cosmology, indicating the interrelationship of all physical planets and suns with other planetary and sun bodies, stretching out and ever-expanding. This is the beginning understanding of the cycular nature of energy, and how the sub-Infinite and the macro-Infinite are joined.

"In this respect, Unarius provides the basic determination for individual scientists to exponentially understand the mechanics of this cycular movement of energy.

"Life will then become the antonym and the synonym of all expressions that are presently the local nature of the physical atom, because the very enigmas of physical life, the material expressions, are a local factor of the Infinite and will give the individual the realization of his so-called beginning and ending! It will remove the enigma of the beginning and the ending of life, of birth and death, and will explain how man is a universal quotient of the universal, intelligent Cosmic Mind, an intelligence that is, at all times, regenerative and expanding the nature of Itself throughout the limitless, timeless and spaceless Cosmos.

"Since there is no length or breadth, no boundary lines, there are no beginnings and there are no endings in the physics of this circular vortexal movement of life. It does explain to man while he is still in a lower atomic frequency, the nature of birth and death as he sees it repeated within the physical appearance of Homo sapiens! Since the planet Earth moves throughout the physical universe in an eliptical manner, it indicates how the Earth reveals the sun rising up on the horizon and how the sun disappears on the horizon. But the sun has not disappeared! The sun has not died. The sun has not been reborn as has been believed amongst the aborigines. That sun is ever-creative and is the basis for the life of the planet. Man will therefore realize that he, himself, is turning, as is his planet, and that he is seeing the sun as the Life Force from a particular vantage point in his evolution.

"The child that emerges from the womb of a woman is, in this respect, like the sun. It is making its appearance and its radiance is reflected into the electromagnetic spectrum of the planet, producing heat, light and all of the other energies associated with life on a planet. The child emerges as a complete physical being, but it already had completed its life; it had never been otherwise. It was a sun. Its energies were the creative energy wave forms that had been projected from the Universal Cosmic Mind!

"Hence, birth as well as death, will be understood to be a cycular movement of life. As the body of man leaves the perspective of the physical appearance of life and no longer can be viewed through the optical lens of the eye, that man or woman has not disappeared, but simply has moved out of the perspective or horizon of that particular earth!

"Man is energy. He is a creative product of Infinite Intelligence. The Unarius physics explains the regenerative nature of this energy system and also provides the means through which the movement of such an energy system as Homo sapiens, can be understood, and in a sense, factored with the recognition that this regenerative spirit of an individual is developing in an evolutionary manner in the recognition of its own basic substance.

"The greater the development, the greater becomes the intelligence of the individual who is becoming that spiritual being. We say 'becoming' because he has not yet developed the necessary physics which has been rectified into a lens where he can see the interior of his own energy body. This is evolution; this is the entire nature of the developmental statement of life that science has given to the viewer, as the observer and the subject, to develop the understanding of his own nascent development.

"So we see in this reflective manner, the purpose and the development of science that reveals the interior nature of energy, where Planck and Einstein have laid down as a basic foundation for the evolving spirit of science, to project as a picture on the physical plane of life. However, as life is a circular movement, the third dimension can be considered to be the far side of the moon, so to say, that cannot be seen by those who are stationed on the Earth. It is always on the opposite side from the view of those Earth observers. In this respect, the fourth dimension is always on the opposite side of the third dimension and cannot be seen unless one makes a voyage and develops the necessary awareness from the realization of an opposite perspective.

"Life itself is a revolving movement of energy, but it is revolving in a dual fashion. This is the greatest enigma that has not yet been conceived within the present theories of scientists, which is the observable nature of the fourth dimension. Each individual does have an awareness that he is a refraction of a universal higher Force. He has information that has not been taught from his earth universites, but is apprized of a higher intelligence that is much wider and broader than any one or many individuals grouped together, whether on one planet or on the interplanetary association of physical planets.

"Yes, some scientists have indicated the metaphysical factors in the equation of life, but have not gone so far as to state they have returned from the far side of life and have gained their greater intelligence while attending the schools on these worlds. They have themselves been teachers, explaining interdimensional physics to those who were yet beginning to understand the diagrammatical nature of this cycular movement of life. These individuals are, in truth, the originators, the initiators who have laid down the format for the new science. Maxwell, Oliver Lodge, Sir William Crookes are some of those who have made definitive statements of the existence of intelligent life on the far side, on the extreme end of the physical universe!

"Now it is the purpose of science to provide full knowledge of the nature of the environment that is both on the north pole and the south pole This is the beginning development in the opening up of man's mind to the nature of his own universal orbit. He has always moved between two statements of life; the reality of the universal constant which is his spiritual awareness of himself as a part of a larger whole, and the reality of a physical, atomic plane which is a temporary picture that loses its firmness, as the illusion of this reactionary nature of life dissolves in his evolutionary development.

"The problem in the understanding of the physics of life is that it has been basically one dimensional. Although this is a three-dimensional plane, the knowledge of the evolutionary development and the shape of the Creative Infinite Energy has escaped most scientists. Laplace and Spinoza specifically described the vortexal nature of the universe. The vortexal nature of the universe was clearly demonstrated by Spinoza, although he gave no specific diagrammatical pictures, nor did he involve himself in the physics of this delineation. But he, as well as those who we have mentioned, were all individual scientists applying the knowledge that they had gained in the fourth dimension, rectifying this information and attempting to move man into a new square on the chessboard.

"This movement is being done with extended knowledge, as the entire complex design of life can only be understood by the individual player through his conceiving of the mechanics of his own energy system, because he is involved to the greater extent in which these changes will occur; making possible for him to complete certain cycles and therefore, to coalesce with a higher state of understanding. The understanding of self, the understanding of nature, and the understanding of the organism of society cannot be accomplished until man KNOWS that he is a product of a Grand Design that is functioning in a developmental manner from a smaller set of conditions to a larger and ever larger continuing complex movement of the very nature of itself!

"Energy is the entire plasma that is life. The Infinite is an ever-moving and infinite movement of energy. Man is energy that has been coalesced out of this great Infinite Creative Intelligence that is known as the Cosmic Intelligence, the Father, the Fountainhead. Therefore, in order for the individual to be aware of his own life force and to evolve into a higher expression of it, he must become aware of the electromagnetic spectrum in which his energy system is inherently fixed.

"Hence, it is important to know to some degree, of the basic physics of the exterior environment on the Earth planet, as a factor of relevance to the physical body, for it is important that this physical body maintain its balance so the instrument which is man, the spiritual self, will be capable of retrieving important information from his involvement in the atomic feature of life.

"But that is only one factor of the involvement of man in his physical environment. The other factor is the distillation of all information so gained, which becomes a basic inventory, to sieve through the experience and retrieve from it certain basic principles. In this manner does man realize in a developmental manner, life to life and day to day, the physics of his own energy system; thus to become involved with the electromagnetic exterior that is the formative nature of physical universes.

"He becomes aware that he can project a picture that has greater detail, a firmer outline and possesses a higher content. This picture is each individual's mind as it is projecting into the electromagnetic spectrum which provides him with feedback to see the exterior nature of his interior development. Man, in this respect, is a camera. His life experiences are the film, and as he exposes himself to the varieties of complex situations in his life from birth to death, he is developing certain understandings gained from this exposure. The distillation of information is each individual's application of the developing kernal of intelligence which is the application of logic and reason.

"Logic and reason are the basic chemicals; both the developing and the fixing fluid where the logistics of his mind become firmly set and become an instrument which can function in both time and space and in the space/time continuum. In other words, this instrument is the mind that functions equally in any dimension, but particularly having its purpose to function in the higher frequency dimensions where the lower physical anatomy is not needed to propel that individual through his environment.

"The difference between the Unarius Science and physical science is that it prepares the individual for his life he will live as he moves around in his evolution from life to death! And as he lives on the other side, he will have to learn how to exist there without the temperature, without the dependency on the grosser factors of material life. He will be able to stand up and move his body according to his knowledge of it and will be able to create for himself his habitation and gain the confidence of his relationship to the new society in which he will find himself. He will either be a misfit, mentally retarded and unable to be a part of society, or he will be a part of society to add to a greater extent, new intelligence, new states of awareness as to his Beingness.

"In this respect then, the mental retardation of man in his physical anatomy is indicative of the lack of development of the physics of life, the physics of reincarnation, the physics that has to do with the preparedness of an individual for living within the broad expanse of society. A mentally-retarded individual is considered such because he is incapable of adding a viable content to society; he is not giving of self. There is a block of one who has lost his bearing, his direction; hence, he does not reflect sufficient intelligence to add to the system of life lived in that particular statement of society.

"In this manner then, mental retardation is a blunting of the logistics that are the refractory development of each individual's mentality. To be mentally retarded is to contain a degree of interference in the nature of the electronic system of the individual. This system of energy then veers in its orbit and does not touch any base. It is in every respect, similar to the astral debris that floats in space, which are the remains of the explosion of a planet.

"As the title of this book implies, man is both a regenerative and an evolutionary development, but that development is neither a beginning nor an ending. That development is an evolutionary movement because man is spirit and spirit is energy that has been held in its constant expression from the outpouring of its Source. The present realization in the community of scientists is that man is a relationship and the evidential nature of intelligence in the universe. And this Spirit is the nature of man who has been rectified to his appearance as a flesh, skeletal, atomic body, and is only one small face or facet of the Infinite! It is the face of the Infinite Creative Intelligence from its lower delineation.

"In this respect, man is a product of the Infinite Mind and is now aware of his finite nature. And over evolutionary periods of time he realizes the infinite nature of himself. This is the entire statement of Spirit. It has been debauched by individuals who have called themselves priests; fanatics in their lack of confidence in themselves. They have attempted to wed themselves to a Supernatural Force, believing that such an identity with such a Supernatural Force would give them the confidence they so lacked.

"These individuals have been the agressors who have attempted to still the 'small, still Voice' which was the beginning amplification of man to his spiritual nature. Although living in a physically structured, atomic body, he is *NOT* limited to the time in which this physical body functions.

"A science must explain the continuity principle of life, the true nature of energy as a cycular structure. However, knowledge of fourth dimensional physics cannot be compressed into any individual's present consciousness, because consciousness itself is the evidence of the design of the Creative Infinite, to provide for each individual the freedom to determine the nature of his own cycular Spirit.

"So as the clock is moving in its constant cycular pattern, the mechanism of life is also moving in this manner. The cycles of life have regenerated evolutionary-wise from epoch to epoch, civilization to civilization, where the appearance of life on planet Earth has given sufficient evidence of the physics that is the basic reality of this interdimensional cosmos. The fall of civilizations and the rise of new ones are themselves the evidence of order coming out of chaos! Out of the destruction of the Roman Empire, the Egyptian Empire, the Persian Empire, have come new orders, new societies, new interrelationships where the customs, folklores and the mores of the people develop into newer perspectives of the interdimensional nature of life.

"In this respect then, it is the true physics of life where there will, as a result, be the restoration of Spirit within the consciousness of mankind; the realization that there are higher and more complex evidences of the fourth dimension. It is the fourth dimension which is the joining of the atomic, third-dimensional state of consciousness with the fourth-dimensional state of consciousness; a concept of life that is a balance of the two polarity factors of consciousness.

"The fourth dimension is the completion of the parts that have been separated in the alternate movement of the forces of the Infinite. The fourth-dimensional concept indicates the completion of the circle. The circle, or the cycular dynamics of consciousness, is the true structure of energy. All energy is a cycular movement. For the purposes of the development of mankind, this energy structure is separated into its two halves or polarities forming the sine wave. Yet, the sine wave is still functioning essentially in a cycular manner as time and space, where the interior structures of the fourth dimension are separated into its positive and negative polarities.

"In this respect, the understanding of the physics of the fourth dimension as an evolutionary development, is coming to a point at this time in the 20th century where sufficient knowledge has been correlated into the life of mankind, where there is the greater evidence of man as a polarity function of the Greater Infinite. How else could life be learned if not through the beating together of opposites; the whole of which is its true intelligence?

"The Creative Infinite, through involving man in the expression of his own evolutionary life patterns, with the knowledge that he lived previously one thousand, eleven thousand, or one million years ago and has lived in these past lives sequentially, will be the new format in the development of the new science; a Science of Life where man is the central pivotal point of life's pattern, evolutionary-wise. Yes, this is true. Man is, in every respect, a sun, and he has within him the destiny of becoming a brilliant sun. He contains in his psychic electronic anatomy the very nature of this brilliance. It must be developed by him with the knowledge of the mechanics; a physics with which he will polish the lens of his spiritual nature!

"Knowing about the past does provide scientists with a greater understanding of their present research, because they must understand their own involvement within the nature of their own subjective bias. Only in this way can they see that they have been functioning for many lifetimes and have come to certain climactic statements in which they are the present, evolutionary development within the sphere of their own specific endeavors.

"As such, these individuals who are spearheading and opening up to man the realization of his interior self, the submicroscopic world and the exterior self, the macrocosmic world, will he be able to truly call himself a scientist; and as such, science will then be the Science of Life! A knowledge of life is the most important basic principle which is the beginning development amongst the thousands of scientists spread throughout planet Earth. But there is not yet sufficient alacrity and capability amongst these scientists to publicize, in their findings, the realization of their own previous involvement in the spheres of material life. They have not done themselves justice, and they have not done service to the people as a whole in holding back this understanding.

"What is conceived as paranormal is within the basic detection of an individual of his own spiritual nature. A scientist, therefore, who can truly call himself such, and is worthy of the name, is one who has the universal principle always in focus, and is looking from the large end of the telescope into the small end and alternately reversing his viewpoint. When he does this, when he has the greater view, the cosmic viewpoint, at the same time he can then respect and be aware of the microscopic view in which he is presently operating.

"But again, to reinstate and reevaluate our previous statements, man is moving into a new cycular movement of the electromagnetic Force Field of the interdimensional vortex and into new pressures. The pressures that are being received from the higher frequency Force Fields from the higher spectrums of information factors of the higher dimensions, are circulating into mankind as new ideas.

"These ideas are a functioning format, containing imprints that change society. At the same time this evolution is opening up man to new ideas of consciousness; an energy system capable of being attained through the individual's own mentality. There is the opposite force that is expending itself into the electromagnetic force that is man. That force is man's past; the past lives and recreates itself but in a dissipating manner. That is to say, it is a past that is, in all respects, the dissociated experiences of people, and this is the retardation force for mankind.

"These are the many explosions that have taken place in man's past history, and as fine pieces of metal debris from the exploding bomb, they can and do slice into the minds of the people who are still in tune with these disastrous, negative, life experiences. It is the past of man that has not been polarized and has not been rectified which is the basic hindrance in the evolution of man. It is this hindrance which is the greater problem in all respects, in facing the new society.

"The hindrance has come to one complete and formed picture, which is the fear of nuclear war. The nuclear arms race, the atomic munitions depots are basically a statement and the substance of man's past. In one manner - and in one manner alone, has man really proven the past history as an attempt to hold on to the material nature of life through force. Atomic weaponry is the negative regeneration of man's fears and his instability in his true understanding of himself as an electromagnetic spiritual unit of the Infinite.

"If man knew this, if mankind were given this information freely through the halls of science, from those religionists who supposedly espouse the spirit of man, and through the policies of government, there would not have been the accumulation of the evidence of man's reprisal nature, recriminatory, revengeful, fearful, and in every respects, guilt-ridden from his acts of his past. So it is in this respect that the present is an expression of the reality of life as a cycular movement, because the past is moving every moment into the present, and the present is moving every moment into the future. So we see that the movement of life must be understood in the true physics which is its basic structure. There is no reality in life, looking on from afar and observing the movement of some microscopic organism through the microscope, or a celestial object through the telescope without the involvement of the individual in the very nature of this movement.

"Unarius is therefore a universal, interdimensional science, providing the basic guidelines for wedding for all time, the separate disciplines of history and philosophy, the physical and social sciences, and above all, their relationship to the inherent immortal structure that is man, who is spirit. Not the spirit that has been tampered with and molested and discolored by certain religious movements that believe that they, and they alone, have the truth of life, such as with Christianity, or with any other system that would decry that their system of dogma must be accepted, else there is no salvation for man.

"Unarius is not a system man-made and misrepresented by the language of rhetoric to provide salvation for any individual or of mankind. The only means of being saved from one's own past is to know of this past. The only saving grace is in the knowledge of the workings of the spirit of man. In this manner does man see the face of his savior. That savior is his own alignment with Infinite Intelligence! There is no God who speaks, who judges and hands down a sentence to man. God is man himself! Hence, science, religion and society as a whole are wedded together, interrelated in such a fashion that it is a necessary fourth-dimensional physics that will cut through all divisions of society that have separated mankind from himself and bring back the essence of life, which has been called, in some respect, the Divine Nature of Creative Intelligence.

"The 'Divine' Nature of Creative Intelligence is the knowledge of the psychic anatomy. In that alone will man truly pierce through the rhetoric of language and the symbolism that has resulted in the attempt to understand the continuity of man's life beyond the physical tenure of his earth planet.

Only in the knowledge of self will man learn of the true self from which and with which he has been created! The Spiritual Self is the 'divine' because it is the instrument through which man gains knowledge of his true identity. He sees from afar and yet, holds within his own mind the effulgence of the Creator as it becomes a part of him. He *BECOMES* a part of the Creator. Whatever this Infinite Creative Substance is, can only be known by an individual who has learned of the physics of his own mind. Let it be then, that each individual learns of his own origin and not tamper with another.

"The entire Infinite lies in its subliminal manner within each individual. For each individual to excavate through the research of his own life, he will then have added a quotient of his divinity to his community, and all will gain by it. This then, is the sum and substance of the Science known as Unarius. It provides each individual with guidelines to discover the nature of his own spirit. It does not enforce or judge, but simply provides the knowledge of interdimensional physics which can be learned by anyone.

"Indeed, this Science of Life is learned at all times in every life and on every level that life is lived; both on the third and the fourth and higher dimensions. The cognition of such an individual who becomes a reflection of this Science, takes on the luminosity of the sun, whose rays are projected to all people throughout a planet!

Such are the directive Intelligent Forces who are Scientists, Brothers of Light, because they have tuned their electromagnetic structures, so they are in tune with the Causal Force.

"This is a time where one has the liberty and the freedom to look deeply into oneself, where the repercussive nature of religion and other types of diatrabs will not interfere in the open mind that holds the reflective nature of life.

"As a summary, science is an understanding of relationships, of cause and effect, because the entire movement of life is a causal and effectual relationship which is ever moving into new relationships of new causes and new effects. The reincarnation statement of life is the basic essence in the understanding of this relationship, and the ever-changing face of man, as he sees greater and greater associations from his life-to-life study of self.

"Life then can be seen to be a grand schoolroom in which each individual is a micro-organism of the Infinite! The individual gains greater and greater understanding of his relationships to each and the other individual. And in this manner does he eventually learn who he is when he sees more clearly his interrelationship with the greater Cosmos. This Cosmos is revealed to man microscopically in his societies and communities, in his nations and on his planets. The organism of Infinite Intelligence makes Itself known to those who have attuned themselves to the higher channel of the mind which provides for this illumination of self and society; of man and Superman; of the Fatherhood of Spirit!

## Chapter 12

## Rational and Irrational Numbers and the Sylogism of Man

"The difficulty in understanding the regenerative, evolutionary development of man and his spiritual nature is due to an inability to cognize the Infinite as an absolute. In every respect, in all attempts to understand the physical universe, there has been little understanding of how this physical universe is itself part of an infinite field, and its Infinity has been proven by its finite expressions in all associations of material life.

"The measurement of Infinity must have some degree of infinite calculation. In other words, there must be a basis upon which any calculation of life is determined; a base plane, a zero. The zero which has been established in previous civilizations, and in fact, has been the basis upon which any derivatives have been received, has given basic understandings in carrying out day-to-day life, the building of technologies which become a reflection of civilization.

"The minuta of putting up a material structure is based upon calculations derived from an understanding of the finite resolution of infinite numbers. Hence it is, that man has a recognition of the Infinite that is his own creative nature; that his finite expression is the association of his life within an Infinite, so associated as one of the finite expressions of Infinity. In other words, the physical universe is both an infinite expression and a finite expression of this absolute Infinite.

"Man, in this respect, is discovering his association and relationship as one of the many fractions that lie between the whole numbers. In this manner, in the mathematical derivative of a ruler, the numbers that are inscribed on a twelve-inch ruler are the whole numbers - one to twelve. But in between these twelve indices are an infinite number of derivatives that are the fractions. They are rational and irrational numbers. It is the irrational numbers that attain that infinite projection, which in fact, is the provision for understanding the absolute nature of the Infinite.

"Hence, the basic mathematics of the third dimension are a calculation that takes into consideration the zero as the infinite base upon which all finite calculations derive their relationship. Transferring this awareness to the understanding of man, he is then seen as a fractional number within the whole numbers which stand for Infinite. He is a developmental factor, regenerating the nature of the fractions that are the structure of himself. These fractions are the basic associations of his life-to-life development.

"The associations are his involvement with other fractions, and fractions are man himself, of the many different perspectives from which he sees his own relationship as a fraction, as a finite factor of the whole number. Hence it is that man at the present time in his third dimensional development, is beginning to see the extent of the infinite nature of his finite universe. To this extent, in all developments in technology and pure science, in social encounters with his family unit, the larger community, the nation and the planet as a whole, man is learning of the additions of the finite fractions and beginning to realize the irrational numbers that are themselves, interwoven within each fraction. Man is, in this respect, coming to the awareness of his association to the wholeness of his own fraction as one, plus the many rational and irrational numbers, add up eventually to two. The two can be seen to be a finite expression but a greater finite than the one. It is an addition of many individual rational and irrational numbers, fractions that lie between these two indices.

"The present regeneration of man can be expressed mathematically as a relationship between the many different expressions that have been the localized statement of life, where man has been separated from his awareness of his relationship to others and to a greater whole number, which is the expression of his individual finite planet.

"The planet as a whole, can be considered to be a universal expression of a whole number, but it is also a finite expression of the total infinite. So in this manner, we can resolve the expression of life into an evolutionary development. The additions of the fractions, both rational and irrational, are evolutionary developments, the building blocks that are the expression of the double helix as the DNA molecular strain that recreates molecular cell structures on a grander scale, which eventually express as a physical anatomy and when coupled with the higher transmitter of a higher frequency energy structure, recreates or regenerates and rejuvenates a new organism that is called man.

"Homo sapiens is not simply a fraction but a totality, a wholeness. This wholeness is known as thinking man. The relationship between his mind and his physical body is an evolutionary development. It is a regeneration process because it is the result of two or more numbers which are basically expressions of the Creative Infinite, which in its expression, is an absolute that cannot be understood except from its local finite expressions.

"The coupling factor of this is the fact that there is a constant catalysis taking place, which is a transceiver mechanism, and it is because of this that man is Spirit. He is a higher note. He carries within him the whole number that has been fractionalized into separate finite expressions as a means for him to add up and catalyze through a psychokinetical means, the true understanding of an infinite whole number.

"In other words, the whole number is a coupling of many individual factors. These are the expressions of life that are contained in man, as he is both carrying the whole number and the fractions within himself. The whole number is his electromagnetic energy system called Spirit. But Spirit itself is an evolutionary development to the extent of its application and use on the base plane factors of finite expressions which is the involvement of man within an environment which is an expression of the integration of the many rational and irrational numbers which are the fractional nature of the Infinite.

"This is the entire expression of mankind in the innumerable methods by which the spiritual self, which is the whole mind, is the whole number, providing the libido and the drive to be understood individually as a whole by man and his society. Society as a whole, is the expression of the finite man so that the infinite nature of man becomes a definite statement of the life of mankind in his communities, in the expression of his social structures and within the planet in which these communities are interrelated in different spectrums of its planet.

"In this manner then, we see a regeneration, a manifestation of the reality of an infinite number. The problem in retrospect is in the knowing and application of the elements of finite life; of the finite factors of each individual's life experiences in which he

gains the understanding of the whole.
If he does not add the fractions of his
own life experiences together where
they become a universal whole, then he
is fractionalized and is unable to complete his spiritual development that
had been so initiated by the Infinite
Creative Intelligence. His god then becomes a minor note, and he thus is interrupted in his journey to add up the
basic indices of his life expressions.
He becomes, in this respect, a retarded
calculation in the infinite note of the
grand symphony; a mote in the eye of
the Infinite, which does not link itself up, to express itself as a factor
of infinite expression.

"In the evolutionary nature of
man is contained the bias of negative
interference to growth which has caused
a degenerative expression to live within the electromagnetic body of man, the
psychic body, to manifest various malfunctions and aberrations, resulting
in the inability of an individual's
spiritual self to manifest in his physical life environment. Because it is in
the physical universe that man learns
to a great degree of the coupling nature
of himself as a factor, to become a
whole note and to see upon a plateau,
the valley lying below, his past is
not now dislocating his view of life's
pageantry.

"He sees now the interrelationship and the addition of all of those
fractions that had been the basis of
his past, not as a land carved by lava
and separated by crevices that were

the results of earthquake and volcanic eruption, but of distilled knowledge gained from his basic life platform as a result of his adding the various fractions that had separated him from the understanding of his own individual spiritual nature.

"The past of man is the evolutionary historical note upon which all peoples must consistently and constantly function. Therefore, it is clearly seen that the present inundation of distortions into the calculation of man of his awareness of who he is and from whence he has come, and the purpose of his life has been cut through by the deep fissures that lay between himself and the whole number which is his spiritual self - the whole number, the expression of the Absolute Infinite that is only knowable through its own fractions, which are the finite fractions of its own expression. Yet these finite fractions, these finite fields, the finite expression of the Infinite Creative Substance are held in abeyance in the knowledge of man until he reaches back and claims for himself his own basic quality and realizes the dissonance caused by his inability to count or to use the ruler which has been built into his psychic anatomy.

"In this respect then, let us realize that the present third dimensional form of life is itself one of the finite and yet infinite fractions of the greater Infinite, and in this manner, receiving the entire imprint of the grander Infinite, which must be and is an absolute number; an absolute number that nevertheless cannot ever be realized by any individual, because if it were so realized, there would be no absolute and the Infinite would Itself cease to exist.

"The Infinite, as man is aware of it, is the expanding nature of his own physical universe. It can be postulated that there is within each individual the product of the Infinite Intelligence, a regenerative factor. And regeneration can only be understood as an evolutionary factor itself. To regenerate is to evolve. There is in this understanding then, within these four words: Man, Regeneration, Evolution, and Spirit - the entire consensus of Infinity!

"At one time in the medieval period of the Earth world, it became a question as to how many angels can exist on a pinhead. These calculations were seriously studied. Some theologians considered there were possibly one hundred thousand angels who could exist on the top of a pin, but how were these calculations derived? Only on the basis that the Infinite contained both the microcosm and the macrocosm or else it could not be the Infinite.

"Man is, in this respect, a syllogism, and in the three-letter word 'man' is a containment of this micro-macro relationship. Spirit is a syllogism. Spirit can also be considered an anachronism and an acronym; a word that contains the entirety of the nature of Infinity. Spirit is a whole number. Man is a whole number; yet man and spirit exist in different levels of finite relationships which are expressions of the greater Infinite. Man is the expression of a whole number and is also finite, yet an infinite relationship - micro-macro, alpha-omega. Spirit is universal and yet is a finite expression of the greater Infinite. It is also the micro and macro, alpha and omega, the beginning and the end because in every respect, these are different expressions of different whole numbers on the ruler of the Infinite.

"Man can be considered to be the number one, and spirit, the number twelve - both whole numbers. Yet they are separated in some respects in the distance frequency that separates them. The fractions and other whole numbers are both finite, yet are finite within their own infinite universe.

"This relationship is similarized to a ruler containing a succession of different markings that are also the nature of the schematic, marking the future properties, that is the extrapolation of man and spirit. Regeneration and evolution are the processes through which man derives his spiritual nature. On the other hand, spirit is also a process from which it gains its manhood. This is to be seen and to be understood as there are many finite and yet infinite derivatives of the greater Infinite.

"The Homo sapiens lives in a physical universe which is bounded by the property of light, pulsing at 186,200 miles per second in its oscillatory movement. The finite-infinite universe that is known as the physical universe is an expression of the greater Infinite. In its circular movement it contains within it the fractions of itself; yet the adjacent fourth dimension expresses in a circular orbit but in a wider circumference, contains the same man as spirit.

"Hence, spirit functions on a wider circumference of the interdimensional vortex which is composed of a higher frequency, where it is a combining and a compounding, to be completely integrated, where time and space, and light itself, are all combined. The higher properties of this fourth dimension provides for a new, finite expression of a greater Infinite! Yet, it is infinite in its own finite expression, because of the many infinite fractions which lie within its order. However, the relationship between these dimensions, these cycular movements of individual finite light forms are at all times, associated in frequency and harmonic affiliation.

"The properties of the atom, which is the base plane frequency of the physical universe and the properties of its higher numbers, its isotopic, causal nature are at all times, functioning in a stable and consistent relationship. These relationships are finitely Infinite and functioning in their local but adjacent unversal wholes.

"In this respect, man is functioning from two different transposed universes; universes that are both Infinite and yet finite. In this respect, the greater understanding of the regenerative factor of life is man, since he is the totality of many whole numbers, having been spawned over evolutionary periods of time to include many of the fractions. He is becoming aware of the infinite nature of himself through the finite life experiences that have been so evident to him as an accumulation of information.

"That information is the beginning knowledge of his infinite expression of life, as additions that are the expression of each individual's own sense of his godlike nature. It is godlike in the sense that it is a total of many different derivative fractions and evidences itself in the expression of an integrated number. That number is his frequency and harmonic relationship to his infinite nature, because the coupling of the organic man who lives in and through his physical expression of life, and the inorganic man who lives from the transposition of his higher frequency expression, become the spiritual man.

"The Spirit therefore, is the higher finite expression of the Infinite; the addition of all of the numbers that add to twelve. That is one indice in the calculations of finite expressions of life but which become an infinite expression, because they are the association of both the physical attributes of life, which is the negative polarity, and the non-physical attributes of life, which is the positive polarity. So in the mathematical derivatives in which many scientists are attempting to work through this forest, this maze of fractions to some fork in the road, where they will see the cause of all of the individual expressions of the fractions in physical life, will they realize the nature of the evolutionary statement of life.

"The stepladder reaches a point at its height. The height is basically the higher expression, the higher whole number. From that whole number all mathematical physicists and all mankind are, as a result, becoming aware that they are derivatives of a whole note but have not been able to calculate this because of lack of instrumentality. Physical instruments have been incapable of providing the complete total which is the nature of all expressions of life with respect to the gestation of the physical anatomy at birth, the completion of it at death, the individual life experiences of each person in between his childhood and his old age, which do not add up to a complete whole number.

"The instrument, which is man's mind, was interrupted and did not contain certain components necessary to complete this evidential picture of the circular nature, the evolutionary nature, and at the same time, its regenerative features whereby in each expression of life, the fraction of the whole number gains for that individual additional knowledge which provides a wider perspective for him to make the next calculation.

"The finite universe in which the physical anatomy is the prime reflecting organ and which basically is the bias of a subconscious note, is the negative note reflected in the whole number that has been given too great a resolution and has been accepted as a real whole note rather than a true fraction, which it is. In this respect then, the instrumentality of the mind has been impaired because man gave too great importance to these negative fractions; the desires for the carnal appetites of the physical anatomy. These carnal appetites are basically the association of all the fractions that have to do with the five senses, and which basically deposit themselves as a necessary regeneration of the physical anatomy.

"The health of the physical organ and its many different other expressions as sex, sleep and the exercise of the body, can be dissonant factors and if given too great attention over and above the positive factors of man, the whole note, the spiritual libido he feels within himself does interfere with and does not allow the instrument to function properly. Therefore, it does have a disclaimer set within itself. That disclaimer is the additive factors or irrational numbers which become, in this respect, unknown and unrecognized and do not provide a completion. The interest given to the physical, sexual excitement of the physical body does not add up to a whole note.

"The physical anatomy is one small factor of the whole and yet, if it is exercised to that extent where excitability of the organs provides some contentment to the individual to stabilize him in his associative learning of self, it acts as a spell and hypnotizes the individual! That is to say, it lulls the mind and dulls the consciousness so that there is no developmental updating of his mental instrument; he is not able to calculate with it and learn of the whole numbers that exist, and to become cognizant of this whole number, which is his spiritual whole note. He may be aware of it in some manner, but not capable of using the knowledge because he is not developing the strength to apply this information.

"He is greedily attacked by the insistent regeneration of habit forms which are localized in the atomic nucleus of his physical anatomy, taking this to be proof of the excitability and feeling of being alive. He loses his mental relationship in the development of his progressive evolution! He becomes digressive as he moves with the force of the physical universe as it is constantly expelling and regenerating itself from the sum and substance of its prehistory.

"The prehistory, of course, is the involvement of man on the various planets that has localized the knowledge of the infinite, progressive future. So this mathematical foray in which we have been taking the reader is to shed additional light on the understanding of man that he is one strong link, because the Infinite is a structure containing infinite-finite structures of itself and these finite structures are links.

"As a man is a structure or system of energy with respect to the nature of this cell structure, he cannot be expected to be capable of understanding the sixty trillion cells that constantly regenerate his physical anatomy! Individually, he is not aware of these cells as they are functioning in an intelligent relationship. He is aware only of the totality of his operative consciousness. Yet, the sixty trillion cells of his physical organism are but *ONE CELL* in the untold hundreds of billions of trillions of cells that occupy the Infinite in one of its finite dimensions!

"Therefore, as man is a product of these cellular structures which are the expressions of the Absolute Infinite, he learns of his identity by learning of his own interior association in the basic finite in which he lives. That finite contains many relationships; that finite is associated with his relationship to his father and his mother, as he matures into an adolescent and an adult. It is another finite relationship between him and his peer group, his family members and others similar to himself from other family structures and other finite groups, and added together become a greater finite and a whole number by which means one attains to a greater understanding of himself.

"Then as the child moves out into his adult years and takes on the responsibilities of his own finite and yet infinite nature, he begins to realize and accept certain responsibilities of himself as a cell in his society; that he is both a micro-organism and a macro-organism, and so on and so forth. Through life to life expressions in the reincarnation process of life, these finite indices of experience are regenerative as he dispels the husk and extracts from it the grain. He gains an additive and another regeneration of consciousness.

"This is the seed that provides him with the ability to couple many different attributes that he has discovered in living his finite statement of life. We see in this manner, through the many associations of experience, the growth of knowledge which becomes wisdom when that knowledge has been so integrated within the individual. His mind becomes a finer attuned, electronic device, and he is thus able to catalyze the expression of the two alternate dimensions that live within him, yet are located on different frequencies. In this respect, they are different infinities.

"Man is therefore both a fraction, a derivative of the atomic plasma of a physical universe, and he is also an infinite derivative of integrated energy which is positively biased and contains its complete component nature within itself. The separation of the different fractions thus have all been completed because the growth of that individual evolutionary-wise, has been attained in his recognition of these dual characteristics that make up the nature of his holistic self.

"He has recognized the fractions over periods of life spans and has calculated the positive expressions in each of these fractions that have been the hundreds of thousands and even millions of lifetimes lived where he has learned to fashion his mental instrument. The mind therefore becomes the means through which an individual attains that intelligence of logic and reason, which is the entirety and purpose of evolutionary life. It is to attain the ability to calculate and use the mental logistics of logic and reason to see the indices that are the reflections of Infinite Intelligence. It is an individual expression that is the responsibility and in fact, a prerogative for man to gain.

"It is not that we are touting Unarius as the all and everything. It is that Unarius is the expression of these basic mathematics, which is the functioning movement of the energy of the field that we call life. Unarius is a basic statement of the higher calculus, the higher mathematical equivalents; the exponential statement of Infinity. It is an exponential calculus. In whatever respect a gain has been made in the understanding of Infinity, as Einstein has related in his concise definition of the cycular nature of the physical universe, these exponential realizations of consciousness must become the higher mathematics for each individual in his day-to-day, life-to-life relationship.

"In this calculus of mathematical infinities is the knowledge that each person is stretched from the finite fractions that have been the nature of his previous lifetime, biased to the physical life, to the positive perspective side of life, which is the infinite expression of life that is biased in a progressive finite manner. That is again the extension of and extrapolation of the movement of the Infinite in its finite regions that may be considered to be finite but are infinite in respect to the individual micro-macro-organisms that live within its universe.

"Man is therefore stretched between two opposite fields and is growing in his understanding of his infinite nature through his finite placement. But as life is a development that must at all times be expanding, the previous finite position is the detrimental factor when not recognized and dissociated or disclaimed by the individual. The past, no matter what it has contained, is therefore but a beginning in the next set of derivatives of the fractions of the greater Infinite.

"Once having gained access to a whole number, the next whole number must be attained, and the progressive development involved in the attaining of that number is the movement forward into the next and adjoining finite expression of the Infinite. One cannot progress if he still looks back over his shoulder and is continually calculating some past error. Hence, he cannot develop a new concept. One cannot be in two dimensions at the same time. One must always integrate the knowledge of some previous information; having added two and two, resolving the addition to four which is represented to the first or to the tenth power, and again use this formula as his basic foundation to move forward.

"To look back is a weakening effort resulting in an inability to gain momentum. This is basic to the psychodynamics of life expression that the bottom line is the reality of the past; a reality and yet an illusion. It is an illusion only when it is understood that this reality is an incorrect estimate, given to such properties that have been resolved into the present. Such properties are the many, many reflections of the emotional characteristics of man. These emotions, as frustrations, are disclaimers to man's whole nature and are basic retrograde factors which impede man's evolutionary progress.

"Although these neuroses and psychoses have been discussed and have been recognized by most all people, the mechanics of the basic physics for a corrective methodology, to cancel these perverse factors in man's subconscious life have not been integrated within the body of man. This corrective and preventive methodology is the teaching curriculum of the Unarius Science of Life!

"Unarius is not a 'holier than thou' statement, but it is a pragmatic application of the higher mathematics of Infinity into the mind of man, to rectify the obsessional factors of the individual, negative, past life experiences. These are the dissonent fractions that have become irrational, hiding man's spiritual seed from himself, causing great tension and blisters to man's mind. How can these various problems that have become the basic expression of dissonence in man's society be resolved? Again, the mathematics for the understanding of their life energy force must be understood; a mathematics of energy as a cycular oscillation, a sinusoidal alternate movement between two polarities - positive to negative and negative to positive.

"In the third dimension, this energy code of the Infinite has been separated from its cycular expression, and time and space is the means for man to learn of the evidence of the consonant note of his own spiritual nature. Time and space is the finite expression, a means for man to learn of self, and is not repetitive unless it goes unrecognized. These life-to-life expressions of man which are not objectified to contain new understandings of the infinite is the eternal disease of man and society, that can only be resolved when the knowledge of reincarnation becomes the accepted format in the curriculum of education and in other fields of man's social expressions!

"The dissonance of life are the expressions of man's past, which are visible and recognizable in the many physical and mental diseases which have fractionalized society. Therefore, the restrictive note of past anomalies of man must be realized as static energy, the additives of different negative fractions from these countless different life expressions!

"The Unarius Science is the stabilizing constant that teaches the basic mechanics of the mathematics of a higher infinite structure. It is the mathematics of time and space synthesized. In other words, time and space, past, present and a future can only be worked with when it is understood to be a whole note and that man is presently living and experiencing its separation as a fraction of the whole number.

"The past is a necessary factor in progressive evolution, but if it is not included in the calculations, the derivation of fractional numbers do not add up to make any logical statement. In this manner then, the mathematics of the Infinite must become a proper education of mankind so that he can function in the New Age where the knowledge of this physics will be the property and expressions of all schools of knowledge. Not knowing the physics of the Infinite will reduce an individual to a mental case because he will not be capable of functioning in the new society and the new society will not be able to express if there are many mental cases of this nature. Those people will gain certain needed healing on the astral or higher dimensions where time and space are completely unified, and will return to integrate this knowledge to a greater extent in the new society.

"This has been the gradual development and the evolutionary expression to be enhanced in the 21st century. Incrementally then, these are the additions that add to the equation of the infinite expression of life and in its finite format in a third dimensional form. So it cannot ever be judged that the new science that is the Science of Spirit has not laid its egg in the Earth plane because this egg was laid some time ago, and the results of it are just beginning to be felt. This development will have great implications in the uniting of man, individually, as a whole to its planets, and the planets to their own recognition in the different placements that they form light years distant from each and the other.

Time and space will take on an entirely different relationship to man in the physical universe because he will see through the artificial contrivance, if it can be called such, that he has accepted as the nature of distance. He will see that time and space is as unreal to him as his physical body. But as he realizes the real nature of his spiritual body and the timeless and spaceless ingredients of it as it is a composite of time and space, then he will conceive a greater Infinite. He will be able to grasp the significance of life on different continents on his own planet.

"The implication of the Science of Unarius is not only international but is interplanetary as well, and interdimensionally to the greater extent. It is the interdimensional nature of life which is man's spiritual foundation, a basic evolutionary format through which means man will lose his restrictive awareness of one life on one planet. The implications are great, and the result of the work of many hundreds of thousands of advanced Intelligent Beings who have attained their infinite mentality through progressive evolution.

"They are known as Unariuns because they practice an infinite mathematics. They are responsible helpers to man over many hundreds of thousands of years as Brothers of Light. They have taken on various names with certain physical anatomies when they incarnated into an earth world. As a whole, of course, it has been the expression of Uriel, who has stabilized the planet Earth by incarnating more often than any other higher Being. The higher Infinite development of Uriel has not incarnated, but the intelligence of the higher Being known as Uriel has regenerated a receiver in a physical anatomy which has and is functioning through physical bodies to stabilize the present civilization of man on planet Earth.

"Evolution, of course, is not a function of any one person, or is it a function of many persons. It is an interdisciplinary function that is the purpose of mankind to understand. The Infinite contains many finite features, and in these finite features is the development of civilizations, containing the accumulated knowledge and expression of man in his perception of his participle relationship in the particular universe in which he functions, on particular planets in which he is gaining his infinite perspective.

"There are therefore higher expressions of man who have attained a coherent relationship amongst themselves in their association with each other in the interdisciplinary cultures of their world. The push and pull of life is at all times a positive and negative oscillation where individuals who have become positively oriented are now functioning positively as the structure of their spiritual anatomy is a greater reflection of the higher Infinite. Therefore, they can and do reflect their intelligence into the dimensions and worlds below them in universes that contain the billions of galaxies! The awesome spectacle of an expanding

Infinite should be a considerable realization and a humble note to anyone striving to know of self; the realization that he must always have the diametrically opposite expression of Infinity's note to give him leverage in his present state of consciousness.

"That is to say, he knows on the one hand, as he peers into the expanding Infinite that there are individuals who have set themselves up as gods and who are opinionated and believe they have the Infinite in their back pocket or on some particular parchment, or in some way attest to speak for the entire Infinite. Such individual must, for himself, gauge the Infinite as a developing understanding and that each and every individual, himself included, who feels he has grasped the infinite nature of life must have the capabilities to live an integrated life, reflected in the works of his present expression.

"In this respect, the instrument which is the ever-regenerative factor of man, his mind, does have the possibilities of recreating true intelligence in the applications of these many composite forms of life, which function through its opposite reflections. It is through the opposite polarities of energy that one develops the logic and reason of himself and of his work for a progressive evolution.

"The positive and negative sine wave oscillation is the expression of the past and the present expression of life, which is the integration of two opposite and opposing statements of being. To attain the balance in this oscillating movement is an indication of an individual's progressive development. In that respect, he is a futurist because one who has been capable of adding the fractions of his own life to gain a greater whole, does not live in the past. He is thus a futurist, realizing the evolutionary design of life for himself, to be expressed to the people on his planet.

"The title of this book attests to the Intelligences who have garnered this higher information. Man, the regenerative, evolutionary Spirit is the higher mathematics and is the spiritual nature of an advanced Homo sapiens. The true man is a generic term for Spirit. Spiritual man will be known by a higher awareness. He will be a Being because he will have attained the composite nature of the fractions which have been his evolutionary developmental design, containing the lower numerical equivalents from his third dimensional development, now integrated in the higher numerical equivalents of his positive self. Thus he becomes a whole note, containing a greater Infinite, which becomes an ever-finite note in the greater abstract Infinite Creative Intelligence.

"Yes, these are abstract statements; yet they contain within them the necessary ingredients to be applied to every individual situation that is materially clothed. The material expression of life is the negative note of the sine wave. It needs its opposite to give it its true tone, since without an understanding of the physics of Interdimensional Science, the material clothing of physical life does hold man to his past. He is thus restricted and is degenerating and cannot reincarnate to a higher base plane frequency which is a higher finite whole note of the Infinite. On this higher frequency note he can see from the top of the mountain and feel the pulse beat of the Cosmic Mind in such a manner that he is himself regenerated!

"His mind, as an instrument of the Infinite, is capable of functioning with a totality unknown in his previous finite expression! He becomes, in this respect, the Being that he has so desired and feels the Breath of Intelligence of the Creative Infinite Pulse Beat!

## Chapter 13

## Man and Spirit — Coefficients of Energy

"A science that is universal has an established framework, its substance constructed from interdimensional principles and containing the inner and the outer relationships of electromagnetic fields of energy. This interrelationship of the complex movement of atoms forms a particular structure regenerating into new structures, spatially extending the boundaries of the first structure and indicative of an interdimensional interrelationship that becomes exceedingly greater and greater as its boundaries expand outwardly.

"With respect to the physical formation of molecules that are relationships of atoms, the tiny amoeba is such a construct of molecular matter to become a particular organ in a physical anatomy as a component structure of the physical body. The regeneration of this physical structure into more physical structures forms a community of Homo sapiens expanding out to become a social system, a nation, a planet, a solar system, a galaxy, a universe, and exponentially regenerating into additional universes.

"This we see in the coefficient mathematical indice, explaining the regeneration of all things. At the present time, man is discovering a basic coefficient in that the solar system is much larger than was first supposed. It had been considered that the planets were members circling their sun. However, man's regenerative intelligence, aided by computer calculations, has estimated that the solar system extends out many thousands of times farther than was first approximated and believed. This again is the coefficency that has been discussed previously of the infinite nature of Infinity; that man himself can expand the nature of his local environment on the premise that at all times there is an unlocalized intelligence.

"That is to say, man possesses a mind that can sweep out into the farthest reaches of the Infinite. He can do this through the development of his coefficients, the electromagnetic energies which are properties of the psychic anatomy. Man's mind becomes the extension of the psychic anatomy; a lens that is shaped by the information which is the sum and total of the structure and function of this electronic or psychic anatomy.

"This is the development of the lens; a mind which is, in every respect, an intelligent program to search out additional information and to find additional interrelationships within the great field that is Life with a capital 'L'. We refer to Life that is ever-expanding and can be sensed in the most minute yet tangible manner; also, in the most minute intangible manner.

"Life is the extension of absolute boundary lines, the tangible expression of man in his ability to conceive the validity of an expanding universe. Mathematics proves and validates the mind as a mathematical pattern, functioning within the higher latitudes of the space/time continuum. That is to say, the mind is not a structure that is limited by third dimensional space and time. The mind is a refracting lens that has formed its characteristics and power from the psychic anatomy.

"The psychic anatomy is itself regenerated from the Infinite Regenerative and Creative Intelligence. The mind, therefore, can at all times, sweep through in a circular manner, into the psychic anatomy, which is to all intents and purposes, a computer containing in a developmental pattern knowledge of the universes in their ever-expanding structure! Those of us who are scientists have extracted from the infinite computer of ourselves greater and greater information that provides us with the ability to scan the firmament of life, to recreate in this manner through individualization of greater understanding, which allows us to speak with the strength of logic and reason.

"It is not that we are making statements which are based upon hopes and aspirations, but these statements are the nature of life in its gradations, as it is experienced by man, so established from contact with the physical structures of life. Each individual who has demodulated for himself the interdimensional nature of the Infinite, is capable of speaking in this clear manner from his knowledge and experience. The interdimensional knowledge is the proviso for wisdom!

"One cannot speak about the fourth dimensional concepts until he sees beyond the linear boundaries of life. This is the basic limitation of Homo sapiens who exists on the opposite side, the third dimensional side of the universe and cannot discern the circular structure of the Infinite. He is therefore living in a time-space universe, linear in nature. It is basic intelligence that one cannot speak without himself having gained the experience of validating the nature of his infinite self by having experienced the opposite side or fourth dimensional side of his universe and had validated the extent of its reality.

"He now has extended his linear ruler which is marked by the indices of one to twelve, but now he has gone beyond the entire length of the ruler, extending its linear nature into its circular derivation. The twelve points on the ruler are only a fraction of the whole; the whole number containing two opposite third and fourth dimensions.

"The joining of time and space therefore validates the reality of life, not as a potential but as an actual living, breathing, vital Force that speaks to the individual who has joined the two halves of himself. As such, one who has been functioning life after life over the many millions of years in the schoolrooms of both the fourth and the third dimensional universities has established through his own individual experience and knowledge of the physics of the linear third dimension and the time-space continuum, to complete the fourth dimension. He can speak more exactly and more definitively about the physics of life because he knows that third dimensional physics is still a developing science that cannot complete the understanding of life to people basically questing answers to the space-time continuum, because they now are aware of a relationship between the physical universe and the non-physical universe.

"Scientists on the third dimension are aware of the positive and negative attributes of energy. In this respect, mathematicians have validated the basic theorem that for every positive number there is a negative number, and it is the junction of the two that forms a greater linkage. So an electron has an opposite nature or charge, which is the positron. If there is any matter in the physical universe, it has its opposite nature somewhere.

"It was established basically in mathematical conceptualization, because man in the highest order has the mental ability to conceive of the fourth dimension, although he cannot live it in the essence while he is in his physical body. He knows it exists because the mind iself is a property of the fourth dimension. It has been established by a Nobel laureate, an Englishman by the name of Dirak, that every whole number has its opposite, negative number. The whole numbers are positive numbers and the negative numbers are their opposite charge. This led to the theory that matter contained anti-matter, that an electron or positron had an opposite structure and has been validated and became the basis for the development of the general and special theory of relativity.

"These theories have been advanced by physicists and mathematicians. Hence, it is of the greatest importance to understand the mind. If it has not fractured itself from a malfunction it can function as a searchlight and can light up the various characteristics of the interdimensional features of the universe! This is being done but can only be realized by individuals who likewise are searching for the relationship of their negative self to their positive self.

"The establishment of the relationship of matter and anti-matter is the basic algebraic statement of Unarius; that man is a dualistic entity; that he contains the positive nature of his infinite, creative potential, plus the negative self of a finite nature. Both are functioning for the purposes of developing a greater knowledge of the relationship in which the structure of the Infinite Intelligence functions as an integrated pattern with the mind of man.

"These abstract concepts are beyond tactile senses of the physical anatomy but are, nonetheless, as real or in fact, more real than these tactile five senses of the physical body! Yet the physical universe and the life that man lives, localized to the extent that he is functioning with his five lower senses, is necessary for the establishment of his reality as a homogeneous being, through which means he realizes the inner structure of himself. The negative universe that is the third dimension is real, to the extent that while man lives in it and is born to it, is at the same time, regenerated to evolve by developing the mental apparatus of himself, to establish a future time when man will be able to cohabit with his higher senses.

"The sixth, seventh and higher senses are the mental logistics, the breath of fresh air blown into the world of man as he lives in his atomic constituent body; in the sense that the electron is at all times, being polarized through the association of the positron. Thus, the relationship between the third and the fourth dimensional development is taking place, to all intents and purposes, on every level of life, and in every conceivable situation where life situations are basic experiences.

"These are leavening programs, which when rectified positively, are inserted into the grand computer or man's electronic anatomy, and he is thus regenerated by a rounded whole note which is forming a higher harmonic, regenerated from life experiences in both negative and positive dimensions.

"In this respect, mathematics and physics contain important logistics that explain the abstract nature of the Infinite, a logic and reason which is the highway for any individual to attain the recognition of his whole note. That is to say, he becomes joined in the understanding that he is living in the negative universe of time and space and is aware of the opposite universe of the space/time continuum, the unified field of the 4th dimension. Although one cannot integrate this unified knowledge of self in any one lifetime, whatever man can conceive is a reality at that point in his evolution. Therefore, the conceptualization of an individual of the interdimensional physics of energy, that he is alive to alternative reflections of the Infinite, in this respect, allows him to make determinations that are based on the two halves of his human nature - the physical and spiritual.

Life after life, the expanded knowledge of evolution brought to mankind by Star Travelers, the Advanced Scientists, had deposited into the scientific community a rounded understanding of the interrelationship matter and its equivalent energy substance. And these higher energy statements of life are the foundation for the progressive evolution of mankind!

"Regeneration, in this respect, takes place on two levels in the evoluting of man into the realization of his true identity as a Spiritual Being.

It takes place in the lower level in which all people are dispersed into the various interrelationships in his planet, to gain the necessary confidence, independence, and strength in gaining a livelihood. Thus, he provides for the physical needs of his body and learns through various life experiences in which these needs are concerned. Learning then through the life experiences in which these needs are manifested, does give certain macrocosmic reflections to an individual as it brings down into himself certain realizations as to the nature of his positive self.

"That is to say, the positron, his higher self, becomes realizable to him through the many life to life experiences, composed of millions and billions of individual contacts of resulting complex variations. The relationships between man and woman in marriage, in developing a family, in their occupation and in their social life, their political and religious interrelationships, and other derivatives, become the means through which the intelligence is established and where the properties of the positron or the higher self becomes known. At all times, the energy of the Infinite is functioning within its duality but has not yet been conceived by the individual in his beginning expression in the evolving of himself to a recognition of his own relationship to the All-Creative, Infinite Mind!

"So at all times, the invisible

anti-matter, truly the opposite factor for the establishment of the third dimension, provides an answer to the enigma of the continuity of life within the interdimensional cosmos. The time and space continuum in this respect, is composed of matter and anti-matter. It is in the joining of the two polarities when the linear meets its opposite polarity that we have the full and complete nature of reality.

"Man is complete in himself when he lives with the understanding of both polarities of himself when so joined to function in such manner to reflect a greater aliveness. That aliveness is the positive regenerative beat or oscillation of his electronic structured body in an integrated and unified pattern, connected harmonically to the Infinite as it functions with other advanced humanity.

"The majority of the population of the world on the planet Earth is living in a physical body, the negative charge from the fourth dimension. Anti-matter is, in this respect, fourth dimensional. Man is living now in his electron body but unaware of his positron body. He is unaware that he has another body that is a completely charged force. This body, known as the psychic body, is an electronic configuration of radiant energy. It is not localized to the extent that it is functioning as coefficients of 92 elements but is functioning on an entirely different dimension.

"It is, to all intents and pur-

"Life can therefore be seen to be a succession of subjects which are presented to the student. Should he qualify in understanding the nature of the information, applying such information as a feedback to himself and expanding his relationship with the universe, of his family, his profession, and in every respect, his association to individuals who have advanced to a higher school in higher frequency planes, he will graduate to a higher consciousness.

"It should be realized that we do not condemn anyone for living in the physical anatomy, nor do we condemn those who have failed the grade by not being capable of extrapolating from their life experiences the existence of the non-material universe or the anti-matter dimension. It is not a premise but is a basic statement that man is an energy system that is bounded by time and space. He is a product of the higher Recreative Infinite Intelligence that is revolving infinitely, in infinite universes!

"We cannot and do not condone individuals therefore, who have completed their examinations, but have falsified their tests and have lied about their ability and have, in this respect, fattened up the appearance of the negative universe, which is the third dimension, and given this universe the reality as a complete and finished product. In this manner then, figures can be interfered with, results can be changed, and the half knowledge can be the means to deceive by hypno-

poses, anti-matter because it is no[t]
binding, nor is it limited to the t[h]
dimension. Although it is functionin[g]
to recreate the negative atom it is
dependent upon it. That is the great
difference! The physical anatomy is [the]
negative atom and is dependent upon
positive atom, or the electronic ene[rgy]
constituents that make up the positi[ve]
body. This electronic body is radiant
energy of an entirely different natur[e]
because it does not have the weight o[f]
the third dimensional atom. Giving it
the name of 'isotope' would indicate
its positive charge.

"Energy is finite and infinite;
it is complete and yet is dual in nature, functioning to equate both its
positive and negative polarities so
there is always a balance between the
two charges. In the physical universe
the two charges, positive and negative,
are separated by the lower frequency
of time and space, as the physical and
the electronic body. Yet the separation
is only with respect to the mentality
of the individual who is living in
these energy structures.

"One can perceive that the Infinite lives within and without all
people when he conceives from the various clues gained by life-to-life experience. These clues are the developmental factors of his life as he extrapolates from his experiences the enigma
of these experiences. He extrapolates
the answer relative to his ability in
completing the subject matter and passing the examination.

tizing any individual from the recognition of his own logic and reason.

"Putting two and two together is, of course, a simplistic statement of logical determination; yet it is the only means by which one can advance out of kindergarten. Knowledge by definition is the ability to add, subtract, multiply and divide; and with this basic development in arithmetic functions he can continue to the higher mathematics of algebra, trigonometry, calculus, to the physics of interdimensional equations. He has then begun to establish a fourth-dimensional physics as a developmental statement of third-dimensional life.

"It is one thing to be able to validate the existence of the fourth dimension, as Einstein and others have done, but it is quite another thing to apply this mathematics in the life of oneself, which is a gradual developing and learning process. Thus, it is an infinite procession where man becomes a number that is progressing infinitely, as the spiral that is the vortex of the Creative Infinite Mind is ever regenerative.

"It is a sinusoidal movement of energy, always moving within itself, expanding and contracting. The contraction, of course, is with respect to the beginning learning of the nature of the developing spirit who is yet unaware of the higher forces from which he has been recreated. Hence, it is not as if man was born out of a vacuum and attains to some capabilities in the environment which he perceives in his life, but that he was born from the mind of the Father, the Creative Infinite Intelligence, and he is developmentally learning of this Mind, the energy which is the substance of himself in its microcosmic structure.

"The great abstract syllogysm is that man is a sinusoidal energy wave form and is moving with reference to the giant vortex that is expanding and contracting. Man is a part of the interdimensional vortex, which is a great infinite structure. Those who have not realized the extent of their relationship to the macrocosm that makes possible this movement which is the breathing nature of the Infinite, are out of alignment with this Force; therefore, they do not receive the Breath which is constantly demodulating itself down from the higher vortex, from the higher dimension, into the smallest end of itself, as the venturi tube demonstrates.

"He may be existing within the microcosmic or equilibrium portion of this expanding and contracting universe, but as a cork on the ocean, is simply being pushed around by forces that are applied to him as an organism of this great energy field. In this respect, he is not going anywhere; he is wavering between the north, south, and then to the west, but is not really moving in a forward manner. He is not adding to or gaining the intelligence that lies within the expanding nature of his evoluting organism.

"Ignorance of the real energy structure of the Infinite, the energy that exists within man, generates a static charge which is a fault in man's energy structure. Hence, man is misaligned to the forward motion that is the prerogative of life. There is a rearward or descending movement of the Infinite which is the expelling of the entire energy structure of the Infinite out into Itself. This outbreathing or discharge is the negative universe. It is an opposite charge of the duality of the Infinite Intelligence. Should this opposite or negative discharge continue, and regenerates long enough, then all factors that are involved in this structure of evoluting Homo sapiens will be discharged in a negative manner.

"The atom will establish itself by recreating its structure in Homo sapiens, but eventually, man must join with his higher or protonic self, which is his infinite nature. He must join the opposite factor of the lower self where another equilibrium line takes place. All information, therefore, that has been accumulated in these two charges is joined to contain a new regenerative statement of a new organism. However, this is the higher physics that can only be understood in the questing and in the developing of greater and greater intelligence into the inner structure of self as it functions from life to life; not on the negative universe alone, but in life to life as it functions alternately from the negative universe and the positive universe or the third to the fourth dimension.

"In some respects therefore, man is learning about himself from the negative charge of a third dimension where he lives in this room of the Infinite Universe, to gain some basic fundamental understanding of the higher or interdimensional physics of life's expression. Such higher physics is learned in a modulated manner when one lives in a charged universe that contains the integral number, which is a synthesis of the energy factors of matter and antimatter. One then applies and thus polarizes certain fundamental principles through objective life experiences in the material life on some earth world.

"He learns to overcome certain recessive factors that are the experiences in the material or atomic life. In other words, in a crude sense, he has banged his head against the wall, as he has not recognized the true nature of matter. He has felt the force of a negative charge and has been awakened to the fact that he is experiencing an opposite charge and does have a mind that can function free of matter.

"The experience of living is therefore a basic format for the understanding of evolution. By experiencing life through living in a dense, compacted, atomic body, one realizes the nature of the lower frequency associated with such a body, and one thus attains certain awareness of the need to use the logic and reason of intelligence rather than of the physical body. He thus has to prove to himself that he has achieved a certain understanding of his own spiritual, non-physical nature. This understanding is the whole statement of evolution and explains the need to incarnate into the schoolroom of physical life again and again and again, so that he can eventually pass his examinations and move out of the sphere of this particular development into the evolving of spiritual consciousness. This is man's goal!

"To become conscious of the reality of life is to become spiritual. Spiritual is not a label for irresponsibility, but is the result of great learning and social responsibilities, similar to the cum laude honors attained by a graduate of a university. He has proven that he no longer needs to depend upon the five physical senses as a means of being alive, but he can now function with his sixth and higher senses that are the true intelligence quotient of the psychic anatomy.

"The World Teaching presently taught by Unarius, is to provide all students with the knowledge of the electromagnetic structures of the psychic anatomy, the positive and negative polarities. The positive structure of the psychic anatomy is the higher body known as the Superconsciousness. The development of the sixth and higher senses of an individual is the result of learning in which one has developed particular intelligence. That means that he knows of the existence of the positive polarity of himself. This input from the fourth dimension has been called the Christ Self, the Father Within; and in every respect, the latter is the truth because it is the Father who is projecting Its greater Intelligence to each of us who are all products of this Power of the Father!

"The higher Self is the joined Consciousness of one who has recognized the dual nature of Infinity. He now has attained the ability to function in a greater integrated manner by having learned to balance the two alternate charges of the Infinite. Therefore, we can clearly realize why the higher Self is the Intelligent Self. This is the logic and reason of Spirit. It becomes the wisdom of an individual who is capable of deciphering from the map of his local environment to select his direction in day-to-day and life-to-life experiences!

"So the individual who would wish to understand and resolve the various problems that have cropped up in his life, must understand that he has made that problem a viable factor of his life because that problem is the product of negative experiences that have given him the belief that the negative world, the world of matter, is the most important world. Therefore, he has piled up from his past-life experiences all manners of insecurities, guilts, and other types of emotional factors that are the phobias and the psychosis which have become the accumulated evidence of a slag heap which is the statement of a static and unbalanced life.

"Such an unbalanced individual has therefore not become aware of his positive self. He had been off balance and is biased in his attempt to create a picture out of material life that is composed of but one-half of the real picture. Therefore, he has not had the ability to see a whole picture on the screen that he calls life. He is an endangered species because such accumulation of negative energy must eventually be pulled into the vacuum cleaner which is the spiralling sub-infinite as it removes all atomic by-products regenerated in the third dimension and restores the basic energy so that it may be joined in full array with the Waters of the Infinite!

"The Infinite is always recreating its progeny as microcosmic regenerations of Itself. Each individual who is regenerated in this structure in the lower universes known as the atomic universe, must determine selectively, through life experience, what direction he will take. In an incremental manner life after life, all human beings live sequentially, dividing their time between the fourth dimension and the third dimenion so they can develop greater access to the fourth dimension as a living, breathing, intelligent organism.

"Alternately, they can bias their evolutionary development with a biased negative charge with the matter of the third dimensional universe. In this respect, they will be pulled back to the alternate or negative polarity of the Breathing Universe and will bias themselves, mentally speaking, to the 'desires' of a physical body in order to experience life.

"These then are individuals who are caught in a bind and can no longer advance into a higher statement of the energy, which is the true nature of their electronic structure. Therefore, they must decrease the higher frequencies that carry the potential of their spirit, to demodulate their mind, which in every respect, is pressed within the four walls of a physical universe, in time and space. They thus become the ghosts, the poltergeists, they become the devils and demons; in every respect, individuals who cannot function with the logic and reason of progressive evolution.

"This is a degenerate development; yet it is evolution devolving the individual intelligence of Homo sapiens. In time, such individuals will be unable to reincarnate into a physical body. Eventually they are propelled in such a manner that they can no longer function in space and time, and are continuously losing their relationship to the mathematics that had been developed to experience a physical body, in a physical universe. This is total annihilation of the individual intelligence once achieved through the hard-won attainment of logic and reason!

"This is a treatment that will, of course, have to be recognized by any individual who has suffered some shocks in his life, the traumas that he and most people have experienced when they have lost their equilibrium and have not been able to function in society. They are separated from humanity and are living in some astral world that contains unsubstantial images. These are individuals who are neurotic and/or psychotic, now experiencing a state of consciousness which seems real but lacks coherency, cogency and intelligence.

"It is this state of consciousness that will eventually result in closing off an individual from necessary and vital life experiences that will initiate him into his evolving spiritual nature.

"Whatever man can imagine is a valid statement of the reality of his life experienced in some one or another dimension. It is man's ability to so-call 'imagine' that provides him with the realization that there is nothing, or no thing that is impossible because man is only learning of the possibility of life in the basic beginning of his gestation into spirit. But since the enigma of life is that man is both spirit and also composed of matter, it is the spirit of man that is eventually resolved into the dispensation of mankind when he discovers that his matter body is the less significant and he learns the greater responsibility for the development of his mind, which is in every respect, directing his physical body.

"Man is the editor and does move the matter in the space that it occupies. It is true that he cannot move his body except through recognition of the third dimensional physics, but he can move his mind without any resistence to momentum, inertia, and gravity when he learns of its electronic composition. Scientists who have learned of the higher physics of the mind, are capable of moving through the interdimensional cosmos.

"The authors of this book, who have established their own credentials, having lived in physical and non-physical bodies for many hundreds of thousands, millions of earth years, they are now capable of functioning in this manner, to direct their minds to an advanced Mind on the Earth plane (Ruth Norman). They establish interplanetary and interdimensional contact in this fashion, explaining and describing the higher physics of life so it can be conceived within the language of a negative universe, because the language of the third dimension is not the same language as the fourth dimension. This is the great difference in attaining the balance with the higher mathematics of the mind!

"The language of the fourth dimension is a complete language. It does not contain rhetoric. It does not contain theories or hypothesis, but is a complete awareness; at least to the extent of the knowledge contained in that dimension. Learning, of course, takes place on all dimensions, but we who are graduates of the universities of the earth worlds and of the Earth itself, of the third dimension, are capable, therefore, of speaking with a factual awareness of the physics of the matter and anti-matter universe. We have attained this understanding within our own life-to-life expressions and are functioning to live our lives within this interdimensional understanding.

"The proof is that there are no hindrances in our movement throughout our environment. We are not dependent upon the local environment but can extend our minds to move backwards and forwards in space-time, as we are doing in your case, and moving backwards in so-called time. We can also move forward and contact the higher dimensions above us because in this respect, we are similar to that one, Ruth Norman, living in a matter body but containing the anti-matter statement of a fourth dimensional consciousness. She can therefore receive our thoughts and translate them into the language of the third dimension in whatever language necessary.

"We make these statements so you will appreciate and understand that there must be a transmitter to transmit information, and a receiver to receive information. That is the learning of man. Ruth Norman, as the transceiver for this advanced physics, the Unarius Science, is in every respect, involved in this teaching or else there could be no diagramatical statements made. The extensive nature of progressive evolution is that man himself will learn how to be able to attune his mentality, likened to a giant radar antenna dish, to contact the advanced Minds of people who had once lived on earth worlds, to share the knowledge that they have gained; both with respect to our fourth dimensional statement of life and the knowledge that was gained by us whilst in the third dimensional environment.

"That is the portrait for the future! It is the great human potential in this New Age of Spiritual Renaissance, the Age in which man will realize the matter and the anti-matter of himself. He will surely be a highly-charged particle, whose brilliance will be seen by those who are seeking for direction in their lives; seeking such information that can be received by them in this polyphase, synchronous attunement.

"A highly-charged particle can therefore function through the smog and through the overlay of dense cloud formations. This is another instance in which the third dimensional, atomic body can be rectified, and the mind that motivates the third dimensional body can also receive evidence of a fourth dimensional intelligence, to regenerate the nature of intelligent life on third dimensional planes. This is evolution! It is being done, not singularly, but by many thousands and hundreds of thousands of people stationed on the higher worlds, on the fourth dimension and the lower third dimensional worlds.

"This contact is the bridge that has been laid down by the Unariun Brothers, and has been completed by Uriel who, in every respect has fastened down the hatches securely so that the bridge between two worlds, between matter and anti-matter provides a basic foundation upon which the knowledge of the higher physics of the Infinite can become a basic curriculum in the gestating life of Homo sapiens who will reincarnate life to life in these physical planets! Man will have a body of higher information to function with, over periods of evolutionary time. This will have great meaning in the regeneration of the material planets so they will become charged with the positive energy of spirit, to regenerate into their fourth dimensional nature as astral planets; planets that contain the balanced charges of their electromagnetic fields.

"Once these concepts are vitalized in the society of man, no man can rest without desiring to attain this knowledge of Spirit for himself. Because he will have, as he reads the texts or listens to a dissertation from more advanced, intelligent individuals who have laid down these foundations of interdimensional life, his mind will be touched, and it will gain a greater reflection which will be the ascendency of that individual over the negative nature of his life. He will realize the wholeness of himself and will be able to express the Science of Life. It will make his life one of peace and harmony. Life will not be a happening without his personal involvement; he will have a balance in the movement and pulse of life and will experience a cool breeze which will alert him to the ever-widening gate of his higher Self, in the realization that there are many Brothers on the inner planes who are functioning to advance the nature of man's spiritual self."

# INDEX

Aberations 125, 293
Aesop 186
Age of Science 174
Age of Technology 183
Akhenaton's teachings 67, 184
Alternate polarities 68-70
Ancient civilizations 66
Apparency of life 1-2, 7, 19, 27, 39, 46, 50, 121, 192
   resolutions of the 56
   the physical body 44
Arms conflict 105, 282
Astral body 260
Astral plane 153
Asymptotic characteristics 85, 102
Asymptotic reflection of life 89
Atom 5, 29, 90, 135
   indivisible 89
   interdimensional 244
   nature of 63, 251
   proton of 139
   the sub-infinite 200, 214-215
Atomic view 267
Atomic weaponry 282
Attunement 50, 78, 106, 180
   lack of 99
Avatars 188

Balance 64, 231, 313
Barriers
   are mentally conceived 49
   of time & space 27, 32

Base plane frequency 85, 91
Belief systems 73, 179, 201
Big bang theory 109
Bifurcation 57-58, 68-69, 110
Birth & death 11-12, 46-47, 241-243, 246, 268-269
   a cyclic movement 33-34
Birth of man 67, 91, 243
Bjornson, Bjornstjerne 147
Born, Max 147
Brain structure 15
Breakdown of society 77, 103-105, 115
Bridge between two worlds 339
Brothers 182, 196
Brotherhood of Man 159, 196, 198, 206

Cacophony of physical life 99
Carnal appetites 300
Carrier wave 246-249, 256
Catalysis 213-217, 222
Casual Mind 28
Cellular structure 13, 89-91, 115, 215
Chaos 60, 113, 116, 118-120, 124-125, 135
   as negative 151
   order out of 113, 129, 278
   seeming 60
Circular movement of life 268-269
Clairvoyant ability 93, 232
Closed system 113, 126, 130

Complexity of life   59-60, 109, 226-267
  the nature of the Infinite   114
Conflicts
  between old & new science
  inner   133, 152
Consciousness   40, 124, 132, 173, 211
  cosmic   100, 106
cycular dynamics of   279
  fourth dimensional   166
  higher   326
  mental   132
  regeneration of   303
  subjective   63, 113-114, 280
Consistancies of life   9
Conspiracy   21
Continuity of man   12, 250
Continuity principle of life   278
Contradictions of life   1-24
  and time   54
  movement of the electromagnetic field   9
  seeming chaos   60
  within himself   41
Corrective methodology   307
Cosmic Consciousness   100, 106
Cosmic design   125
Cosmic egg   23-25, 28, 309
Cosmic Mind   71, 91, 174, 201
  attuned with   106
  opposite nature of   29
Cosmic pattern   137
Cosmic viewpoint   281
Cosmic Visionaries   226-228, 233
Cosmological view   267
Cosmology   253-254, 268
Couplng of polarities   64
Coupling factor   85, 291-292
Creative Infinite Mind   28
Crookes, Sir William   198, 272
Cycle of birth & death   33-36
Cycles of life   278
Cyclic evolution   118-128
Cyclotrons   63
Cycular dynamics of consciousness   279

Cycular relationships   119
Darwin, Charles   109, 225, 231
Death   47, 118, 131, 153, 204, 239-2k40, 250
Degeneration   175, 334
Descartes, Rene   83, 86
Devils & demons   334
Dirak, Paul   319
Disease   308
Disharmony of life   104-105
Disintegration of civilization   124-125
Dissociation of man   201-203
Dissonance in life   308
Dissonent factors in man   300, 307
Double helix as DNA   179, 291
Duality   12, 56
  in nature   12, 56
  of energy   64
  of the Infinite   96, 201
  that is man   94, 201, 241

Ecology of earth   236
Education of mankind   k308
Einstein, Albert   147, 155, 198, 212, 267, 270
Einstein's Equation   94-95, 116
Einstein's relativity theory   81, 108, 144, 199, 320
Elder Brothers   129, 169-170
Electromagnetic energy field   9, 18, 37, 40, 56, 61, 72, 101, 121, 135, 201, 205, 207
Electronic body   45, 121, 137, 140, 204, 325
Electromagnetic envelope   61
Elements   5, 58, 204
Embryo   244
Emotional characteristics of man   306
Emotional factors   332
Emotional reactions   73
Energy
  a cycular movement   34, 279
  and evolution   115-116
  duality of   64
  is finite & infinite   325

man is  68, 273
out of tune  126
proof of  68-69
plasma that is life  273
polarity nature of  229
reconversion of  143, 153
Energy body of man  74-75, 95, 121
Entropy  109-110, 118-120, 135, 169
Escape techniques  238
Eternal Force  36, 76
Eternal life  22
Evidence of man's past  127
Evolution  51-52, 179, 181, 204, 270, 311, 338
  a regrouping of finite quantas of energy  115-116
  a spiritual development  68
  an association between polarities  69
  and bifurcation  57-58
  cyclic  118-128
  hindrence to  282
  progressive  152-153, 206
Evolutionary cycles  10
Evolutionary development  97
  finding the Father  62
  mind / body relationship  291
Excitability  301
Expanding universe  213
Experiments  217-218
Extended knowledge  273

Family  4
Far side of life  271
Father  62, 76, 194-195, 201
Field equation of life  88
Finite universe  300
Five senses  14
Folklore  140, 197, 278
Fountainhead  28, 201, 273
Fourth dimension  37, 42-46, 70, 95-97
Frequency & harmonics  119, 152, 174

Galaxies  5
God  128, 134, 161, 284

Godhead  230
Grand Design  103, 125, 154, 205, 220, 273

Habit forms  301
Harmonic affiliation  85, 297
Harmonics  101, 119
Harmony  102, 104
Health  300
Healing science  172
Heaven  56-57, 76, 245
Heisenberg, Werner Karl  108
Higher consciousness  326
Higher intelligence  64
Higher Self  323,332
Higher senses  232, 321
History of life  231
History of man's past  140, 168, 178
History of science  146-148
Homo sapiens  17, 20, 33
Homo Spiritualis  42, 166, 176
Homonide  17, 20, 24
Humanists  129
Hysteresis  61, 62, 221

Ignorance  329
Individuality  85, 89, 122, 192
  and base frequency  85
Infinite Creative Intelligence  201
Infinite, The  13, 132, 195
Infinite-finite relationship  84-85
Infinite nature of man  58-59
Infinity, measurement of  288-289
Inspiration  207, 232
Inspirational Forces  169
Integration  97, 306
Intelligence  35, 37, 66, 90-91, 266, 270
  higher  271
  Unlocalized  316
Interdimensional
  atom  244
  life is  244
  mind is  65
  nature of life  262
  physics of Unarius  138, 172

principles 315
Interference to growth 293
Interpretation of life 49
Interpretive concept 7, 12
Interpretive values 2
Interrelationship
   man & environment 65, 77, 104
   mind & body 291
   science & religion 137
Isotope 23, 139
Isotopic body 260
Introspective research 62

Jesus of Nazareth 163, 167, 187-188
Jesus of Nazareth's teachings 67, 162, 184-185, 187-188, 193-194, 226

Kepler, Johannes 225
Knowledge
   of the nature of life 30
   of the psychic anatomy 284

Laplace, Pierre 272
Larning 17
   by overcoming 167
Leibnitz, Baron Gottfreid von 83, 86
Lens 35, 316-317
Libido 71
Life
   a grand schoolroom 286
   a revolving movement of energy 271, 283
   after death 248-2k50
   examinations 261
   is interdimensional 244
   problems associted 50-51
   purpose of 23, 205, 111
Life cycle
   of the atom 39
   of the physical anatomy 39
Life experience 111, 289, 330
Light Forces 130
Limitations of man 34, 49-50
Literature of man 186
Lodge, Oliver 272

Logic & reason 153, 162, 183, 275, 312, 322

Macrocosm 210, 214-217
Malfunctions 125, 293
Man
   a derivative of the atomic plasma 303
   a duelistic entity 320
   a spiritual force field 33, 291-292
   a system of polarity relationships 204
   a transmitter & receiver 170-180
   a universe 215-216
   an egg of the Infinite 3-4
   an individual beat frequency 27, 122
   as a synthesis 253
   as energy 68, 277
   dissonent factors 308
   emotional factors 73, 306, 332, 335
   must choose 229-230
   Infinite nature of 58-59
   limitations 34, 49-50
   purpose of 10-12, 15-17, 40
   retardation of 276
Man's birth 67-68, 244
Man's interpretation 49
Man's mind 65-66
   an instrument 299
   becomes a lens 316
   is 4th dimensional 95
Man's potential 201, 205
Man's purpose 10-12, 14-17, 40
Man's relationship to the whole 136
Masters 3, 45, 124, 167, 170, 188
   teachings of the 184-189
Material achievements 239
Material expression of life 314
Materialism 20-21, 175
Matter & anti-matter 23, 320, 324-325
   of himself 338
Maxwell, James 272
Mechanics of his energy system 273

Mechanistic view of life   108-110, 118-119
Mental disease   308
Mental instrument   87
Mental consciousness   132
Mental retardation of man   276
Metaphysical factors in life   271
Metaphysical poets   27
Metaphysics   224-226
Microcosm   210, 214-217
Microcosmic viewpoint   281
Mind   18, 40, 47, 49, 61
  a refracting lens   35, 316-317
  attunement of   123
  body relationship   291
  Causal   28
  Cosmic   71, 91, 174, 201
  formative nature of   217
  is an anatomy   100-101
  is interdimensional   65
  most important vehicle   256
  superconscious   228
Mitosis   90, 110
Music   32
Myths   140, 197

Nature   195
Negative forces   151-152
Negative polarity   37, 68
Neuroses   306, 335
New Age of Spiritual Renaissance   169
New paradigm   234
New Science   158-182
New World Teacher   159-161
New World Teaching   331-340
Newton, Sir Isaac   147, 155, 225
Newtonian revolution   108
Norman, Ernest L.   138
Norman, Ruth   233, 337
Nuclear armament   104, 282

Obsessional factors   307
Occult derivative   184
Opinions   22, 225
Oppenheimer, Robert   198

Optical illusion   88
  as positive   151
  out of chaos   129, 278
Overall plan   266

Paranormal   224-226, 281
Parent atom   10
Particle physicists   136, 139
Pascal, Blaise   198
Past life experience   78, 125-127, 139, 294, 307, 332
  evidence of   141-143, 152-153
  unacknowledged & inaccepted   176 177
Peace of mind   157
Phobias   332
Physical anatomy   15, 19, 60-61
  a secondary anatomy   74, 204
  a composition   91
  a receiver   246-249, 253
Physical body   33-35, 39, 44, 89-90, 274, 204, 247
Physical evolution of man   15
Physical sciences   62, 65, 264-265, 275
  basic problem   72-73
  revolution in   144-145
Physical universe   29, 32, 325
  a gigantic egg   9
  the negative polarity   23, 68, 114
Physics   55
  of his own energy system   274
  revolution in   206
Pioneers   56, 72, 73-74
Plank, Max   108, 147, 267, 270
Plank's constant   210
Poetry   26-27, 31
Polarities   70
  alternate   68-69
  association between   69
  coupling between   69, 85, 281-292
  separating the   57
Polarity nature of energy   229
Polarization   37, 49, 70, 79, 197, 227
Positive polarity   37
Priests   277

Progogni, Ilya   113, 117-118
Progression   105, 124
Progressive development   152-153
   indication of   313
Progressive evolution   206
Proof of energy   68-69
Psychic anatomy   46, 70, 154, 205, 217
   a computer   317
   a transmitter   178-180, 247
   man's spiritual body   18-19
   positive polarity   70
Psychic body   324
Psychics   245
Psychoses   306, 332, 335
Purpose of life   23, 111, 205
Purpose of man   10-12, 15-17, 40
Purpose of science   272
Pythagoras teachings   67

Quantum mechanic theories   108, 144, 199, 214
Questioning   31-32, 66, 94

Radial lines of force   28
Receiver   247, 253
Reconversion of energy   143, 153
Rectification   189
Regeneration   6, 189, 204, 291, 315, 322
Regeneration of man   6, 205
Regeneration of consciousness   303
Regenerative nature of life   198
Regression   105, 124
Reincarnation   276, 286
Relationship to society   133, 302
Religions   184-185, 190-194, 201-203, 245
Researcher   113-116, 211-212
Responsibilities   303
Restoration of spirit   278
Restrictions of life   49-50, 142
Retrograde factors   306
Rivalries   43
Russell, Bertram   81

Sages of old   184-189
Salvation for man   284
School of life   261
Schrodinger, Erwin   212
Science (see also physical science)
   62-63, 79-80, 236-237, 251-252, 266
   a universal   55, 77
   conflict between old & new   223-224, 239-244
   of life   111, 129
   purpose of   272
   the next step   75, 151
Science & religion
   joined   207
   relationship between   137
Science of Life   129, 236-238, 283
   implications of   310
   that unites   111
Scientists   73-74, 80, 113-114, 138, 211, 263-264, 267-268
Sentient factor of man   17
Second law of thermodynamics   134-135
Security   21, 51
Separation
   of man from himself   193, 236-237
   of the continuity factors of life   192
   of the individual with society   229
Shakespeare, William   27
Shankara   159
Sine wave   279
Singularity   43, 161
Society
   breakdown of   77, 103-105, 115
   patterns   41, 136
Socrates' teachings   67, 162, 167, 184, 226
Solar systems   5
Space-time continuum   139
Special theory of relativity   320
Spinoza, Benedict   272
Spirit   244, 298
   an elecyromagnetic forcefield   70, 207
   an interdimensional Force   13, 70

an evolutionary development 291-292
is energy 277
nature of man 277, 313
psychic anatomy 70
Spirit Self 45
Spiritual birth of man 13-15
Spiritual being 17, 67, 250, 270
Spiritual body 18-19, 47
Spiritual Force 14
Spjiritual man 38, 42
Spiritual Renaissance 130-131, 205
Spiritual self 285, 292
Spiritualists 245
Static energy forcefield 177, 329
Subatomic particles 133-134, 214-215
subconscious affiliations 186
Subconscious self 228-229
Sub-infinite 200, 214-215, 267, 333
Subjective consciousness 63, 113-114, 280
Superconscious Mind 228
Supernatural 184, 199
  force 201-203, 277
Symbolic logic 86
Symbolism 164-165, 169, 194, 284
Synthesis 97, 176, 215-217, 254-255

Technological achievements 239
Technological developments 236
Technology of television 247
Television set analogy 174, 246, 249
Tennyson, Alfred 186
Theory of relativity 81, 108, 144, 199, 320
Thinking man 55-56, 291
Third dimension 30, 37, 70-71, 95
Time 112
Time & space 53-55, 57, 75, 139, 224, 307, 309
  joining of 318
  resolved 173
Transceiver mechanism 291
Transmitter 61, 97, 137, 178-180, 247
Travelers between dimensions 98-99, 198

Truth 76

Unariun Brothers 127, 310
Unariun Scientists 149-151, 164, 226, 267
Unarius 55, 77-78, 155, 268, 283-285
  a fourth dimensional physics 163, 171
  a synthesis of all disciplines 254-255
  Brotherhood of 159, 206-207, 227, 252, 265
  intention of 255
  Science of life 206, 241, 257-262, 308
  the new science 145-149, 156-182, 171-173, 206-208, 223
Uncertainty principle 108, 116
Unification theory 44
Unified field 29, 172-173
Unity 111-112
Universal science (see Unarius) 55, 77
Universe 29
  a biological plasma 9
  expanding 213
URIEL 132, 310
  Cosmic Visionary 233
  Emissary for planet earth 232
  New World Teacher 159

Validation 209
Venturi tube 213, 220
Vinci, Leonardo Da 146
Vortexal nature of the universe 272

Wealth 13
Whitehead, Alfred 211, 225
Wisdom 318

Zero 288-289

# Suggested Reading In The Unarius Library

## Pulse of Creation

Voice of Venus
Voice of Eros
Voice of Hermes
Voice of Muse, Elysium & Unarius

## Dissertations From Advanced Masters

Tempus Procedium
Tempus Invictus
Tempus Interludium,          Volume 1
Tempus Interludium,          Volume 2
Infinite Contact
Cosmic Continuum
Infinite Perspectus
Tesla Speaks,          Volume 1
Tesla Speaks,          Volume 2
Tesla Speaks,          Volume 3
Bridge To Heaven
Tesla Speaks,          Volume 6
Tesla Speaks,          Volume 8, Part 1
Tesla Speaks,          Volume 8, Part 2

## The Science of Self Discovery

The Psychology of Consciousness
The Infinite Concept of Cosmic Creation
Tesla Speaks,          Volume 9
Tesla Speaks,          Volume 11
Man, The Regenerative Evolutionary Spirit
Interdimensional Physics, the Mind and the Universe

## Parables of Light

Whispers of Love on Wings of Light
Elysium
Anthenium
Glowing Moments

## The Extraterrestrial Connection

The Truth About Mars
Underground Cities of Mars
Tesla Speaks,                        Volume 7
Tesla Speaks,                        Volume 4-1
Tesla Speaks,                        Volume 4-2
Tesla Speaks,                        Volume 4-3
Tesla Speaks,                        Volume 5
Have You Lived On Other Worlds Before, Volume 1
Have You Lived On Other Worlds Before, Volume 2
The Restoration,                Volume 1
The Restoration,                Volume 2
Roots of the Earthman
The Restoration of the Interplanetary Confederation,
The Grand Design of Life for Man
Communications From Outer Space
Preview for the Space Fleet Landing
Exploring the Universe with Starship Voyager
Preparation for the Landing·
Monuments of Mars
The Night Sky

## Life-Death and Immortality

Conclave of Light Beings
Rainbow Bridge to the Inner Worlds

## True Stories of Reincarnation

The Visitations, A Saga of Gods & Men
The True Story of Jesus of Nazareth
The Story of the Little Red Box
The Story of the Little Red Box
Return to Jerusalem
The Confessions of I, Bonaparte
My 2000 Year Psychic Memory as Mary of Bethany
Apology of John the Baptist
Yamamoto Returns
Ra-Mu of Lemuria Speaks

## The Saga of Orion

The Decline and Destruction of the Orion Empire, V. 1
The Decline and Destruction of the Orion Empire, V. 2
The Decline and Destruction of the Orion Empire, V. 3
The History of the Universe,     Volume 1
The History of the Universe,     Volume 2
The History of the Universe,     Volume 3

## Past Life Therapy

The Principles & Practice of Past-Life Therapy
Lemuria Rising,     Volume 1
Lemuria Rising,     Volume 2
Lemuria Rising,     Volume 3
Lemuria Rising,     Volume 4
By Their Fruits Shall They Be Known,     Volume 1
By Their Fruits Shall They Be Known,     Volume 2
A Beginners Guide to Progressive Evolution
Return to Atlantis,     Volume 1
Return to Atlantis,     Volume 2
Return to Atlantis,     Volume 3-1
Return to Atlantis,     Volume 3-2
Return to Atlantis,     Volume 4
Effort to Destroy the Unarius Mission Thwarted
Past-Lives, Dreams & Visions

## Summary of the Unarius Science

New Hope for the Drug and Alcohol Abuser
Facts About UFO's
On Future Changes for Planet Earth
Man's Endless Journey to the Stars
Biographical History of Unarius,       Volume 1
Biographical History of Unarius,       Volume 2
Satan is now a Light Bearer
Testimonials of Unarius Students
Pictorial Tour of Unarius
Life-Death & Immortality
A Brief Description of the Unarius Science
Who is the Mona Lisa?
Introduction to Unarius
Unarius Light Magazine, Quarterly